Linux® System Administration

Linux® System Administration

M Carling
Stephen Degler
James Dennis

New Riders

201 West 103rd Street
Indianapolis, IN 46290

Linux System Administration

M Carling, Stephen Degler, James Dennis

Copyright © 2000 by New Riders Publishing

International Standard Book Number: 0-56205-934-3

Library of Congress Catalog Card Number: 98-85926

Printed in the United States of America

First Printing: August, 1999

03 02 01 00 99   7 6 5 4 3 2 1

Interpretation of the printing code: The rightmost double-digit number is the year of the book's printing; the rightmost single-digit number is the number of the book's printing. For example, the printing code 99-1 shows that the first printing of the book occurred in 1999.

Trademarks

Warning and Disclaimer

Publisher
David Dwyer

Executive Editor
Laurie Petrycki

Acquisitions Editor
Katie Purdum

Development Editor
Jim Chalex

Managing Editor
Gina Brown

Project Editor
Alissa Cayton

Copy Editor
Gayle Johnson

Indexer
Ginny Bess

Technical Editors
Richard Muirden
Becki Kain

Composition
Paul C. Anagnostopoulos, using ZzTeX

Coniugibus delectissimis

Contents

IV   Appendix

Foreword

Nearly from its beginnings, LINUX has found a natural home on server machines at large sites—business data centers, campus networks, research clusters. LINUX's high reliability, coupled with the guarantee that if something does go wrong you can fix it yourself, has given it a strong appeal to overworked and underbudgeted system administrators.

For all its utility, LINUX's infiltration of serious iron has been a rather stealthy process until recently. Often, system administrators would replace machines providing Web service or mail or DNS or file-sharing services under other operating systems without their management being aware of the change. In most cases, the resulting dramatic improvements in performance and uptime would be taken for granted by everyone except the sysadmin, who would be grateful enough for getting fewer 3:00 AM beeper calls.

This book is an indicator of the un-stealthing of LINUX. Over the last eighteen months, LINUX has earned enough good publicity to join the official toolkit that management will sign off on. The savvy administrators who have been using it all along are pulling LINUX machines out of closets, and many others are giving it a first look.

This book is a reference for experienced LINUX administrators and a guide for new ones. It distills the authors' extensive rubber-meets-the-road experience with real-world challenges—including all the expertise Jim Dennis has built up in his "Answer Guy" persona at the *Linux Gazette*.

Armed with the knowledge in this book, you should be able to configure, deploy, and secure LINUX machines like a pro. This will make your life easier. And it will speed the day when you can say to your boss "NT? Windows? Novell? Time to get rid of all that legacy software; it just doesn't perform . . . ."

So go forth and conquer. And have fun, too!

Eric S. Raymond

Preface

The world is even more full of technical books for technical readers than it is full of technical books for non-technical readers. Being technical readers, system administrators have an abundance of technical books on system administration from which to choose. But these books do not suffice because only half the job of system administration is technical.

This book addresses the need for a non-technical book for technical readers before delving into the technical details of system administration. Part I surveys system administration from a bird's eye view, scanning requirements analysis, recovery planning, capacity planning, network principles, and security policy. The intended audience is the professional system administrator. However, it is essential reading for managers of system administrators who come from other backgrounds, such as programming or finance.

Part I is accessible to any reader with a curiosity about system administration. As such, it is ideal for computer programmers and other users who wish to know what their system administrators are doing while they are out of sight, and for the parents of any system administrator who wishes better to understand what their child does for a living.

Part II takes a worm's eye view of the technical aspects of system administration. It is a practical guide written for system administrators without regard to accessibility for others. Some programmers, network administrators, and database administrators may find Parts II and III of interest, but non-technical managers and others without responsibility for hands-on administration of LINUX systems may do well to skip directly to the Glossary.

Part III provides an overview of the major services upon which systems and applications depend. Most system administrators will find these services essential to the performance of their duties: Email, Printing, NFS, NIS, and the myriad range of network services.

Finally, a guide to the emergencies that may arise in the course of LINUX system administration is included as an appendix. We hope that most readers will rarely need it.

Acknowledgments

I'd like to thank Laurie Petrycki, Executive Editor at New Riders, for allowing us to produce this book using Open Source software. Katie Purdum, our Acquisitions Editor, attempted to keep us motivated. Jim Chalex, our development editor, provided useful suggestions along with a calm when the publisher otherwise seemed tortured. Gayle Johnson and Audra McFarland, our copy editors, meticulously improved the book, line by line, despite my paranoid insistence on reviewing every change. Ginny Bess indexed the book while learning how to do so in LaTeX. Alissa Cayton proofread the manuscript.

Paul Anagnostopoulos of Windfall Software offered several valuable suggestions while laying out the copy.

Our technical reviewers, Becki Kain and Richard Muirden, provided many valuable suggestions.

Heather Stern of Starshine Technical Services provided an abundance of useful technical feedback.

Karl L. Swartz reviewed the manuscript for both readability and technical content. His feedback improved both.

I thank Cynthia Garb, who edited the chapter drafts and created the illustrations. Her organizational insights enhanced the clarity of the book.

Don Lee Miller edited copy and provided a generous contribution of commas.

Professor Angelo Codevilla, then of the Hoover Institution and now of Boston University, taught me to write. Master Seargent Charles Cantwell, then a Senior Instructor at the US Army JFK Center for Unconventional Warfare and now a Professor of Fine Arts, taught me discipline. Without them, I would not have been able to complete this undertaking.

It is too late for me to thank E.C. Carling, my late grandfather, who first taught me engineering. I acknowledge him here, though he will never know. It is not too late for me to thank the other members of my family for suffering my intolerance of interruptions. I should remember to do so while they are still alive.

I thank Beth, Connie, Irma, Kellie, Miesha, Rena, Sheri, Shirley, Stacey, and Victoria for relieving my physical stresses and keeping me fit enough to write day after day.

Recurrent Technologies graciously donated a SPARC5 which was used in the production of the manuscript. They are friends to the LINUX community.

Those who use Open Source software and, even more, those who write it deserve the thanks of all of us, for they help us to live free.

All three of us thank the Degler family, Sara, Kara, and Madelyn for their patience, encouragement, and understanding.

Also, thanks to Catherine Pavlov for Mr. Degler's photograph.

Finally, I must thank my coauthors, Steve Degler and Jim Dennis, without whose contributions this book would be vastly inferior.

Responsibility for any errors is mine.

M Carling, *Paris*

About the Authors

M Carling consults at the intersection of system administration and investment banking, having managed system administration projects for large banks in New York, London, Tokyo, Toronto, and Zurich.

Stephen Degler has been administering UNIX systems for major financial firms for the past 8 years. He currently manages systems administration for the FAST (Financial Analytics and Structured Transactions) group at Bear Stearns.

James Dennis holds the position of Senior Reseacher at Linuxcare. He writes the "Answer Guy" column for the *Linux Gazette,* and has performed system administration for Fortune 100 corporations.

About the Technical Reviewers

Becki Kain is president of Furph Incorporated, an e-commerce house, in Livonia, Michigan. She has previously worked as a UNIX administrator for Environmental Reseach Institute of Michigan and Ford Motor Company, specializing in very large email systems. She lives with her husband, five ferrets, and three cats.

Richard Muirden obtained his degree in Applied Science (Computer Science) from RMIT University in Melbourne, Australia in 1992. At that time he had already been working as a System Administrator. Since then, he has worked on UNIX-based systems from PC's to Cray Supercomputers. More recently he has worked in the field of SAP R/3 and acted as a consultant in the areas of UNIX System Administration.

Tell Us What You Think!

As the reader of this book, you are our most important critic and commentator. We value your opinion and want to know what we're doing right, what we could do better, what areas you'd like to see us publish in, and any other words of wisdom you're willing to pass our way.

As the Executive Editor for the Linux team at New Riders Publishing, I welcome your comments. You can fax, email, or write me directly to let me know what you did or didn't like about this book—as well as what we can do to make our books stronger.

Please note that I cannot help you with technical problems related to the topic of this book, and that due to the high volume of mail I receive, I might not be able to reply to every message.

When you write, please be sure to include this book's title and author, as well as your name and phone or fax number. I will carefully review your comments and share them with the author and editors who worked on the book.

Fax: 317-581-4663
Email: newriders@mcp.com
Mail: Laurie Petrycki
      Executive Editor
      Linux/Open Source
      New Riders Publishing
      201 West 103rd Street
      Indianapolis, IN 46290 USA

I

Principles

*Friends don't let friends use
closed source software.*

1

The Prime Directive

TO PROVIDE AND MAINTAIN ACCESS TO SYSTEM RESOURCES is the system administrator's "prime directive." Ultimately, all of our professional activities stem from or relate to this goal. Regardless of the computing platform involved, all operating systems provide mechanisms to manage resources. These resources include files, applications, peripherals, services, bandwidth, CPU cycles, memory, and storage space.

Identifying the resources, their owners and users, and defining the forms of access and the authorities involved is a process of requirements analysis. System administrators must transform this generalization into specifics for their systems, their users, and their management.

Maintaining access to a system's resources transcends the maintenance of access to the system itself. If the system fails or is made unavailable due to some disaster, the system administrator will be expected to restore normal operations in a timely fashion. Most people think "doing backups" fulfills this requirement. However, our focus will be on recovery planning—which usually includes doing backups but also entails risk assessment, testing, and more.

During normal operations, and especially as organizations grow and adapt, the utilization of resources changes across systems. When the attempted utilization of any resource exceeds capacity, it is likely to be viewed as a disaster. The system administrator will have failed in his prime directive to provide the necessary access. One failure may also cause the failure of other services. For example, if system logs fill a disk partition, this can prevent the delivery of email through that system. These disasters must be avoided through capacity planning.

Security is the corollary of our prime directive—to deny access to system resources, as well as to ensure that services are provided appropriately even during and after attacks by outsiders or insiders. Security involves both policy management and enforcement.

Appropriate forms of access must be provided, as authorized by the owners of each resource. The processes of defining and enforcing these policies are the two essensial components of system security. Security issues permeate every aspect of system administration. So, although we include a chapter on each of these security topics, we also refer to security implications throughout every chapter.

These topics—requirements analysis, recovery planning, capacity planning, and security—are the core of the system administrator's job and constitute the first part of *Linux System Administration*. Throughout the discussion of these topics, Gnu/Linux-based examples are used, but most apply to other variants of Unix. The concepts apply to computer systems generally.

The rest of this volume covers practical details of administering Linux systems, including booting and shutdown, the kernel, network profiles, and sample configuration descriptions for the most common types of servers and workstations.

Why Do Systems Need Administration?

With Linux we have a version of Unix that is so easy to install, on such a wide variety of commonly available (and inexpensive) hardware, that relatively inexperienced users can install and use it themselves. Current versions of the popular Linux distributions are easier to install than the versions of MS-DOS that were sold by the millions less than a decade ago.

However, it is one thing to install Linux on a PC and run typical applications on it. Almost anyone can do that. To do this in a way that meets the specific business needs defined by management requires a professional.

Those who have become accustomed to home computers naturally might ask, "Why do these systems need constant maintenance?"

The fact is that many systems do not. There are "embedded" and "turnkey" systems that function like appliances. These need even less maintenance than a toaster or refrigerator (which have to be cleaned occasionally). Some of these computing appliances, like the Igel Ethermulation X terminals, the Cobalt Networks Qube, and the Corel Computing NetWinder "network computer," are built around customized versions of Linux. Some organizations purchase these, plug them in, and use them with no system-level changes throughout the lifetime of the product.

However, the computer systems in most organizations are much more dynamic. Computers are general-purpose devices, and most operating systems and widely available software are written for general use. Thus, it is the system administrator's job to adapt these tools to the specific needs of a given organization. Those needs change over time and differ among departments within an organization.

Who Administers Linux Systems?

If you're reading this, chances are that you're professionally managing at least one LINUX system, or you expect to be responsible for one or more LINUX systems in the near future.

Perhaps you've been administering a LAN full of UNIX workstations and servers, and you're adding some PCs to the network. This might be motivated by their low cost, their ubiquity, or any number of other factors. You might also be considering the SPARC or MIPS ports of LINUX on some older Sun or SGI workstations left unsupported by recent versions of Solaris and Irix.

Perhaps you're approaching LINUX from the PC world. You've been managing NetWare, LAN Manager, or WINDOWS NT servers and you need to augment or replace these with some form of UNIX.

Perhaps it isn't even the servers that you're concerned about. Some of your users may be demanding access to applications and tools from the UNIX world.[1] The release of WordPerfect for LINUX and recent upgrades to that package, and the maturing Applixware and StarOffice commercial applications suites, as well as the ongoing development of free applications like LyX, SIAG, and the GIMP, are contributing to this demand.

It may also be that your management requires more centralized control over and security for their desktop systems than is possible using more common PC and Macintosh operating systems.

Perhaps you are an experienced LINUX user and the professional administration of these systems is new to you. The management of multi-user and network systems is much more complex than maintaining and using home systems.

Linux System Administration addresses these cases and many others. Naturally, it can't be "all things to all people." We assume that you are a reasonably advanced LINUX user— and we won't waste your time with "blow by blow" monographs on how to install LINUX on a PC, how to use a command shell, or how to edit files.

System administrators are advanced computer users. Although a majority of LINUX *users* had no previous UNIX experience (some estimates suggest as many as 75 percent), most LINUX system administrators have experience with several forms of UNIX.

---

1. This is more likely for some specialized scientific applications and, of course, by many programmers. Surprisingly, the 1997 IDC survey showed that LINUX was used for *workstations* almost 2:1 over WINDOWS NT and almost 4:1 over all of the traditional variants of UNIX.

Titles and Roles

Many people whose primary job responsibilities include the administration of a UNIX or LINUX system don't have the title *system administrator*. In fact, system administrator doesn't appear in the *Dictionary of Occupational Titles* [26] at all. According to a survey done by *SysAdmin Magazine*, over 70 percent of their subscribers who were primarily responsible for managing one or more UNIX systems had other job titles.

SAGE, the System Administrators Guild, discusses this in some detail in their *Job Descriptions for System Administrators* [28]. SAGE is a special technical group within the USENIX Association. Its mission is to promote the recognition of system administration as a profession and to develop standards of nomenclature, training, and possibly certification within the field.

Looking at the SAGE *Salary Survey*,[2] we find that their membership lists over a hundred job titles. In some cases this is due to simple bureaucratic nomenclature, while in others it reflects real differences among system administrators' responsibilities.

We define some titles and corresponding roles that will be used throughout the text. In addition to system administrators, these include database administrators, network administrators, operators, and managers. When we use a particular title, its implied role will be as we define it here.

System Operators and Managers

Many organizations put their system administrators, network administrators, database administrators, and related staff into an Information Systems (IS) or Information Technology (IT) department. To this group they may also add systems analysts, web authors and webmasters, possibly a Help Desk team, and some management, of course.

Some organizations have enough system administrators to form a loose hierarchy, with system operators at the bottom, junior system administrators and senior system administrators above them, and an "IT Manager" or "Director" in charge. Larger organizations are even more hierarchical.

In other cases, the system operators work on mainframes and minis (such as VAX clusters), the network managers and network supervisors are responsible for the NetWare LANs and servers, and the system administrators are in charge of UNIX and LINUX hosts. In yet other cases no distinctions are made among these titles.

There seem to be no standards that are widely observed with respect to these job titles. However, it is useful to distinguish among different roles in the organization— even if the same person wears many or all of these hats. We therefore make the following distinctions:

The operator follows a written set of procedures to perform routine maintenance and operations on a system and handle well-defined eventualities. These typically include:

---

2. This is an annual survey that is available exclusively to SAGE members via their web site at http://www.usenix.org/sage/salary_survey/salary_survey.html

- Perform system and data backups
- Monitor systems, particularly servers and routers
- Test recovery procedures ("fire drills")
- Add new users
- Change user passwords
- Restore accidentally deleted or damaged files
- Remove access for former users
- Troubleshoot, document, and resolve problems on any of these systems' subsystems
- Help users with routine issues
- Recover from various lesser disasters
- Prepare and configure new client systems
- Perform minor repairs and upgrades on systems (adding and/or replacing hard drives, memory, and so on)

The system administrator is charged with the conception and implementation of these procedures. He interprets policy, recommends and implements the plans, and researches new technologies—often with hands-on testing and evaluation of tools and applications. And the good system administrator documents the environment.

The typical responsibilities of this role include:

- Perform risk assessments
- Prepare recovery plans
- Implement backup and test procedures
- Monitor and tune performance
- Plan for necessary increases in and adjustments to system capacity
- Create scripts to abbreviate or automate some operations; delegate and regulate others
- Select monitoring software and equipment
- Review and recommend system security policies and procedures
- Select, install, and configure security tools
- Assist operators and Help Desk staff with extraordinary issues
- Install and configure new software and hardware
- Upgrade existing software (or test and prepare transition plans for major upgrades)
- Recommend server configurations

We use the title of network administrator to refer to those who are responsible for network infrastructure, including routers, switches, hubs, and wiring. System administrators are the customers of the network administrators.

Theoretically, policies are handed down by management to be implemented by the administrative staff. A manager or director gets (or negotiates) a set of directives and/or objectives and translates these into requirements or policies. Ideally, managers also act as mediators to provide their IT department with the necessary resources to do the work—and as liaisons to other managers to deal with interdepartmental issues.

Typically the system administrator and his manager must negotiate a service-level agreement or specification. This might be very informal, or it could be in the form of quarterly and/or annual objectives. A properly agreed-upon service level specification is of great benefit both to system administrators and to management because it helps the system administrators prioritize conflicting responsibilities, and should provide a reasonably unambiguous reference as new and unexpected goals are assigned or delegated.

The nature of IT departments makes them a scapegoat for other departments. Frequently departmental managers will engage in "turf wars" and "job dodging." The debates and negotiations that follow from these aren't always unnecessary—the distribution of responsibilities does genuinely differ from one organization to another and changes over time.

A good manager will deal with those issues while allowing the system administrator to focus on more technical and specific issues. A good system administrator will understand these issues and account for them in his recommendations and planning.

As we'll see in Chapter 2, identifying the involved parties, their priorities, and the lines of authority throughout is a vital part of the requirements analysis process. That process is crucial to the work of everyone in an IT department. Less obvious is the work that goes into accomplishing these tasks.

A big part of being a good system administrator is knowing what is possible and what is being done by others in the field. In smaller organizations, for example, system administrators who don't know about IP masquerading or proxying may be constrained in their ability to consider and offer options. System administrators in large organizations who don't know about DNS round-robin load distribution and who don't understand the principles underlying a VLAN (virtual LAN), may be constrained similarly.

Thus, the system administrator must be a forager, periodically wandering a number of fields surrounding his "core competency" to find the fruits and nuggets that are growing and ripening thereabouts. He must also be a hunter, describing the user's and management's desires in terms that are likely to find matches in Internet search engines and generate responses from the mailing lists and newsgroups.

Overlapping Duties

Experience has shown that system administrators are rarely dedicated to a specific platform. Most sites use several different operating systems. This extends beyond the obvious cases for system administrators supporting desktop systems running MS WINDOWS or MacOS.

In particular, many system administrators have to manage routers, telephone switches, modem pools, tape libraries, specialized fileservers (like those from Network Appliance and Auspex), and other equipment that is often not thought of as being a "computer."

Many of these have embedded operating systems that only offer the vaguest semblance to UNIX.

Beyond the range of environments with which they work, system administrators are often given responsibility for any roles for which an organization has no specialists. Sites that have no dedicated DBAs (database administrators) generally have one system administrator who manages any local database systems. At sites that have only one DBA, a system administrator is likely to cover for him and is likely to manage many technical aspects of any database servers that the DBA works on. Similarly, at sites that have no dedicated network administrators, the system administrators manage the hubs, routers, and switches and often maintain the network cabling. At sites that have no Help Desk, the system administrators usually provide all of the on-site end user technical support. For sites with a Help Desk, the system administrators are nearly always the ultimate point of escalation for technical questions. A system administrator is usually a "jack-of-all-trades."

The "Vendor" Documentation

The primary source of information for any operating system or software package should always be its own documentation, whether printed or electronic. It includes the help pages (traditionally provided by the man command in UNIX and LINUX, and supplemented by the texinfo program and files that are part of the GNU suite), help screens, menus, and other features within the programs themselves.

Since LINUX isn't the product of a single "vendor," we find that the documentation for different GNU, LINUX, and other Open Source packages comes from diverse sources and in many formats.

The documentation for LINUX is developed by the same process and distributed in the same ways as LINUX itself. The Linux Documentation Project is a collaborative effort by many individual volunteers and various interested organizations. It includes over a hundred HOWTO documents on specific topics and packages, a number of FAQs, and a set of guides (full-length books).

These are the "vendor" sources for LINUX documentation. The place for LINUX novices to start is *Linux Installation and Getting Started*. From there a user might progress to the *Linux User's Guide*, while the aspiring system administrator will certainly want to peruse the *Linux Network Administrator's Guide* and *Linux System Administrator's Guide*.

In addition to these sources, most distributions of LINUX come with their own documentation. Some of it may be printed (as with Red Hat), some may be included electronically (Debian), and some may be included in both forms (S.u.S.E.).

In all cases refer to your distribution's documentation. Some packages change as they get upgraded and ported. *The map is not the terrain*. If our examples disagree with the man or texinfo pages at your site, it's probable that a program's behavior will match its documentation. Ultimately it is the program itself that is the "terrain." In some cases it may be necessary to test the program or read its sources, in preference to relying on the documentation that came with it.

Other Books

The vast majority of information about LINUX is available on the Internet. LINUX was built as a collaboration over the Internet, and its documentation has followed the same model.

Ultimately LINUX is an implementation of UNIX. Thus, most books on UNIX apply as much to LINUX as to any other flavor of UNIX. Much of the documentation that is written specifically for LINUX can be applied to any other UNIX—especially since almost all of the programs that run under LINUX are portable to most other UNIX platforms. This is why so many UNIX professionals on other platforms routinely subscribe to the *Linux Journal* and refer to Linux Documentation Project HOWTOs for their work.

There are only two noteworthy books on general UNIX system administration that we recommend:

- *Essential System Administration, 2nd Edition*
  by Æleen Frisch

- *Unix System Administration Handbook, 2nd Edition*
  by Evi Nemeth *et al.*

One of the more frequently asked questions (FAQs) in the USENET `comp.unix.admin` newsgroup is "I'm a new system administrator; what books should I read?" The answer invariably includes these two titles (and will hopefully come to include *Linux System Administration*).

Many of the topics covered in a single chapter here are the subject of whole volumes. Mail handling and domain naming services, for example, are special issues that require separate books. Other specific needs will also require more specific books. Most chapters include an extensive suggested reading list for exactly this reason.

Linux System Administration on the Web

Linux System Administration is dotted with URLs. LINUX is a product of the Internet, and almost all of the information about it is primarily available via the World Wide Web. However, the web is *huge*. Even with search engines like google, Yahoo!, and Alta Vista, it can be difficult to find what you're looking for. Also, the web is constantly changing. People change hobbies and/or ISPs, ISPs go out of business, and so on. As a result, the best URL on a subject today is the "Error 404" of tomorrow.

You should have to type only *one* URL from this book into your browser. So, rather than hunting through the pages of this book and retyping the URLs listed in the footnotes, just bookmark the following:

> *Linux System Administration* errata, annotations, and links: `http://www.linuxsa.com/`

Any correspondence regarding this book can be sent to:

> `lsa@linuxsa.com`

When you're up to your waist in alligators, it's easy to forget that you're there to drain the swamp.

2

Requirements Analysis

AN ELEGANT APPROACH TO THE WRONG PROBLEM yields the wrong solution. Users and managers who make demands of system administrators often present the wrong problem because they lack the perspective to see the forest past the trees. It is easy for a system administrator to lose sight of priorities and objectives when he's too busy solving apparent problems and reacting to superficial symptoms. Thus, it is a system administrator's responsibility to have the depth and understanding of the business to discern the real problems underlying the complaints that queue up.

Requirements analysis is a process of translating *desired results* into specifications. Management sets policy, and system administrators translate policy into procedures and plans (for operators) and make recommendations (to management). The system administrator's input is necessary to provide management with the right information on which to base policies.

The key to requirements analysis is to really understand the desired results of our managers and users, even when they do not, and to manage those expectations or meet those needs. Doing so precludes many problems.

Ultimately, any job or project is about what a set of people *want*. Identifying the set of people to be satisfied is the first step toward figuring out what needs to be done. Then we can ask what it is they really want. For example, users often want new computers, complaining that theirs are too slow. The real problem may be that insufficient memory is causing the computer to swap pages to disk, creating the appearance that it is slow. In such cases, adding memory will generally satisfy the user. Note that even this simple case requires some investigation and analysis.

The System Administrator's Job Requirements

Most professional system administrators want to get or keep a job in the field, to progress in their careers, or possibly even to move into another field for which system administration may be a stepping stone. Most system administrators prefer working with the latest technology, and derive satisfaction not just from doing a good job, but from solving problems or keeping an organization running smoothly.

The preliminary requirements analysis is a matter of determining whether you have the prerequisite skills for, and interest in, a given position. You may decide that you don't have the necessary expertise—and be offered the position despite that. Expertise may be the most obvious prerequisite for the system administrator, but it's not the most important. The ability to recognize the limitations of your own knowledge, and the willingness to ask, to research, and to recommend further consultation will often be far more valuable than fluency in shell commands or Perl scripting.

Alternatively, you may come to the conclusion that a given position doesn't interest you. Requirements analysis will almost certainly help you discover this more quickly than on-the-job experience. In some cases, you may even be able to isolate the specific aspects of the position that you dislike, and get them changed, delegated, or reassigned.

Most books for system administrators start with a list of duties and responsibilities that are typical for the position. As we've discussed, there are a variety of titles under which system administrators work. In addition, the actual jobs vary considerably from one position to another and over time within any one of them. The problem is that this list of "typical" duties won't cover all or even *most* of the duties of any particular system administrator. For the exceptions, the extraordinary, and the rest, we have a process to explore the requirements and negotiate among possible solutions.

Ideally, you want to perform some analysis of the requirements for your potential role as a system administrator even before you accept the job. Asking appropriate questions to that end in an employment or promotion interview will probably increase your chances of getting the offer. Good questions demonstrate experience and knowledge far more effectively than testimonials or anecdotes about past performance, and will demonstrate your interest in the position.

Here are some questions to ask before accepting a system administration position:

- Who would you report to?
- Who, if anyone, would be reporting to you?
- What were the duties of your predecessor?
- Under what circumstances did your predecessor leave?

- Will it be possible to contact your predecessor?

- Does the site use some sort of "issue tracking" system?

- Are there defined escalation procedures for technical and policy issues that you can't resolve directly?

- Is there a Help Desk or internal technical support department at this site? Are you on the escalation path for that team? Are you going to *be* the Help Desk?

- Do current policies exist for the site's security and acceptable system and network use? Have they been published? Are they available on the intranet?

- Has there been a recent site security or administrative audit?

- Does the site have disaster recovery plans? How comprehensive are they? Have they been tested? How recently and regularly?

- Is the site currently experiencing any performance or capacity problems?

- Does the manager to whom you'll be reporting already have a defined set of performance metrics that relate to your prospective position?

Assumption of Responsibilities

Taking over the administration of a new set of systems can be a scary experience. Ideally you'll work with the system administrator who initially set up this system—or who has used and managed it for awhile. Sometimes you may be forced to take over a system completely—with little or no support from the previous system administrator.

In the worst case you'll be taking over a system that has not been properly managed—and one where your predecessor left on hostile terms. In these cases you'll be faced with the very real possibility that your predecessor has left backdoors and/or logic bombs on one or more systems, which we'll discuss further in Chapter 8, "Enforcing Security."

Your Organization's Requirements

What does your boss (or prospective boss) expect from you? How does he define *system administration*? As we've discussed, this term covers a range of jobs and titles that mean different things to different organizations.

Requirements analysis is about answering these questions and many more like them. Typically, requirements analysis is studied by programmers and engineers in the context of product design. It's unfortunate that the subject isn't discussed more broadly. At its core it is simply a matter of clarifying problems at hand. In other words, it is making sure that you really understand the problems before committing time and resources to misguided effort.

The usual product of a requirements analysis process is a manufacturing requirements document or a product specification. This is essentially a set of criteria by which management can determine the extent to which the program or product that's delivered to them matches what they asked for.

This is a bit different for the system administrator, who is not delivering a "product" or a "program" and who is not normally involved in a single, well-defined project. The system administrator is usually either a permanent member of the staff or a long-term consultant who will be involved in various projects during his tenure. Indeed, it is common in smaller organizations for a system administrator to be involved, at least peripherally, in every project and aspect of an organization's operations.

Performance will be measured in some way, and there are some failures for which you'd certainly be fired or at least moved into another position. This is true for any job, of course. However, the need to define, clarify, and (to some degree) *negotiate* the system administrator's responsibilities is more acute because of how broadly the work crosses hierarchies within most organizations. IS departments and MIS staffs are notorious scapegoats for a variety of failures and disasters. In many organizations, every department is dependent on the "IS team" or the "operations group" for a variety of computing and communications resources—so the natural tendency in any crisis is to point to any deficiencies and performance problems in the computational infrastructure.

On the flip side of this coin, any server, network, or telephone system failure can paralyze a department or a whole company. Although the phrase mission critical is overused in modern business, it does convey its original meaning: If a mission critical component fails, the whole mission fails.

Requirements analysis is about discovering these dependencies and priorities. As you discover your organization's requirements, you'll naturally start to ask about the consequences of various failures and disasters. You'll be engaging in risk assessment, which leads to recovery planning. As you define these criteria and write them down, you'll have created a service-level specification (sometimes called a "service-level agreement").

The Service-Level Specification

This is the product of the initial global requirements analysis. Hopefully you were able to start that process before you even took the job.

To develop a service-level specification, you have to gather much information and ask many questions. Here are a few to get you started:

- Who do you work for?
- Who works with and for you?
- What systems are you responsible for?
- Will 24/7 on-call support be required?
- What training is available?
- Who uses these systems?
- What applications and services are in use on them?
- What policies and procedures existed for your predecessor (or still exist for your associates)?
- Who sets these policies, and who has the authority to revise them?

It is possible, of course, to just jump right in and learn as you go. You can use your best judgment at every turn and guess what your priorities should be. You can also seek out your boss and coworkers and ask these questions as you go. You'll certainly need to do these things in any case. However, creating a service-level specification and clarifying these things early—and negotiating a set of priorities among them—can save quite a bit of time and result in far fewer mistakes.

As an example of setting priorities, it is likely that you'll be responsible for a number of different services. If some users do transaction processing (like phone orders) using a corporate database system, keeping that server and the networks and/or terminals connected to it up and running is likely to have a high priority.

In most organizations, company email has priority over Internet web access, which probably has precedence over Usenet news. Most of that is a matter of common sense.

Of course, it's often not that simple. For example, most applications and services require access to DNS (the domain name service), and many services and applications depend on consistent timekeeping across all systems on a network (such as accounting systems). Almost everything on a network depends on the basic routing and lower-level protocols. Therefore, maintaining these subsystems usually is a very high priority—though most users aren't even aware of them as distinct aspects of your work.

Initial Requirements Analysis

Your first opportunity to perform requirements analysis is when you're considering a new job or an offered promotion. The purposes of the initial requirements analysis are to create the service-level specification and, ultimately, to gather enough information to decide whether or not you're willing to take on that specific set of responsibilities.

To summarize the process of determining requirements, we outline some processes appropriate to every organization. Before beginning the process, ask whether any other processes may be required by the circumstances of the organization.

- Identify the involved parties: you, your boss, his management, your users, your assistants, and so on
- Clarify the lines of authority
- Inventory the resources for which you're responsible:
  - Networks
  - Servers (hosts)
  - Peripherals and other equipment (hubs, routers, and so on)
  - Services (file sharing, printing, email, and so on)
  - Applications and subsystems
  - Phone systems, if applicable
- Poll the users—learn what representative members of each group *do* on each of "your" systems

Ongoing Requirements Analysis

From the initial requirements analysis, there will be ongoing opportunities to practice these skills. We suggest viewing every request by managers and users as a set of requirements that need some level of analysis.

For example, if a manager suddenly comes in and asks about setting up a web server, one could just enable the copy of Apache that probably came with LINUX, or just point him to any suitable server on which LINUX is installed.

However, asking a few questions might reveal that a much different approach is needed. Here are some questions to ask in this scenario:

- What information or resources are to be made available?
- Who should have access to it?
- Where are they located?
- What sorts of connections do they have?
- What speeds and protocols do these connections support?
- How sensitive is the data?
- From whom or whence will the information come?
- What are the risks associated with corruption or unauthorized revelation of these data?
- How much money, personnel time, and other resources are available?
- Who will control the content?

These are just a start. The answers to these questions will likely lead to other questions. Note the concern for security and ongoing management of the site emerging from these questions.

Obviously the situation might call for a common, publicly accessible web server, or it might be sufficient to just have it virtual hosted (maintained on an ISP's shared machine) or co-located (where one of your systems is placed at an ISP's location). These are all appropriate for some kinds of public web sites.

If the need is for internal use by employees while they are on-site, the system is an intranet server. This is where many of the more complicated issues about document sensitivity and access control are usually encountered. However, authenticated and differential access to private resources by authorized representatives of other organizations define an extranet. This entails very nearly the same security concerns as an intranet server.

What is less obvious is that a completely different solution such as an automated mailing list or mail responder mailbot may be required. You might even find that the web, for all its popularity and ubiquity, is not appropriate to your manager's requirements. Granted, these days it's hard to imagine any business or institution that has a good reason *not* to hang out its "cyberspace shingle," but you'll never know unless you ask. This example was chosen precisely because it initially seems like such a "no-brainer."

The Process

The process of transforming a request into a specification should be simple, quick, and easy, yet thorough enough to ensure that meeting the specification will solve not just a symptom but the real problem at hand.

This process may vary somewhat from one organization to the next, but it will generally involve most or all of the following steps. If the project is urgent, these may all be taken in a single day. Emergency projects may condense the process to a quick discussion among the most senior system administrators. But the objectives of the process remain invariant—to determine the real problem at hand, and what would constitute a solution.

Abstract the Problem Description

Often a request or requirement will be expressed as a directive to implement a specific approach or proposed solution—for example, "We need to install a new web server." You'll want to abstract from that to find out the desired results. "What information are we trying to publish, and to whom should it be accessible?"

We can, of course, just do what is being asked of us. In some cases *that* is what is required. However, if we understand more about the desired results or the intended goal, we are far more likely to offer good recommendations. Even when we consult with others (such as by posting to a newsgroup), "Which is *the best* web server?" is likely to yield a less useful answer than "Which is the best web server *for* . . . ."

Clarify the Authorities

The first thing to be done is to know whose requirements are to be met. Ultimately there is a person or group of persons who judges whether an effort has been beneficial or detrimental to the overall mission of the organization. It will usually but not always be appropriate to define the problem in terms of their requirements.

A system administrator who understands the business as well as those who will judge his performance may seek to meet the requirements of the shareholders above the parochial interests of managers. While doing so may be the most ethical thing a system administrator ever does professionally, the risks should not be taken lightly. It will usually suffice to point out to a manager that a particular path of action does not appear to be in the interests of the shareholders. A manager intent on doing the wrong thing may sometimes be dissuaded by nothing short of a senior system administrator offering his resignation. If the resignation is accepted, it would not have been a good environment in which to work anyway.

Even after identifying the group whose requirements are to be primary, it will usually be necessary to consider the requirements of various secondary and tertiary groups. For example, in investment banking the needs of the traders are paramount, but the needs of bureaucrats and others must also be satisfied.

Define Metrics for Success

Having selected the persons whose requirements are to be met, the next step is to determine exactly what constitutes success in meeting them. In other words, a set of metrics must be found by which one may readily determine the extent to which efforts have been successful. For example, if the requirement is fewer workstation crashes, the metric could be mean time between failure or number of crashes per unit of time.

Ask Open Questions

It will often be necessary to survey the persons whose requirements are to be met—both in order to understand the real requirements and in order to define metrics for determining success. While many questions will be specific, even having "yes" or "no" answers, some questions should be open-ended, such as "What are your concerns?" "What could we do to help you be more productive?" "What about our operation causes you the most grief?"

Write the Specification

Each specification should be formalized in writing. This will ensure that everyone has agreed to the same thing. Unless the specification is for a particularly important project, it should probably be written by a mid-level system administrator, with guidance from senior system administrators or a manager if necessary.

Once a draft has been written, and the system administrators who may be involved with the project are satisfied with it, it must be submitted along with cost estimates to the users for approval.

Implicit Requirements

Now that we've covered the process of determining your site's specific requirements, we can make the observation that all sites will have some requirements in common. These are issues that every system administrator will almost certainly have to consider. These are the implicit requirements of the job.

Maintain System Resource Availability

This is, in our opinion, the system administrator's "prime directive." The most obvious of the implicit requirements that follow from the prime directive is "don't break the systems." Or, from a different perspective, "keep the systems up and running." Of course, these two statements don't carry quite the same implications.

The most common cause of system downtime for LINUX and UNIX systems is operator or administrator error. We've all heard of the hapless system administrator who typed `rm -fr *` from the wrong directory. It doesn't take anything nearly so dramatic or obvious to "break" a LINUX system when logged in as `root`.

System administrators frequently have to install or upgrade new system software (such as new kernels, security patches, and so on). Ideally, you would like to rehearse each of these major system upgrades in a staging environment prior to "rolling them out" to production. However, time constraints frequently don't allow everything to be done twice, and budget constraints limit how closely staging environments can duplicate production environments.

In addition, the system administrator is expected to be able to maintain the availability of the system's resources even in the face of various disasters—ranging from data loss to accidental deletion and corruption to the destruction or theft of whole systems. So, recovery planning is another set of requirements that follows from our first implicit requirement.

When we examine the term availability and broaden our concept of system resources to include CPU cycles, network bandwidth, and disk space, we find that our management and users are likely to consider a wide variety of capacity planning failures to be disasters. So, performance monitoring and capacity planning are also implicit.

In summary, we've found a cascade of requirements that result from our "prime directive:"

- Maintain system resource availability.
- Design, implement, and test recovery plans.
- Monitor and tune system performance.
- Plan for necessary capacity.
- Provide a logical network organization.
- Monitor and preserve system security and integrity.

These requirements are explained in the other chapters of Part I.

Facilitate Upgrades, Expansions, and New Installations

Just maintaining existing systems should usually be less than half of a system administrator's job—or the job of fewer than half the system administrators. As organizations change, so do their systems and networks. The entire commercial software industry is devoted to convincing users to change their systems (via upgrades as well as new purchases). That's in addition to the many other causes of network and system change.

In 1991, the web was a novelty—a set of tools and protocols used by some physicists to facilitate sharing of technical documents with easily followed cross-references. Now it is the core of many businesses. You'll probably end up putting your organization's policies and procedures manuals on an intranet web server (if they aren't there already).

A few years ago the notion of telecommuting was practically unknown. We may soon see businesses that perform the majority of their operations via remote links. We're already seeing the emergence of virtual offices—where all the employees work from home and/or in the field. These environments present new challenges to system administrators.

Every upgrade, expansion, and new system installation follows from some requirement. The analysis of each set of requirements that leads to these expansion and upgrade plans is fundamentally similar to the process you use in creating your service-level specification. You identify the involved parties (that is the manager whose department needs to do more printing), clarify the lines of authority (who approves the plans, purchasing, and other decisions), and so on.

Operational Analysis

Ideally, in your role as a system administrator you'll find creative opportunities to fundamentally improve operations for your organization. You may be able to eliminate repetitive typing by writing a script to feed a report into another database or transaction system. You might be able to reduce the consumption of paper and toner by providing the staff with better previewing tools (or training them in the use of those already installed).

In a typical case you might find someone printing a set of reports from one system or application and then re-entering some of the data into a set of forms in another. This risk is as prevalent today, with intranet thin client applications using HTML forms and CGI scripts as the middleware between browsers and various sorts of database and custom work-flow management applications on the back end, as it was when minicomputers started performing some of the tasks once performed only by mainframes. The initial volume of transactions handled in these situations may make the forms-based interface the right choice. However, it's easy for that to change without layers of management noticing how much employee time is spent on the processing.

There are specialists who analyze an organization's operations in order to design and implement these sorts of improvements in work processes (not surprisingly, they're called operations analysts). It is the opinion of the authors that all employees and participants in all rational organizations should strive to do some "operational analysis"—to ask "Why are we doing this?" and "Is there a better way to do this?" System administrators are uniquely positioned to perform such analyses because they are already involved in such a broad range of operations and analyses.

Decisions and Recommendations

LINUX system administrators are constantly called upon to make decisions and recommendations. LINUX has the legendary power and flexibility of UNIX, embodying a "toolbox" approach to computing. It provides a set of "mechanisms" from which site-specific solutions may be built, freeing organizations from policies conceived by software vendors. This flexibility and power are both blessing and curse to the LINUX system administrator.

LINUX and UNIX are less constraining than other operating systems. Because they don't set our policies, we must select the tools and methods that match our requirements. To do this we must understand our requirements and know our options.

That's what the rest of this book is about. As described in Chapter 1, "The Prime Directive," one of the themes in this book is "There are usually other options."

Further Study

The topic of requirements analysis is worthy of an entire book, such as *Exploring Requirements: Quality Before Design* by Donald C. Gause and Gerald M. Weinberg.[1] Although it is written for software developers, it is an excellent resource on the topic.

Learning requirements analysis might profoundly affect your personal life as well as your career. Learning to distinguish between requirements and preferences, to identify the involved parties in any problem or process, to define the constraints, to set priorities, and to enable yourself to "think outside of the box" by deferring commitment to any proposed solution until you understand the problem—these are the seeds of success in any endeavor.

---

1. © 1989, Dorsett House Press, New York, NY.

Chance fights ever on the side of the prudent.

~Euripides

3

Recovery Planning

MAINTAIN ACCESS TO SYSTEM RESOURCES: With that as part of our Prime Directive, it logically follows that we must prevent disasters to the extent possible, and be able to recover from as many others as are unavoidable (or unavoid-*ed*, as the case may be).

Every responsible professional and publication advises users and administrators of computer systems to do backups. On the surface, this seems simple enough—a backup is basically a copy of a data set that promises a way to recover it from loss or damage.

However, backups are only a tiny portion of the problem; in fact, the focus must be on recovery. The recovery scenarios you plan will dictate how your backups must be done—and a lack of planning and testing may mean that any erroneous decisions made during the creation of backups won't be understood until it's too late.

Moreover, data recovery is only a facet in a broader process of disaster recovery planning, risk assessment, and operational analysis.

Here are some questions to ask:

- What is the total volume of information that you have?

- How much of it changes over various intervals (per day, per week, per month)?

- Are there any availability considerations that limit when and how long your systems can access the data for backup and restoration?

- Are there any dependencies or synchronization issues? What are the risks of having related files "out of sync" with one another?

- How quickly do you need to be able to restore selected files?

- What is your disaster plan for complete system loss or failure? For destruction or loss of access to your site (computing center)?

- What are the expectations of your management and users?

- What resources do you have available (Remember: system administrator time, system administrator expertise, media/drive capacity, I/O bandwidth, vendor support, and so on)?

The point of these questions is to differentiate between your needs and the mythical "standard backup procedure." The first problem for system administrators charged with developing backup strategies is overcoming the common user and management misconception that there is some widespread convention that covers *everyone's* backup needs. To do so we shift focus to recovery. Usable data recovery plans should be derived from an overall disaster/recovery plan. That, in turn, should come from comprehensive enterprise risk assessment.

Although making backups is an important part of most recovery plans, it is only one method toward the real goal. Sites that don't periodically perform recovery drills usually find that their backups are useless. A backup is a complex process regardless of the specific tools used—software, tape drives, or other media. It is easy to misuse or misconfigure even the simplest and most straightforward programs. It's even easier to miss the implications that some system upgrades have for recovery plans.

For example, sites using dump may find that they've forgotten to account for a newly added drive. Sites may elect to skip backups of some filesystems that are used for temporary files, news spools, and so on, and find that some user or system administrator has been using some of that space for more important files (through a symlink, perhaps).

The only absolutely reliable way to ensure that backup procedures, scripts, and media are all working is to periodically restore an entire system, and place it in production. This carries obvious risks, and should be done carefully and only as often as is necessary.

Performing more limited recovery tests (for instance, by selectively restoring a few files) on a production system still has risks. That's why it's preferable to have a separate system that can be used for this purpose. An ideal time to do this is while receiving new systems and deploying full system upgrades. This can briefly delay the production deployment process—but it ensures that recovery processes are sound and well-understood.

Restarting from Scratch

The default recovery plan is to start from scratch. Those who suffer a disaster for which they have not prepared are left with this "last resort."

In many cases, recovering from scratch is the best plan. As systems are used and upgraded, they tend to accumulate clutter (*cruft*), and an organization may make a business case against devoting administrative resources to performing backups for *some* systems, such as client workstations, instead ensuring that they can be built anew. It's also reasonable for redundant clusters of servers. For example, a large software company distributing its shareware via ftp chose this model for a group of several ftp servers.

The recovery plan was the same as that for installing an additional server: replicate any of the properly working servers by copying the system files through a network link, and push the data to the new server (automatically done from a "master" server for all the other servers as part of the normal publication and release process using `rdist` and/or `rsync`).

This example demonstrates one of the key advantages of LINUX on commodity PCs over traditional server and network operating systems. It's often more cost-effective to deploy redundant systems, which are likely to provide better performance as well as fault tolerance. Many of the common TCP/IP protocols and services, such as DNS, SMTP, and NIS, are naturally scalable—providing support for "secondary" or "slave" servers by design. As discussed in Chapter 4, "Capacity Planning," many other services and protocols are readily scaled with simple round robin DNS.

The "no backups" model is used by many ISPs and academic computing facilities. Their users are expected to maintain backups of any data that they care about (mail folders, virtual-hosted web documents, files in their FTP directories, and so on). In the event of a failure, the ISP will bring up a new machine (or one with a newly installed operating system) and notify the affected customers of the need to restore their content.

The Rescue Disk

The first step in recovering from most catastrophic system failures is to boot into some system where diagnostic, repair, and restore commands can be issued.

The LINUX system administrator's toolkit should include a boot/root floppy for every major type of system supported. It is often possible to build one with sufficient drivers to work in all LINUX machines within an organization, particularly if the boot diskette just needs enough access to the network to mount an NFS exported (read-only) partition with a full set of recovery tools.

There are many "microdistributions" of LINUX—whole systems that fit on one to three floppies and that run completely from RAMdisks. The most popular is probably Tom's Root/Boot,[1] created and maintained by Tom Oesher. This one is fairly easy to customize and is sufficiently "complete" to allow full network client access. Thus, one can customize a Root/Boot with a DHCP client or with a static "recovery" IP address and set up an `rc*` script that mounts an NFS partition and performs an automated reinstallation and/or recovery over the network. Another popular package is YARD (Yet Another Rescue Diskette), which is a set of Perl scripts for creating rescue diskettes.[2]

---

1. `http://www.toms.net/rb/`

2. `http://www.croftj.net/~fawcett/yard/`

Automated Installations

As discussed in Chapter 15, "Automated Installation and Upgrade," the Red Hat distribution supports a KickStart feature (conceptually similar to Sun's JumpStart), which allows the system administrator to write a script that automates the entire installation process, including drive partitions, filesystem creation (mkfs), package selection, installation, and configuration. This can be used to create a "no hands" installation diskette for new systems. Other forms of automated installation are also discussed in Chapter 15, "Automated Installation and Upgrade."

For many systems, an automated installation process may provide more effective recovery than traditional "backup/restore" plans. On a typical workstation, far more space is devoted to "expendable" files (those included on the installation CDs for the operating system and applications, caches, and so on) than to the system's data. Knowing this, a system administrator can focus on protecting the data. There are a number of ways to do this.

The Rescue Root Partition

In addition to maintaining rescue diskettes, it is wise to create an additional small partition on each system drive for a kernel and a full suite of repair tools and configuration snapshots—100MB is plenty of space. Then, if a root partition becomes unusable, it may be possible to boot into this rescue partition and repair or replace the root partition. Naturally there are some forms of disk failure and/or corruption from which this will not recover, so a recovery diskette may still be useful.

Auto–Rescue Configuration

There is a tricky way to set up a system that can automatically recover from some classes of damage to the root filesystem. Set up the production root and the "rescue root" and copy all of the basic files between them. On the rescue root, put an additional copy (perhaps in a .tar file) of the production root's /etc files.

Then modify the /etc/rc.d/rc.* files on the rescue root to perform fsck of the production root—with an error handler and timeout that can abort the filesystem check if necessary; an expect script is a good way to do this. If the fsck fails, you can have your script just mkfs.ext2 the production root and restore it—copy the whole rescue root over it, and then extract the production-etc.tar.gz file to overwrite the appropriate files that differ between the two filesystems. The result is that the "rescue root" can automatically restore the filesystem that's used in production mode.

The next part of the trick, which makes this *automatic,* is to make the rescue root filesystem the default in /etc/lilo.conf. Now a normal boot will bring up the kernel on the "rescue root."

However, it's best not to do that every time the machine boots—only when there is a problem and the system is reset abnormally. So change the "normal" shutdown sequence to include a command such as:

```
/sbin/lilo -R prod root=/dev/sda3
```

This command will set the default command line for the next reboot without affecting subsequent reboots or defaults. So, if the system is shut down normally, it boots from the production root filesystem. If it is reset in some other fashion, it defaults to the "auto-rescue" mode.

Partition Tables and Bootloader Code

Under LINUX it's easy to ensure recovery from corrupted partition tables and damage to a system's master boot record (MBR). The MBR is the first sector on the first track under the first head on any PC hard drive. It consists of two parts: some bootloader code and the partition table.

The bootloader code is supplied by any OS that runs on the system. Most LINUX systems use LILO (the LInux LOader) installed on the MBR of the primary hard disk. Some others might use GRUB (the GNU GRand Unified Bootloader). In other cases, one might use System Commander[3] or the WINDOWS NT or OS/2 Boot Manager on the MBR and run LILO in the logical boot record (or superblock of your root filesystem—or any of the LINUX filesystems, for that matter).

There are a number of common situations where the bootloader code may get replaced or damaged without affecting the partition tables, despite the fact that both share the same sector. Most boot sector viruses and the installation software for many operating systems replace the bootloader code located in the MBR with their own version—typically moving any existing bootloader into another "unused" sector on track zero.

So, there is a common need to restore the bootloader code when it has been overwritten. The easy way is to simply run /sbin/lilo.[4] This will read the /etc/lilo.conf file (by default) and build a new boot record as specified therein. It will append the existing partition table to the bootloader code and merge in the BIOS disk address of LILO's map files. These maps enable the LILO bootloader code to find kernels, boot messages, and other files without any "knowledge" of the filesystems on which they are stored.

So, to restore bootloader code after it's been replaced by, for example, the latest reinstallation of WINDOWS NT, just run /sbin/lilo with no arguments (assuming a proper /etc/lilo.conf file).

One could be defensive and rerun lilo during every shutdown, for example. However, this might be riskier than having the system simply fail to boot on the rare occasions when

---

3. A commercial boot loader and partition table manager that is especially useful for booting multiple different versions of MS-DOS and/or other Microsoft operating systems—which normally can't coexist with one another.

4. Note the distinction between LILO (the bootloader package) and /sbin/lilo, the command that generates boot blocks. See Chapter 9, "Booting and Shutdown," for more detail.

the kernels, partition tables, or boot message files have been changed. In any event, there is no defense as effective as maintaining a well-tested rescue floppy and recent backups.

As noted, lilo doesn't modify or restore the partition table. That can be done manually with fdisk. However, there's an easy way to automate that. Use the dd command to take a snapshot of the whole MBR (or even just of the last 66 bytes—which is the partition table of four entries of 16 bytes each and its "signature" 0x55AAh). Then use dd to restore these.

Here's an example of saving the whole MBR on a system's primary IDE hard disk to a file under root's home directory:

```
dd if=/dev/hda of=/root/recovery/mbr.bin count=1
```

Note that we use the device node for the whole disk, not /dev/hda1, which is a node that refers only to the first partition on that disk. For the primary SCSI hard drive, we'd use /dev/sda as dd's if (input file). GNU dd defaults to a block size (bs=) of 512 bytes, though we could also be more careful by supplying that parameter.

To restore this MBR to a system, just reverse the if and of parameters on the dd command:

```
dd of=/dev/hda if=/root/recovery/mbr.bin count=1 bs=512
```

and run /sbin/lilo in case the kernels or other file-to-disk-block mappings might have changed since our mbr.bin snapshot was made.

Of course, we could also save *just* the partition table using a few different parameters to dd:

```
dd if=/dev/hda of=/root/recovery/ptable.bin count=66 bs=1 skip=446
```

which we would restore with:

```
dd of=/dev/hda if=/root/recovery/ptable.bin count=66 bs=1 skip=446
```

In these latter cases we shouldn't have to rerun /sbin/lilo since we haven't touched the bootloader code in the first 446 bytes of the MBR.

Either of these techniques is easy enough for manual operations or scripts that will be run manually. The latter form, which copies only the partition table, would be better for a cron job—taking a new snapshot of the partition table once a day, running cmp between it and the original, and sending out alerts if there is any difference. One could also test the integrity of the whole MBR—though it should be noted that /sbin/lilo seems to include some sort of timestamp in the boot code it generates. Thus, any run of lilo will result in a change to LILO's portion of the MBR, even if nothing has changed in any of the related files. One could certainly write two separate portions to this check script to report changes to the MBR as a whole and to the partition table specifically.

When restoring a system from a catastrophic failure, one can skip the manual fdisk execution entirely and just use dd to put a new partition table into place. Although in theory this should only be done with drives of the same geometry, it works on most modern drives (SCSI and IDE) regardless. Indeed, the internal geometry of a modern drive is increasingly meaningless to the host system, since zone bit recording is used to achieve varying numbers of sectors per track, auto-translation, linear block addressing, and other abstractions that make the traditional "cylinder, head, sector" model obsolete. In any event, for similar-sized hard drives, the dd command can automate the process of preparing the partition table, and a command like:

```
for i in hda1 hda3 hda4; do mke2fs -c -q /dev/$i; done
```

can be used to make new filesystems on selected partitions. In this example we assume that /dev/hda2 might be a swap partition, and show a list that might perhaps be for /, /usr, and /var.

There is a utility that may help those who hadn't the foresight to backup a partition table before it became damaged. Gordon Chaffee wrote a little tool to create partition tables. It may be found at

```
http://bmrc.berkeley.edu/people/chaffee/fat32.html
```

Filesystems

Filesystems should be robust enough to obviate the problem of users and system administrators deleting and overwriting needed files. Most current filesystems lack such functionality, although several types of filesystems are capable of providing it.

Each time a file is written to disk, the previous version of the file should not be marked for removal. Rather, it should be marked read-only and hidden from ordinary viewing. A command such as ls -a could be used to view these previous copies along with other hidden files.

At the time of this writing, a filesystem expected to provide such functionality called ext3 is under development for LINUX. LINUX kernels numbered 2.4 and higher are expected to include ext3.

An alternative to such a filesystem is the snapshot filesystem. Snapshots of the filesystem are taken periodically (such as hourly or daily); these comprise read-only copies of the inodes as they existed at the time of the snapshot. An example implementation is Network Appliance's WAFL filesystem.

There are no snapshot filesystems for LINUX, but, a crude approximation may be implemented in user space by the system administrator. Doing so is a matter of copying an entire filesystem or directory structure to another filesystem.

Snapshot Partitions

These days, hard drive space is inexpensive, so it's easy to justify additional filesystems and/or partitions on which to periodically place snapshots of selected production files. Although such pseudo-snapshots are not as efficient as snapshot filesystems and lack some features of traditional backup to a tape or removable medium, they can be more expedient for many situations.

Tape drives are often slow, and at many sites their expense justifies sharing them across internal networks. A restore that's needed in the middle of the day will often be slow in its own right and will possibly consume quite a bit of network bandwidth as well. Worse, the user who needs one tree of files will usually not have sufficient permissions to access all of the other files on a given tape. So a system administrator is usually required to restore files from tape servers and on multi-user hosts.

Most data loss is caused by accidental deletion by users or system administrators. Often the loss is noticed within minutes. If there is a copy of the file that's only one day old and is readily retrievable by a simple sequence of mount and cp commands, such a restore will save quite a bit of time and really impress the users. This may be implemented with a nightly cron job that mounts the pseudo-snapshot filesystem, runs an rsync script to synchronize the pseudo-snapshot with the production filesystem, and dismounts it.

Note that this is completely different from RAID mirroring with the md driver and commands or with hardware RAID controllers. Those are solutions to a different problem. If someone accidentally deletes a file on a RAID filesystem, it will almost certainly be removed from both disks before any recovery effort can be undertaken. RAID is intended to protect against hardware failures—the loss of a hard disk, the crash of one of its heads, or (in some configurations) even the loss of a disk controller.

Our pseudo-snapshot model relies on the fact that most accidental deletions are detected by the end of the day—usually within moments after the user presses the Enter key. However, it is possible to maintain multiple snapshots taken at various intervals.

Of course, one can use RAID mirroring, striping, and redundancy on these production and snapshot filesystems in conjunction with such scripts and in just about any configuration.

A different variation of this trick is to use "blank" partitions and/or whole hard disks with no filesystems created on them. You can use these as the targets to a tar or cpio command. Since the ext2 filesystem has a 2GB limit[5] as the maximum size of any single file, it is convenient to use the "raw" disk partitions for these sorts of "snapshot" archives.

One major advantage of exporting snapshots to the workstations of power users is that it enables the system administrators to provide direct user access to recent files. One can mark these snapshot filesystems as user-mountable in the /etc/fstab file (man mount(8) and fstab(5) for details). This allows users to recover their own files without system administrator intervention and without raising additional security and access concerns (assuming replication of directory trees rather than use of tar or cpio to raw partitions).

One easy way to take a snapshot of a full directory tree is to use the -a (archive) option with the Gnu cp command. This is equivalent to a combination of other options that recurses the directory structures, and preserves ownership and permissions. It's often useful to also include the -x option to prevent the directory recursion from traversing filesystem boundaries (down into other mounted filesystems). So, to make a snapshot of

---

5. This limit applies only to 32-bit systems. The Alpha and UltraSPARC versions of Linux don't suffer from this limitation.

the root, /usr, and /home directory trees onto a secondary drive, we might use a script like:

```
mount /dev/sdb1 /mnt/tmp &&
        cd /mnt/tmp  &&
        cp -ax / /usr /home .
umount /mnt/tmp
```

In this example, we use conditional execution to ensure that the cp command is *not* executed if the mount or cd commands fail for any reason.

A more elaborate script might check the available space and make a directory (based on the date name, for example) with a command like date+%Y%m%d. This date format is preferred by system administrators because it is Y2K-compliant (providing a four-digit year, followed by month and date) and because the normal sorting done by ls and similar commands will show these in proper date order. That script would also have to "age" the older directories, check available disk/free space, and so on.

Another way of replicating a filesystem tree is to use the GNU cpio command's -p (pass-through) option:

```
find / /usr /home -mount ... | cpio -p /mnt/tmp
```

This can be used with any set of parameters to the find command to control the exact list of files to be passed through to the snapshot. It's possible to use multiple different find and other commands using shell command grouping such as:

```
(
 find /   -mount ...
 find /usr  -mount ...
 find /home -mount ... ) |
        sort -u |
        comm -13 - /root/snapshot.exclude |
        cpio -p /mnt/tmp
```

In this example, we apply different sets of options to the different invocations of the find command. These are run in a subshell, forcing the output from all of them to be funneled into one common stream for the pipe. We pass the resulting list through sort (removing duplicates with -u), preparing the list for the comm command, which filters filenames *common* to both the list generated from our find commands and those listed in our "exclude" file. Finally, any files that aren't filtered out are passed to the cpio command, which reads the list and performs its "pass-through" archiving.

System Documentation

One of the most frustrating and time-consuming problems encountered during system recovery is the need to research the system's hardware and low-level configuration.

Getting all of the IRQs and other settings right is often a nuisance in the first place—or a series of nuisances encountered over several months as the system evolves. Good documentation precludes the need to duplicate all of that work during an emergency.

Therefore, it's a good idea to keep a summary of each system's hardware and software configuration handy. Then, if the operating system needs to be reinstalled from scratch, you'll know what kind of video card is installed and what selection it requires in the Xconfigurator menu; what SCSI card is installed and which kernel, drivers, or modules need to be enabled to use it; and so on.

We recommend keeping an online set of notes in /etc/README (or /etc/README.$hostname, as the case may be) and printing two copies: one for the regular filing system, and one set to tape *inside the case* (possibly with an extra boot diskette).

This README file should also contain information about software configuration, especially any deviations from the organization's standards, as well as information such as who built the system and when, who are currently responsible for it and how they may be contacted, what systems depend on this one and on what systems this one depends, during what times it may be taken down for maintenance, and who needs to be notified beforehand. Additional information may be needed by some sites.

It is important to keep the README file up-to-date. Another good idea is to require that changes be logged with a timestamp and the name of the system administrator who made the change, along with the version and location of the package that can restore the change if the system needs to be rebuilt. Changes are usually made for good reasons, but the reasons are not always immediately obvious to other system administrators.

Hint: Keep a Printed Partition Table Handy

One lifesaver for a damaged partition table is to have a printout of what it's meant to look like for each system. Then, one can use the LINUX fdisk command to rebuild the partition table from scratch and run lilo to rebuild the bootloader block (the "other part" of a master boot record). Often one can recover a non-booting system with no data loss and no need to restore from backups by simply rebuilding the MBR.

Risk Assessment

The first step to take before planning for disaster recovery is to list the threats. Many sorts of disasters may befall a system administrator. Try to think of as many as you can, and then survey your users to find all the things they think could go wrong. They will usually come up with some that you overlooked. We'll discuss some common disasters, which you may want to add to your list if your survey didn't produce them. Then you'll need to assess the risks posed by all the conceivable disasters in terms of likelihood and consequences in order to prioritize them. Once your management has approved a prioritized list of disasters for which you need to be prepared, you can examine recovery options and plan recovery strategies.

Note that these risks must be assessed from the standpoint of the impact they will have on the business, not just the impact they will have on the computer systems.

Here we list some common risks that system administrators face. Most system administrators will require a plan for coping with all of them, but some will find that the need for preparedness for some kinds of disasters doesn't justify the cost.

User Error

The most common disaster from which recovery is needed is the deletion or overwriting of a needed file. In an ideal world, this would never be a problem because all filesystems would support journaling, and users would then be able to recover from these errors themselves. The good news is that progress is being made toward journaling filesystems for LINUX. But in the meantime, system administrators must be prepared to recover files for users who delete them. In large organizations, the system administrator's department could bill the user's department for each such restore. This encourages users to be careful, and to only request files that are really needed, which is an economy for the organization as a whole.

Administrator Error

Nearly as common as accidental deletion by users is accidental deletion by system administrators. While system administrators are generally far more careful than ordinary users, they use commands that are inherently more dangerous. Thus, when a system administrator errs, he often does so on a grander scale than any user could. Again, better filesystems will help here, but not necessarily to the extent as with the sort of single file deletions that beset users.

System administrators should be in the habit of stringing together commands using double ampersands rather than semicolons. This ensures that, for example, if a cd fails, the following rm will not execute in the wrong directory.[6] As we discuss in Chapter 11, "Scripting," scripts are an even better way to reduce the likelihood of a typo causing a disaster.

Also, system administrators should *always* use absolute pathnames.[7] Some commands may have different instances in different locations in the filesystem, and invoking the wrong one may be consequential. The use of absolute pathnames also affords some protection against Trojan Horses.

---

6. Some versions of UNIX have included implementations of cd which did not return a failure exit status. This should not be a problem with LINUX, but it is always appropriate to test such things before relying on them.

7. Like most absolutes, this has exceptions. Consider a link foo -> ../usr/bin/foo in the /bin directory. An absolute link does the wrong thing if this system disk is mounted under /mnt, perhaps for recovery or building.

To reduce the likelihood of administrator error, it is important when making any sort of change to a production system that there is a plan for testing, deployment, and regression. You should have the plan checked by others and then follow the plan.

Hardware Failure

Hardware failure is another common cause of crises. The best defenses against hardware failure are redundant systems and having spares on hand, along with a practiced procedure for replacing the failed hardware. When a hard disk fails, the procedure will sometimes be complex, and should always be well-documented.

Utility Outages

Everywhere in the world, utilities such as power and telecommunication are less than perfectly reliable. In some places reliability is worse than in others. But one must always consider the impact that a utility outage may have on the business, and what may be done in preparation and in response.

Power outages generally shut down LINUX systems uncleanly. At least in the case of servers, most organizations will want to have enough UPS capacity to perform a clean shutdown. Many organizations will have emergency power from their own generators, with batteries to cleanly handle the transition. This emergency power is not without cost, so determine which systems are critical to the operation of the business, and see that continuous power is available to them.

Many data centers have two separate power sources (fed from different utility substations), with cabinets having a power strip fed from each source. One runs up the left side, and the other runs up the right. Systems with redundant power supplies, such as routers and major servers, are plugged into each. Frequently, at least one of these two power sources will be backed up by generators and batteries, because utility outages often affect more than one substation.

An interruption in external data communications is not as catastrophic as a loss of electricity, but it can still shut down operations for some businesses and impair the operations of others. If loss of telco would cost the business enough to justify it, redundancy is called for. One may order lines from different demarcation points in the building, running along different trenches, to different telco central offices. All of this costs money and is fundamentally a business decision. The role of the system administrator is to help document risks, options, and their costs so that management may make an informed decision.

Software Defects

Many disasters are caused by software defects, particularly with closed, proprietary software. These disasters involve the loss of data, so a system administrator can protect against them (to a degree) by ensuring that copies of the data are available somewhere safe from production software. Then, if data are corrupted by a software bug, the correct data can be restored.

Security Breaches and Sabotage

It is often important to protect data against intentional destruction by both authorized and unauthorized users—even against destruction by root. If a disgruntled employee who either knows or acquires the root password erases everything at his disposal, what will it take to recover, and what will it cost the business?

Obviously, prevention is important, so it is covered from two different perspectives in Chapters 7 and 8, "Security Policy" and "Enforcing Security." But consideration must be given to recovery if prevention fails. In some cases, it might be justified to have two system administrators sign off that redundant sets of tapes or CD-Rs contain correct copies of important data and then to store them in different safes to which the system administrators do not have access. Sometimes there will be legal requirements to ensure that data are available; even stricter protocols may be required, possibly involving armed guards in extreme cases.

But the principle is the same—ensure that data remain available even in cases of a malicious or incompetent system administrator.

Key Personnel

The loss of key personnel may be just as disastrous as loss of data. Of course, good management always seeks to prevent the loss of key personnel, but sometimes disaster strikes despite the best attempts at prevention. Thus, planning the recovery from the loss of a person is no less important.

There are four general areas of preparation to protect against the loss of experienced key personnel: documentation, cross-training, satisfactory compensation, and ensuring that personnel do not "burn out" or suffer from stress-related health problems.

Environmental Disasters

Floods, fires, and earthquakes routinely damage businesses in a variety of ways. One way is by interrupting computer operations. If necessary, steps may be taken to ensure continued operations even during an environmental disaster. One of the authors was responsible for building a computational infrastructure for a large investment bank that would generate a set of government-mandated reports every night—no matter what. Three sets of servers were set up—two in New York and one in London—with four transatlantic connections along different undersea cables, and with well-backed-up power sources. Most businesses do not have such extreme needs, but this example illustrates the sort of preparations that can be made for environmental disasters.

Other Disasters

Many organizations will face other kinds of disasters not listed here. Thinking about the possibilities and then asking users and management will go a long way toward making the list complete. Of course, if some unforeseen disaster does strike, it should be added to the list for the future.

Accordingly, it may be worth considering how to recover from a complete disaster—that is, everything is simply gone or destroyed, including archives and key personnel. Giving this some thought may help in preparing for lesser disasters.

Assess Costs and Consequences

Once all the different sorts of disasters have been enumerated, it is time to assess the cost of preparing for and recovering from each sort of disaster. This process will typically include both your management and your users' management.

The first step in assessing cost is evaluating (literally *placing a value on*) resources. Data files are only one of many sorts of resources that this would cover, though they are most relevant to this discussion.

Obviously each system is a resource. Less obvious is the value of each system's configuration. How much does a system cost to configure? Do you have a standard workstation configuration (such that you could automatically install complete software on a new system and drop it on an employee's desktop)? How much does it cost to install and configure each service on a server? Has everything been packaged for automatic installation and configuration?

A part of this process relies on operational analysis. For example, a programming team or Help Desk might be able to function for some time without a printer—most of their work is on-screen, and quite a bit of their interaction is via email. However, an accounts receivable department might be crippled without access to the printers and forms that produce the bills that are sent to customers.

Having assessed the costs, management will need to decide which preventative measures will be taken, and how much to budget for recovery if prevention fails.

Data Resources

In the context of data recovery, we focus on the data resources. We divide these into software (excluding software in development), configuration data, and transient data—including both data that are generated internally and data that are obtained from external sources—data that are under development, data that are the product of business operations, and databases. For most organizations the most valuable data are those which they've generated and/or gathered themselves—databases in particular.

Software

The disk drive in a typical workstation contains a large body of data that was included with the system and the applications. For most sites, these data are available via the original installation media (operating system and application CDs). These data are "valuable" in one sense—other data cannot be accessed in any meaningful way without the appropriate applications, which in turn can't run without the operating system. However, the cost of such a loss is low because reinstalling the operating system and applications should be easy. However, the risk of corruption for many of these files can be significant, particularly in cases of intentional corruption (such as Trojan horses and logic bombs).

Configuration Data

A typical system also includes site-specific applications and configuration files. On client systems, these generally represent a low risk. Presumably the original sources and binaries for custom applications will be available on a server, and most sorts of configuration files are easily regenerated. Ideally, they should all be packaged. With the advent of inexpensive CD-ROM writers, it is now common for sites to "cut" CDs containing packages for all their applications and templates.

Configuration data usually represents a medium level of value—it can be regenerated at the cost of a system administrator's time. Often (particularly with Microsoft WINDOWS and WINDOWS NT systems), configuration files are concealed within an application and can't easily be isolated and restored separately. This is one of the egregious deficiencies of those systems. Configuration data should always be packaged so that they may be automatically reinstalled after (or along with) the base system software.

Transient Data

There is a tremendous amount of transient data flowing through most organizations today. NetNews articles, browser cache files, and other temporary files are typically of almost no value, although they do represent some risks other than simple loss or even corruption. The loss of a whole news spool filesystem or a directory full of temporary files usually represents only a minor inconvenience. In the exceptional cases of applications that require access to temporary files for days at a time, it is worth requiring that they have "checkpointing" features that allow processing to continue after an interruption. These are the sorts of temporary files that are worth including in your recovery plan.

Then there is email. This is a special case that straddles the line between transient and persistent data. Some email, such as spam and common "Hey, let's do lunch" chatter, is of very low value. However, increasing numbers of email messages are vital to an organization's operations. Many individuals use their email as a personal information manager (PIM) and as a project management tool.

Thus, the value of most email is moderate if it has been retained at all. Loss of individual unread messages or spool files is usually easily remedied because most people archive their outgoing mail and can easily resend a failed or lost message. Also, the majority of email users expect occasional failure. Here's a case where user expectations work in our favor: If a message requires some response and fails to generate it, the sender will usually resend the request without much fuss.

One company we know routinely cuts a pair of identical CDs for anyone who leaves the company on good terms. These contain that employee's mail folders (archives) and home directory; one is given to the former employee, and the other is retained by the company.

Developmental Data

The next sorts of data on a typical system are "developmental" in nature. These could be sources for site-specific applications, drafts of ad copy and graphics being prepared by marketing and/or publications, sales proposals and contracts, or fiscal reports for the next quarterly or annual report. These are typically important files and documents. The risk of loss is quite high (particularly due to user error since these files are being edited/created). Loss of these data is also likely to be expensive—particularly in terms of personnel stress and frustration.

In the case of programming source code, there is reasonably widespread use of "revision control" software to manage the data by replicating files from a central repository to a developer's "working directory." This reduces the risk of data loss for each of the clients—and increases the value of the file server and the source code control systems.

Hopefully, we'll see these techniques applied to developers of other sorts of information—and we'll see the integration of revision control into "editors" of all sorts (including graphics and photofinishing applications). Just noting that "developers" can describe people other than programmers—that sales and marketing people are "developers" of other sorts of "sources"—may encourage IS managers to demand these features from software vendors.

Production Data

Flowing from this "developmental" data are "production documents" which usually should be archived. In many cases there are specific legal requirements for the retention of such documents and products. In many other cases the requirements stem from conventions of "best practice" and "due diligence" (particularly in the cases of financials and personnel records).

Traditionally, most of this information has been handled in paper form. The electronic forms of this information have often been supplemental. However, there is a trend toward implementing electronic document management systems. WORM and CD-ROM are often the technologies of choice here.

Databases

Finally, we have databases. Of course, we include any client/server and relational database systems in this category. However, we also include other aggregations of data—such as password/account files (NIS maps and so on), DNS zone tables, and `aliases` files.

Databases are often the most valuable data a site entrusts to its computing systems. They are also the most difficult to incorporate into a disaster recovery plan, because a running database will not maintain data integrity long enough for the data to be copied by traditional tools. Unless the filesystem provides snapshots, special tools provided by the database vendor must be used.

System administrators will have to work with the database administrators (DBAs) to develop a recovery plan for the databases. If the organization lacks DBAs, the system administrators will have to learn from the database vendor about the utilities available to safely back up a live database, unless backups can always be done while no one has write access to the databases. Typically, the system administrators will perform the backups, and the DBAs will perform the tests to verify them.

Those are the common types of data resources. Evaluating the risks associated with each type of data depends on the nature of the organization. We can identify classes of risks (security, which includes confidentiality, integrity, and access; recovery, which includes backup, restore, and corruption detection), but the costs of each must be determined for each site.

The Easy Cases

An important result of this risk assessment is that we may find that the most effective recovery strategy for many disasters doesn't involve traditional file or system "backups" at all. For example, a public web server that receives all of its data and configuration information via `rdist` from an internal staging host might have this recovery plan:

- Pull the preconfigured spare system from the shelf.
- Power it up.
- Set the IP address and so on, as necessary.
- Test it for functionality.
- Connect it to the network.
- Initiate an "update" push from the staging server.

The recovery plan for the failure of any individual client workstation should be to replace it with a spare. The failed machine can then be diagnosed and repaired later. Once repaired it should be added to the pool of spare clients.

In the case of a set of DNS name servers, the recovery plan might be to do a manual zone transfer from one of the other servers (secondary or primary). A set of SMTP/POP mail servers might have a similar plan: The server for the next available MX record starts receiving the mail automatically after a failure, and an administrator issues an `ifconfig` command to set an IP alias to re-enable POP for the affected clients. Part of that recovery plan might even include a mass mailing to a list of clients to warn of potentially lost mail.

Plan Recovery Strategies

Now, equipped with a prioritized list of the disasters for which preparations are to be made, and a budget for doing so, the strategies must be planned, for both prevention and recovery. The prevention strategies should be defined first, and then the recovery strategies.

Prevention strategies will include the following:

- Defining wise security policies
- Enforcing the security policies
- Keeping hardware spares on hand
- Putting in place redundant networks, power sources, and servers
- Keeping client machines free of data

Recovery strategies will include the following:

- Defining standard configurations for clients and for various types of servers
- Preparing one or more kickstart servers capable of building any standard configuration
- Preparing one or more packages that install all nonstandard files for any peculiar servers that must deviate from the standards
- Documenting the procedures for recovering from the various types of disaster that may occur

The strategies listed here are likely to meet the needs of most organizations. However, some sites may employ additional strategies. There are many possible strategies, most of which will not work. A particular strategy may seem sensible, but until it has been tested, it should not be relied upon.

Testing the Recovery Plans

Obviously most recovery plans depend on the data being available *somewhere*. In many cases the easiest way to ensure this is to perform regular backups and to regularly transport some of those to an off-site storage location—perhaps an underground vault in another state.

Focusing on "recovery" rather than "backups" makes another factor more obvious. It should raise questions like these:

- Do we have an inventory of spare parts?
- How long will it take to get necessary replacement equipment?
- Do we have reserve capital in place for this?

- Is our staff trained in these procedures?
- Have we verified that this plan will work?

This last question is the crucial one. *Have you tested the plan?* When was the last time you performed a recovery drill? How much of the plan did that drill account for? How much of the recovery plan does the recovery test plan cover? How many of the risks does the disaster plan cover?

One of the authors used to work in the technical support department of a large software company that produced a popular backup product. It was heartbreaking to talk to so many people who'd had the foresight to do backups but lacked the skepticism to test them . . . until it was too late.

Frequently these people were stressed because they had been doing backups for months or years and didn't know how to do a restore—until they lost a file. Occasionally their attempts to do a selective restore were frenetic enough to cause even more damage to their systems. In the worst cases, someone had decided to override the software's default and skip the verification pass (in order to halve the time it took for each backup), only to later find that none of their backups was readable.[8]

Obviously most of the questions raised here are beyond the simple technical question of how to back up and restore files to a UNIX system. However, we can view our role in the broader context. We should ask about the big picture and recommend solutions that fit into that puzzle. Thinking beyond the technical questions and considering the real requirements of our users is what distinguishes the professional system administrator from the "whiz kid" or "tape ape."

---

8. Sometimes the plights of these callers held a certain sad humor—like the guy who habitually stored his QIC-80 tapes in a "wooden box" under his desk. The box turned out to be an old speaker cabinet—with the large speaker and its powerful magnet still in it.

Performance optimization is 15% brains, 85% black magic.

~Linus Torvalds

4

Capacity Planning

Running out of steam is a disaster. If users are suddenly complaining about system response time, or if they are unable to complete their work due to a lack of disk space, then their system administrators have failed.

Our prime directive emphasizes the "availability of resources" to remind us that just maintaining existing systems is not enough. As an organization grows and changes, its resource utilization generally increases. We have already seen the difference between resources and systems—and have ensured (through recovery planning) that the current set of resources can be readily restored after various disasters.

Capacity planning ensures that resources will remain sufficient to meet future needs. It is the process of measuring and monitoring utilization of each resource, managing and possibly budgeting the consumption of those resources, and recommending upgrades, additions, and enhancements. As in recovery planning, we are concerned with a whole range of resources: CPU cycles, memory, disk space, local and gateway bandwidth, and even intangibles like IP addresses and UID space.

Capacity planning ties right back into requirements analysis. We must have a list of resources of interest to us, and we must have priorities among them. Although this could be done rigorously, with advanced metrics, graphs, and statistical analyses, most system administrators use "rules of thumb" and their intuition and experience to resolve most capacity issues.

While successful recovery planning is the mark of a competent system administrator, it is capacity planning that distinguishes the superior system administrator.

A favorite management buzzword is "proactive." Being proactive entails capacity planning and making recommendations before complaints come rolling in to the Help Desk. Tracking baseline performance and analyzing the capacities of systems and subsystems facilitates projecting when upgrades and additional systems will be needed, and proactively recommending specific types of upgrades (more RAM, more disk space, additional servers, and so on) to management.

Monitoring

There are a number of tools to provide the system administrator with utilization data for various resources. The most common are the ps, top, uptime (load average), free, iostat, netstat, and vmstat commands. The output from these commands is difficult to interpret. It is particularly difficult if these commands are used only after problems have arisen.

vmstat can be used to isolate memory shortages and excessive disk activity—the swap in and swap out columns for the former and the block in and block out columns for the latter. This makes it possible to determine whether a memory upgrade is needed, or a faster CPU. Swapping should happen only under unusual circumstances. Any system that swaps routinely should have its memory upgraded.

Here we consider a system overloaded nearly to paralysis. The output of vmstat 5 is:

procs						memory		swap			io		system		cpu		
r	b	w	swpd	free	buff	cache	si	so	bi	bo	in	cs	us	sy	id
2	0	0	12904	208	412	5560	42	64	67	39	473	109	89	7	5
1	0	0	12980	1048	424	5476	6	16	18	22	213	96	92	4	3
1	0	0	12380	1600	456	5460	277	0	267	33	1116	162	56	7	37
1	0	0	12880	416	416	5040	0	105	48	54	446	148	83	6	11
1	0	0	12864	1380	448	5340	49	0	25	0	240	115	94	6	1
2	0	0	12676	940	472	5284	97	91	224	73	978	146	57	6	37
1	0	0	12384	496	420	6124	153	0	437	26	1257	178	37	4	59
2	0	0	12996	1260	400	5796	38	194	62	52	678	178	78	9	13
1	0	0	13208	1116	408	5056	5	65	17	54	347	116	82	7	11
1	0	0	12616	688	552	5920	168	0	150	0	652	165	69	6	25
4	0	0	12600	3240	452	4916	0	6	41	33	257	152	94	5	1
1	0	0	12568	1868	568	5308	20	0	73	25	326	138	70	6	25
0	1	0	13472	3736	488	5780	22	462	88	153	1309	142	60	8	31
1	0	0	13116	376	440	5552	104	64	127	37	634	152	83	10	7
1	0	0	12580	3856	528	5820	54	0	97	0	426	150	84	5	11
0	1	0	12784	388	532	5412	0	202	71	107	739	167	60	7	33
1	0	0	12740	164	476	5228	41	40	46	31	369	129	88	6	6

r	b	w	swpd	free	buff	cache	si	so	bi	bo	in	cs	us	sy	id
1	0	0	12728	1316	440	5156	22	0	121	5	414	112	85	4	11
2	0	0	12724	2380	476	5320	5	0	26	18	196	112	91	5	4
1	0	0	12980	1180	480	5348	0	75	3	25	271	107	92	5	3
1	0	0	12888	872	420	5668	107	45	248	35	894	135	88	8	5

Note the si (swap in) and so (swap out) columns. They should both be 0 during normal operations. This machine is in desperate need of additional memory, so we increase the memory available from 16MB to 32MB and run the same processes. Now the output shows a reduction in swapping:

procs			memory				swap			io		system		cpu	
r	b	w	swpd	free	buff	cache	si	so	bi	bo	in	cs	us	sy	id
2	0	0	4716	648	756	13756	0	139	835	80	2142	153	41	19	40
2	0	0	5232	456	752	15792	0	103	1419	69	3232	137	21	26	53
2	0	0	5232	1228	864	15240	0	0	714	42	1614	173	45	13	43
2	0	0	5508	472	728	16256	0	55	1543	52	3375	136	14	28	58
2	0	0	5712	1288	796	15936	0	41	681	43	1612	192	50	14	36
2	0	0	5720	1204	912	15728	0	2	756	45	1706	187	43	14	43
2	0	0	5720	552	1012	15824	0	0	391	6	895	220	66	9	25
1	1	0	5820	556	1160	15800	0	20	392	76	1052	200	50	10	40
2	0	0	5900	728	1284	15964	0	16	512	47	1257	178	52	10	38
1	3	0	5900	1372	1376	16068	0	0	455	0	986	183	56	12	32
2	0	0	6016	4900	860	12952	0	23	468	72	1244	158	29	4	66
2	0	0	6016	592	836	12608	0	0	88	6	290	122	79	7	14
3	0	0	6016	3644	856	12440	0	0	11	25	173	127	92	8	1
2	0	0	6016	1700	884	12520	0	0	14	21	171	115	94	5	1
2	0	0	6016	2696	912	12608	0	0	15	5	141	149	91	8	1
2	0	0	6016	1408	1008	12976	0	0	57	21	258	118	88	8	4
2	0	0	6016	792	856	11268	0	0	32	54	272	95	93	6	1
2	0	0	6648	2652	860	11752	0	126	40	32	434	72	93	6	1
2	0	0	6976	680	836	11920	0	66	0	40	279	35	98	2	0
3	0	0	6956	2548	844	11540	38	0	15	0	258	244	95	5	0
4	0	0	6952	5624	888	11648	6	0	18	0	224	547	94	6	0

The system now has reasonable response, but some swapping is still indicated, which means that processes require more time to complete than they should. Therefore, we increase the memory again, this time to 64MB. The vmstat output shows that the system is not currently swapping:

procs			memory				swap			io		system		cpu	
r	b	w	swpd	free	buff	cache	si	so	bi	bo	in	cs	us	sy	id
2	0	0	5032	1508	5188	40804	0	0	315	33	871	191	49	9	41
1	0	0	5032	1572	4952	40944	0	0	499	0	1099	208	69	11	20
1	0	0	5032	1600	4816	41208	0	0	453	0	1007	211	60	14	26
1	0	0	5032	992	4600	41668	0	0	694	0	1489	189	60	16	24
2	0	0	5032	1372	4440	41612	0	0	414	159	1246	207	33	7	60
1	0	0	5032	1512	4348	41748	0	0	271	60	764	167	53	8	39

1	0	0	5032	632	4188	42296	0	0	499	0	1099	182	68	13	18
1	0	0	5032	1684	3832	42552	0	0	466	0	1033	203	66	14	20
1	0	0	5032	2220	3832	42780	0	0	156	0	413	228	34	8	57
2	1	0	5032	980	3420	43904	0	0	878	0	1858	171	26	12	61
1	1	0	5032	1456	3000	43716	0	0	187	151	779	198	1	2	97
1	0	0	5032	736	2460	43008	0	0	346	0	795	243	21	3	76
1	0	0	5032	5280	2396	41284	0	0	109	112	544	338	67	11	22
1	0	0	5032	2236	2400	40568	0	0	26	0	153	85	95	5	0
1	0	0	5032	1460	2424	40144	0	0	43	0	187	114	91	6	3
1	0	0	5032	3648	2448	40176	0	0	15	0	132	114	94	6	0
2	0	0	5032	5844	2464	40180	0	0	3	76	258	146	94	6	0
3	0	0	5032	5032	2472	40240	0	0	24	0	150	146	89	10	1
2	0	0	5032	2180	2472	40252	0	0	2	0	106	77	96	3	1
1	0	0	5032	2328	2488	40292	0	0	20	18	178	241	89	11	0
2	1	0	5032	5280	2504	40320	0	0	11	0	124	147	93	7	0

With such vmstat output, adding yet more memory will not significantly improve the performance of this system under its current load. However, note the swpd (swapped pages) column, which indicates that pages have been swapped out. Thus, a further increase in memory would still be of occasional benefit. A LINUX system that always shows 0 in the swpd column will not benefit from additional memory unless its utilization increases.

The current load average on a given system doesn't tell much. However, knowing the system's usual load average provides a basis for comparison. If the system seems slow and the load average is about the same as usual, it suggests that the "slow" processes are blocked, waiting for a resource other than CPU time.

So, it's important for system administrators to check and document utilization parameters periodically—to get a sense of the baseline utilization for each resource. On some systems, that may be done manually and informally. In other cases, it makes sense to run cron jobs and/or dæmons that take snapshots of various metrics and store them in a suitable format.

There are several tools that automate this reporting and logging function. One is the multi-router traffic grapher (also known as MRTG[1]). Despite the name, this tool can track many sorts of resources, turning the numbers into neat graphs wrapped in HTML for display via a browser. A couple of other popular packages are Big Brother[2] and mon.[3]

There are many tools for monitoring various system parameters and for providing alerts when any of these pass set thresholds.

1. www.mrtg.org

2. http://maclawran.ca/bb-dnld/

3. http://www.kernel.org/software/mon/

Disk Space

As disk space is used, we must plan to add more (or to remove or shrink some files), possibly migrating them to a hierarchical storage management or HSM system.[4]

Just about every new system administrator eventually writes a script to check filesystems and warn when any approach capacity. Here's a sample of one such script:[5]

```
#!/bin/bash
 # SLEW: Space Low Early Warning
 # by James T. Dennis,
 #  Starshine Technical Services

 # Warns if any filesystem in df's output is over a certain
 # percentage full -- mails a short report -- listing just
 # "full" filesystem. Additions can be made to specify
 # *which* host is affected for admins that manage
 # multiple hosts

 #  Change Tue Jul 22 16:52:03 PDT 1997
 # patch to filter out filesystems that are
 # mounted read-only (such as CD-ROMs).

 #  Change Tue Feb 23 12:12:40 PST 1999
 # patch to detect inode shortages

adminmail="root"
         # who to mail the report to

threshold=${1:?"Specify a numeric argument"}
         # a percentage -- *just the digits*

# Now filter fs' that are mounted read-only (ro)
rofs="$(echo -n '('; /bin/mount |
         gawk '$NF "[^a-zA-Z]*ro[^a-zA-Z]*" {print $1}' \
         | while read i; do echo -n "$i"; done;
         echo -n '/proc)' )"
# This creates an egrep regular expression which
# can be used to filter the output of the df command.
#####
```

---

4. Unfortunately there are no popular HSM systems currently available for LINUX. These would be of great use, but this may remain the domain of custom scripts and *ad hoc* methods for some time to come.

5. Originally published in the *Linux Gazette.*

```
# catch the disk space utilization
fsstat="$( /bin/df  | egrep -v $rofs )"
fsistat="$( /bin/df  | egrep -v $rofs )"

# cat the inode utilization
fsistat="$( /bin/df -i | egrep -v $rofs )"

fullfs=$( echo "$fsstat" | gawk '$5 + 0 > '$threshold )
ifullfs=$( echo "$fsistat" | gawk '$5 + 0 > '$threshold )

[ -n "$fullfs" -o -n "$ifullfs" ]  && {
   echo "To: $adminmail"
   echo "Subject: SLEW Alert"
   echo -e "\n\n Warning: some of your filesystems are" \
           "more than $threshold% full (blocks): \n" ;
   echo "$fullfs"  \
       | while read each ; do echo "  $each"; done
   echo -e "\n\nor more than $threshold% full (inodes): \n" ;
   echo "$ifullfs" \
       | while read each ; do echo "  $each"; done } \
 | /usr/lib/sendmail -oi -oe -t
```

Close inspection of this script will reveal that the basics are quite simple, and that it is almost as much work to filter out read-only filesystems (such as mounted CD-ROMs) and format the email as it is to do the real work at hand.

Bandwidth and Latency

The critical network parameters to monitor are bandwidth and latency. Checking these periodically with about five pings and setting watcher to warn when the latency gets too high or the throughput gets too low would help ensure that users are not waiting too long for their traffic.

MRTG was written to take its input from SNMP (for LINUX, typically the CMU SNMP). However, SNMP is not strictly required to run MRTG—various commands may be used to provide it with statistics to graph.

Diagnosis

The major challenge of capacity planning is determining which resources are at critical utilization thresholds. A specific application or symptom often doesn't correlate to a given resource.

The resource requirements for a given application or subsystem can involve complex interrelations with other systems. For example, an application that seems too slow may be suffering from delays in DNS lookups (a common problem for web browsers).

Apparent application slowness might also be due to a lack of available memory—or a disk drive that is also home to a busy filesystem (perhaps used by some other application). It could be that the system has a slow video card. For X WINDOW applications, the video card may be more important than the host's processor and memory. Slow rendering of web pages is often incorrectly blamed on slow downloads.

Solutions

Capacity problems have three general solutions: optimizing performance, adding resources, and reducing utilization.

One solution to slow DNS lookups may be to provide a caching DNS server on the local LAN segment or on the local host. The trade-off is that this increases the utilization of memory, CPU, and disk space on the DNS server. Another solution may be to reconfigure a web server to not perform reverse lookups on each client for the log files. Yet another solution may be to upgrade the network. The best solution depends on local circumstances and the possible effects on other parts of the computing environment.

Performance Optimization

Often, performance problems are not caused by hardware. Sometimes the application is working "harder" rather than "smarter." For example, a web server may be spawning a copy of perl to generate almost every web page. Many sites have made their document trees "dynamic" at great expense of CPU and memory. Some of these sites could provide the same information by generating static web pages once or twice per day (via a cron job) rather than by dynamically rebuilding each page for each access. Another approach is to use the mod_perl module for the Apache web server. This loads the perl interpreter once and handles the scripts internally. Indexing, hashing, and caching may also be used to reduce the CPU overhead of many processes.

Optimization of business practices and IT procedures can also greatly increase the efficiency of systems and obviate or delay the need for greater capacity. For example, some sites use a central database to distribute their employee phone list. Some have provided a CGI/web front end to this database via their intranet web servers. In most cases, the data that a given user wants hasn't changed recently, so the more efficient method for providing this information is to periodically generate static web pages from the databases.

In our web/CGI-based example, there might be a link that allows any user to force a check against the database. So, if an unexpected answer is received from the static pages (which may be a day old), the user can query the live database. Most requests would still be handled by the static pages, and only exceptional cases would impact the server's load. Additionally, the statically generated pages can be cached throughout the organization, while replicating "live" databases is far more complex and costs a great deal more in terms of CPU cycles and (more importantly) administrator overhead.

Static pages can be indexed (for example with `glimpseindex`) and searched online (for example with GlimpseHTTP). However, they can also be accessed by simple web browsing and bookmarking. Generating multiple versions of the same information—a hierarchy by department and a set of pages separated by the initial letters of the last name—is also effective.

In general, having many small HTML files in reasonable directory hierarchies provides greater web site capacity and usability than having a few larger files in proprietary formats (such as PDF).

The logging of fully-qualified domain names, rather than IP addresses, by web servers involves reverse DNS queries that consume more bandwidth and CPU time. This can be exacerbated further in cases where the web server is also performing ident queries—requesting the "user identity" (usually the login name) that owns the socket on the remote system making a given request. Disabling these features (as well as cookies) are simple steps that yield appreciable performance benefits. This is not to say that webmasters should *never* enable these web server logging features. Consider the cost and value of these extra data. It is also possible to have a separate log host perform the reverse lookups during off-peak hours.

In most cases, "many smaller" will be more effective than having a few much larger, more expensive systems or peripherals. For example, several smaller SCSI disk drives (more spindles) will usually outperform one large one because each drive can service requests in parallel and provide results asynchronously to the CPU. One disk drive must (internally) handle requests one at a time.

Note that it is not necessary to use special drivers (such as the `md` RAID package for LINUX) to benefit from multiple disks. Considerable performance benefits may be gained by carefully distributing filesystems across drives. For example, on a typical web server, putting the access logs and the web documents on separate drives will have a significant effect. Having multiple drives also reduces downtime on the rare occasions when the systems have to be rebooted. For example, `fsck` on two small filesystems is considerably faster than on one filesystem of twice the size. Backup and recovery processes are also often much quicker.

Another instance of this principle occurs when we deploy separate intranet servers in each department and when we use whole groups of servers in "round-robin gangs" to provide various services. A number of Internet protocols and systems are designed to work gracefully under these conditions. For example, it is easy to deploy multiple mail exchange hosts and add additional MX records to DNS zone maps. The mail receipt load will then be distributed over all of those systems, and the failure of any one system will have very limited effect on the overall service availability. The final delivery load is balanced by having each MX host dispatch its mail to departmental POP (post office protocol) or IMAP (Internet mail access protocol) servers. IMAP is more robust than POP. Using this simple architecture, it is possible to provide tremendous capacity and very robust service for relatively modest outlay. Indeed, this email handling architecture is modeled after the largest email system in history—the whole Internet. Protocols such as NIS, Kerberos, DNS, and some filesystems, such as AFS and Coda, are similarly robust and scalable.

In other cases the scaling issues are more complex. For example, while it is easy enough to provide redundancy for basic TCP/IP routing (and normal practice in some industries, such as banking), it is somewhat more difficult to provide load-balancing.

LINUX is an unusually frugal operating system. An old 386 with 16MB of RAM can easily handle mail, web, print, and file services for a small company or department (up to about 25 users). A 486 with 32MB can provide the same combination of services to at least 100 users. So, in contrast to conventions in the rest of the industry, it is often effective to deploy the slowest systems as LINUX servers and save the faster CPUs for use as workstations. Many of the most important network services require very little processor power and are I/O bound (where the CPU is usually waiting for disk or network data).

As the number of systems grows, the network will need to be segmented to maintain a low collision rate. Ensure that servers are local to the segments that make the heaviest use of their services.

Adding Resources

Of course, a CPU could just be too slow, a disk too small, or bandwidth too little. In these cases, the system administrator must be prepared to make prioritized recommendations for increasing the capacity of each of the affected resources.

At a site where one of the authors was the system administrator, the requirement was to increase the capacity of the FTP servers. Installing a newer host with more RAM and a faster processor allowed an increase in the number of concurrent FTP sessions from 100 to 300. Round-robin DNS was later introduced so that clones of this server could be installed.

The next problem was that this site was fed by only a single T1 leased line. This meant that all Internet activity at the site had to share 1.5Mbps of bandwidth. All email, web surfing, incoming requests to the company's web site, and outgoing and incoming FTP sessions were sharing the same bandwidth. Unsurprisingly, SNMP statistics from the routers at this site showed that the T1 was overutilized. Increasing the FTP limit (in the wuftpd configuration) only exacerbated the problem. Hundreds of users could connect and start their file downloads (this company distributed some popular shareware). However, each session would take much longer than it had previously.

The requirements of telephone support staff were met—they stopped getting calls and complaints that the site was "always busy." However, many of the customers weren't satisfied with the throughput.

One recommended approach was to add another T1. This is more complicated than one might think. The manager at that site initially wanted to add the new connection to a second ISP. The idea was to supplement the added bandwidth with some redundancy, so that any service interruptions from the first ISP would be less likely to shut down the whole site. That's a worthy objective—however, Internet routing is not so simple.

That plan would have required the site to peer with both ISPs—usually over the BGP protocol. In other words, the site would need an AS (autonomous system) number, and the routers would need to be configured to exchange routing tables and updates with both ISPs—who would have to reciprocate by recognizing the routes that were being published by that site.

This was all eventually done (over a year later). However, to meet immediate needs, the new T1 was placed between the site and the original ISP. In particular, it was installed such that at each end, both T1s were plugged into the same router. Both routers were of the same manufacture, which permitted load balancing across both T1s.

This solution neatly avoided the routing and IP addressing issues that would later be raised when connections were established to multiple ISPs, or even to multiple points of presence (POPs) at a single ISP. The latter configuration, where a site is concurrently served by multiple sites, is called multi-homing. However, the term can be confusing since a multi-homed host is one that contains multiple network interfaces (like any router), while a multi-homed site is one where the whole LAN or WAN is served by multiple ISPs.

It is possible to connect concurrently to multiple ISPs without peering. However, the routing and load balancing will have to be done somewhere. For example, if all internal hosts are using private network addresses (as described in Chapter 13, "Network Technologies") or are otherwise accessing the Internet through proxy servers, groups of them can be configured to use different gateways.

One of the biggest problems with throwing "more" at capacity problems is that you often run into more substantial limitations as you attempt to resolve the obvious ones. For example, adding more disk space is straightforward. However, an IDE system with no SCSI controllers can quickly exhaust the (typically four) available interface connections. Even SCSI offers only seven or fifteen devices per interface. So, sometimes smaller drives must be replaced with larger ones. In other cases, more interfaces will need to be added. However, interfaces need slots and possibly other resources (memory-mapped reserved addresses, IRQs, I/O port ranges, DMA channels, and so on).

Situations may arise where there are no available resources to add interfaces to a system, necessitating replacement of complete systems. Similar considerations apply to increasing memory and adding more printers.

Reducing Utilization

Some resources are wasted. When a resource shortage appears imminent, it is often worth considering whether that resource is being used wastefully. The elimination of waste is sometimes a quick and inexpensive solution to capacity problems. The most obvious example is the use of compression to reduce the utilization of storage or bandwidth or both. There are also more subtle methods.

For example, in 1996, one of the authors was responsible for providing home directories for a team of ten programmers and their manager. An 8GB partition was provided, without quotas. Code repositories and work areas were provided separately, so this 8GB was largely for personal use. After three months, the partition reached 95% of capacity. It would have been possible to procure more disk space, but doing so did not appear to be in the interests of the company or a good use of the system administrator's time. Instead, the system administrator sent a message to the users, asking that they clean up their home directories. Utilization fell less than 1%. The next day, the system administrator sent another message to the users, warning that if sufficient disk space did not appear within the hour, he would remove any pornography found in the home directories. Utilization quickly fell to 80%.

Overengineering

One of the most common strategies for avoiding capacity-related failures is to overengineer each system at purchase. Most managers and even most home users do this to some degree. It is common to spend a little more on a more powerful system than one currently needs—in anticipation of greater future needs.

We overengineer despite the consistent trend for more powerful systems to be released for about the same price or lower year after year. The early PCs cost about $5,000 (US) back in 1982. That was for a system with 64KB of RAM and no hard drive. Just a decade ago, a 386 with 8MB of RAM and an 80MB hard disk cost about $3,000. Five years ago, a 486 with 16MB of RAM and a 200MB drive was about $2,000. Current Pentium II systems with 32MB of RAM and a couple of gigabytes of disk space sell for well under $1,000.

Personnel Capacities

System administrators are also a resource—and have limited capacities as well. Include the time and capabilities of system administrators in capacity planning models, as well as that of DBAs, network administrators, and other IT personnel.

Because system administrators are more expensive than hardware, and degrade more with excessive use, opportunities to reduce the load on the system administrators by acquiring or upgrading hardware should generally be availed.

Conclusion

When considering capacity planning and performance tuning, here are some principles to follow:

- Get baseline performance metrics.
- Identify bottlenecks.
- Consider methods to conserve or reduce utilization.
- Try trading off a dearth of one resource for a surfeit of another (caching, indexing, and so on).
- Provide management with a specific, prioritized list of requisite additional resources.

5

Help Desk and Escalation

THINGS GO WRONG. No matter how well one anticipates the future, it will present unexpected setbacks. Bugs will corrupt files, users will erase data they need, and hardware will spontaneously combust.

When such things happen, you will not always be the first to know. However, you should endeavor to monitor your systems such that when users call you with a problem, you can tell them that you already know about it and are working on it—or better yet, that you've just fixed it. In the best cases, it will be fixed before users notice that it was ever broken.

Even so, users must have a well-defined procedure for reporting problems and requesting help. In a small organization, this may be as simple as each user having the email address, phone number, and pager number of the sole system administrator. In large organizations, it will be more complex. This chapter offers principles for the operation of Help Desks in large organizations, most of which are also appropriate for smaller organizations.

Firefighting

Many system administrators spend much of their time "fighting fires"—that is, responding to crises. As with real fires, an ounce of prevention is worth a pound of cure. While too much time spent reacting to crises often indicates poor management or too few sufficiently experienced system administrators, we'll look at specific strategies for enabling system administrators to more effectively prevent crises and to more efficiently respond to the crises that do occur.

These strategies include the reporting of problems, the escalation of difficult problems, the logging of the problems along with their resolutions, and the analysis of the log data. All of these things will be done keeping in mind the goal of precluding future troubles.

Dispatch

Where there are several or many system administrators, not everyone will be equally skilled, and a division of labor will naturally occur, with or without direction from management. It might be tempting to assign the most junior system administrator the role of dispatcher, answering the Help Desk and sending others to solve the problems reported by users. This would be a mistake. Junior system administrators should be sent to resolve problems that are within their abilities (unless much would be lost each minute the problem persists). However, the dispatcher must be qualified to assess each report and determine which person is best sent in response. This assessment requires not only skills, but familiarity with the skills of the other staff, that are beyond those of an entry-level system administrator. The minimum qualification for a dispatcher is, in addition to basic qualification as a system administrator, several months of working the Help Desk as a troubleshooter.

Diplomacy

Communication skills in general, and diplomacy in particular, are essential qualifications for members of the Help Desk team. Members of the Help Desk team will often assess a particular problem as being caused by ineptitude on the user's part. Experience shows that this is usually a correct assessment. But it will almost always be the case that the problem will be better solved (and repeat calls avoided) by something other than explaining to the user his lack of competence. Two of the authors have worked with a senior system administrator of exceptional technical competence who gained notoriety for telling the vice president of a large investment bank, "The problem is not that the printer doesn't work; the problem is that you don't know how to print."

Better tactics for dealing with users include suggestions of training, gently reminding the user of the FAQ and how to find it, and patient explanations in terms of concepts that the user understands. It may take time for the members of the Help Desk team to learn the (often strange) concepts by which users think about their computers, but doing so will slowly pay off. Therefore, personnel should be assigned to the Help Desk only if they have the diplomatic skills necessary to solve problems without digressions that cause the users grief. Training the Help Desk personnel in diplomacy may not only make them and their users happier in their interactions, but will likely reduce the time needed to resolve the technical problems that arise.

Reporting Systems

It would be nice if we could require all problems to be reported via a database accessible from Mozilla.[1]

However, some failures will render such a reporting system unusable. This is no reason not to implement a browser-based reporting system. But the Help Desk must be willing to accept failure reports by other means, such as phone and fax, if the online reporting system has failed.

The web page for reporting a problem should also include a FAQ. This should include phone numbers, pager numbers, fax numbers, and any other contact information for the Help Desk, as well as the circumstances under which it is OK to report a problem other than through the web-based application. The FAQ should include a primer on how to report problems in a useful way, including examples showing information that is useful and information which is not. And, of course, it should include answers to the questions that are most frequently asked in the organization. The FAQ should help users solve problems themselves, by gently leading them through some elementary diagnostics.

There are several reasons for insisting that problems be recorded into a database, even if the nature of the problem precluded the user from logging it via the Help Desk's web page or if the problem was fixed before ever being reported by a user. Therefore, the dispatcher will have to make the database entries when automatic logging doesn't work, such as when the web page is inaccessible. Recording problems helps ensure that they are resolved. It also ensures that a record is kept of who asserted that a particular problem was truly fixed. And statistical information becomes available both about how many problems each system administrator resolved (and whether they were resolved satisfactorily) and about the relative frequency of different sorts of problems. The former will help the manager of the Help Desk to manage his employees. The latter will help the senior system administrators determine how to allocate resources toward prevention.

Some types of information, including some statistical reports, should be widely accessible. This will help engender confidence among the users that the Help Desk really does take care of their problems. But more important, it ensures that real problems with Help Desk operations are not ignored, which is of benefit to the organization as a whole.

The Help Desk's home-page should include a list of whatever problem types require their own form, along with a general form for other problems. Each form could require

---

1. The only IT reporting systems we know of that come close to meeting the requirements we describe are Frontdesk and Remedy. See http://admin.gnacademy.org:8001/uu-gna/tech/dbedit/frontdesk.html and http://www.remedy.com/ for more information.

the user to indicate whether or not he has read the FAQ, a link to which should be prominent. When a user reports that he has read the FAQ and doesn't understand the answer, or the problem persists, the dispatcher should send someone to help and then verify that the FAQ entry is clear and up-to-date.

One example of a problem that justifies a special online reporting form is requests for restoration of deleted files. The form should request enough information for the restore procedure to be automatically run, with a dynamically generated web-page indicating which tapes need to be loaded (if restoring from tapes). Of course, this requires that the application authenticate that the request is being made by the owner of the file to be restored. This way, the junior system administrators assigned to load tapes need only check this page (perhaps from a machine in the data center) to see which tapes need to be loaded. All other parts of the restore procedure should be automated. Note that this level of automation would be impossible if restore requests were made using a generic form.

In some environments, some users (such as stock traders or medical doctors) will be too busy to fill in problem reports. They will make a phone call indicating that they have a problem and will reasonably expect someone to show up within minutes to fix it. In such cases the dispatcher will have to make the entry and should try to get some useful information about the nature of the problem so that he can select the right person to send. When such a person calls it may not be appropriate to send someone junior. Quite the contrary: In some situations, it may be best to send one of the most senior system administrators, even if the report is "the printer doesn't work."

Automated Monitoring: Alerts

Monitoring is an essential task of system administration. But it is a task for which men are notoriously ill-suited. Fortunately, computers are well-suited to monitoring each other and to alerting humans when an anomaly is discovered.

Note that more than one computer must be configured to perform monitoring, because any computer doing monitoring will itself need to be monitored, preferably by a computer on another subnet. One of the things they should check is that cron is working correctly on the other monitoring hosts.

The common means by which computers may alert humans to a potential problem are displaying or sounding a warning (or both) on a system administrator's workstation, paging one or more system administrators, logging the problem to a file, and sending email to one or more system administrators.

The selection of alerts will depend on the nature of the particular problem. For example, notice of a file system nearing capacity might be emailed to the senior system administrator responsible for the filesystem. A network printer that doesn't respond properly to pinging might alert the Help Desk dispatcher, while a file server that doesn't respond to pinging would probably set off pagers. All of these would be logged.

Which alerts a script should select to respond to any given problem will often depend on the time of day. For example, some problems will justify paging system administrators during business hours, but not at 2:00 a.m. Other problems may justify paging one or more system administrators, even at 2:00 a.m.

The scripts by which computers monitor one another and alert humans when they discover a problem are normally run from cron. How frequently they need be run will depend on local circumstances but will normally be at least once per hour. More on scripting may be found in Chapter 11, "Scripting."

Evaluation, Prevention, and Documentation

It is important for the senior system administrators (perhaps with their managers) to periodically review the problems logged in, and statistical reports generated from, the incident database. The main purpose of this is to find persistent or costly troubles that can be obviated by automating (or better automating) a task or set of tasks. This database should be the principal basis for decisions about which tasks the senior system administrators most urgently need to automate.

Managers of system administrators should also examine the database. This will be one of the sources of information available to them about both the quality and quantity of work being performed by the system administrators. Managers may glean hints about which system administrators need commendation, training, and discipline. Final action will of course depend on a broader review of the evidence.

As they look through the database, the senior system administrators should also be thinking about opportunities to better document procedures so that users and junior system administrators can avoid problems in the future. Keep in mind that better tools are to be preferred over better documentation. But sometimes the tools are as good as they can be, and the best course of action is to better document a procedure. As the Help Desk gains experience, historical information gleaned from the incident database should be used by the senior system administrators to update the user FAQ, as well as to better document procedures for junior system administrators.

Escalation Plan

Sometimes a system administrator will be dispatched to solve a problem beyond his abilities. When this occurs with an impatient user, it is important that the system administrator on the spot know to whom he should turn. This is a good reason why the most junior system administrators should not be sent by themselves to help users whose work is mission-critical. For example, if the problem is due to an incorrect entry in DNS, the system administrator on the spot should at least know that is the nature of the problem, even if he cannot correct it. Then he must know who among the more senior system administrators are DNS wizards, as it would not do to page a mail specialist.

In very large organizations, there may be a need for a very formal and detailed escalation plan. This should be available on the web to all system administrators. But even when this is the case, there must be flexibility, and mid-level system administrators must be encouraged to call the person best qualified to fix the problem when circumstances are urgent enough to justify setting aside the plan. No one should get in trouble for disturbing a busy, highly-paid senior system administrator if doing so significantly benefitted the company's bottom line. In other words, system administrators should be empowered to use their own judgement and should be rewarded or punished on the basis of the results. Persons with poor judgement will inevitably be poor system administrators.

A pint of sweat will save a gallon of blood.

~George S. Patton (1885–1945)

6

Network Computing

A HEALTHY NETWORK COMPUTING ENVIRONMENT resembles a healthy living organism: it is resilient to the failure of individual components, it can adapt to rapid changes in the environment, and its competitive effectiveness is greater than the sum of its parts.

When computing environments attain this state, several concrete results are achieved. Data are always available to those who are intended to have access and are always unavailable to those who are not. Redundancy is built into the environment so that the failure of one component or service does not affect other components or services. Other machines continue to provide the affected service so the failure is invisible to end users. Finally, the environment lends itself to collaboration, because an arbitrary group of functionally identical computers can be chosen to contribute to a particular task. They have the same configuration, the same filesystem hierarchy, the same set of shared user accounts, and equivalent network connectivity.

Purchasing 100 copies of WINDOWS NT or LINUX and 100 computers does not purchase a network computing environment. It purchases some of the elements of network computing. An overall systems design is still needed. In this chapter, as well as in Chapters 14 and 15, "System Profiles" and "Automated Installation and Upgrade," we present the concepts and practices needed to complete an architecture. It is our hope that the material presented leads to a component-based approach to network computing, in the same way object-oriented and component-based programming methodologies contribute to application architectures.

Architectural Objectives

The obvious requirement for a systems architecture is to build an infrastructure that provides desktop computers with a standard set of services. This accomplishment alone is deserving of merit. Unfortunately, it is not sufficient. The method of service delivery itself is a key feature of network computing. Several key requirements distinguish an architecture:

- It must be reliable.
- It must be maintainable.
- It must be scaleable.

Meeting these requirements is a lofty goal. Due to the limitations of system technologies, there are no perfect solutions. The following list is a series of guidelines that help achieve these goals:

- All desktop computers are generic, have the same software installed, and store no user data.
- All servers conform to a well-defined system profile, as detailed in Chapter 14, "System Profiles."
- Servers use RAID to attain higher availability.
- Network hardware is deployed in a redundant fashion.
- Software is distributed in a controlled fashion. If an organization has multiple locations, all sites should contain the same suite of applications.
- Every desktop computer sees an identical file hierarchy.
- Each user account appears identically on every system within a department. Typically, user home directories are made available to every system via the automounter or Samba.

Larger organizations with multiple departments should utilize a number of senior system administrators to collaborate on the systems architecture for the entire organization. If standardization exists among departments, system administrators responsible for one group can administer systems in another department when the need arises. Also, custom applications developed by one department are easy to integrate into another.

Standardized solutions save an organization real money. Nothing scales better than a solution that can be replicated arbitrarily. Even if the initial investment in time seems large, the recurring cost savings in deploying a well-architected environment will quickly outweigh the initial expense of design and documentation. Additionally, a growing organization that adheres to an architected environment will amortize the engineering costs over a larger number of desktops.

Conversely, network computing environments that are allowed to grow in an uncontrolled fashion become exponentially more expensive to maintain. Eventually, almost all system administrator resources will be consumed by problems that crop up due to unanticipated incompatibilities, dependencies, and the dire consequences of short-term solutions.

This leaves the organization unable to respond to needed changes in a timely fashion. Network computing environments that have not been built with an architectural model always have this problem. Some reach a state of total paralysis. The only solution at this point is to create a totally new environment and migrate users and hardware to it. Worse yet, if the new environment is also not architected, the same degradation will begin anew. This is a huge expense to incur, yet many organizations pay the price repeatedly due to a simple lack of vision.

Some IT managers excuse themselves from planning by asserting a need to maintain flexibility. Networks that grow without planning impose constraints as surely as planned networks. The difference is that planned networks impose planned constraints and unplanned networks impose unplanned constraints.

A Few Words Regarding Namespaces

A namespace refers to a system of mapping symbolic names to objects. Within the scope of system administration, we define a namespace to be the set of names that exist within a particular network naming protocol. The most important objects to be named are hosts, but namespaces apply to every network resource.

Name services insulate network services from details of the network environment. Hosts providing network services can be moved to different physical locations of the network yet retain the same symbolic name. This dramatically reduces the work required to make changes in the network environment, since all of the references to the host do not need to be changed.

As the world stands today, there are many name services that provide overlapping functionality. Proprietary operating system vendors have worked to ensure that no one name server will be able to provide naming for a large organization. In fact, any organization with a heterogeneous environment will have to take special care to load all services with the same data, and more importantly, to ensure that the data stay synchronized as changes are made. It is the network architect's responsibility to solve this problem.

A new generation of name servers, known as directory servers, is being developed. Directory services can contain arbitrary data, and could potentially be used to combine all namespaces into one unified service. Unfortunately, operating systems vendors have been slow to integrate directory service access into their products.

Within LINUX, there are three basic naming services, two of which are associated with network protocols: NIS and DNS. LINUX also can use the /etc/hosts file to resolve names. Use of the latter should be restricted to host names needed for booting. LINUX manages access to these name services via the /etc/nsswitch.conf file. Configuring this file, by modifying the order in which the name services are accessed, permits each computer to have a customized namespace. Do not do this. Every computer must have an identical namespace in order to avoid creating an unnecessarily complex environment. Choose one nsswitch.conf configuration for the environment and deploy it to all hosts.

Network Services Overview

The network is merely the conduit through which data travel. The actual services provided on a network are hosted by the organization's servers. A typical organization will offer the services outlined in Table 6.1.

The services visible at the application or user level depend upon lower-layer network services. These are described in detail in Chapter 17, "Network Services." These lower-level services must be rock solid, since the entire computing environment depends upon them.

Table 6.1 **Typical network services**

File Services	Transparent access to remote files
Print Services	Access to printers as network objects
Fax Services	Transmit documents via a networked facsimile facility
Electronic Mail	Internal mail systems with connectivity to the Internet
NetNews	Access to the network news service. Also permits system administrators to define local news groups.
Web Access	Access to both internal web sites and the Internet
Applications	Applications are installed on servers and accessed by the clients via file services
Database Access	Database access via applications and ad hoc reporting tools
Time Services	The Network Time Protocol allows system clocks to be synchronized to within a few milliseconds of Coordinated Universal Time (UTC).
Distributed Management	Whether an organization employs network management protocols like SNMP or utilizes a simple set of homegrown scripts, facilities exist to manage the environment as a whole rather than as isolated computers.
Remote Access	Members of the organization have access to all services whether they are at home or on the road. The remote access mechanisms support authentication and encryption to ensure the privacy and security of data.

Buzzwords

Some buzzwords have arisen recently in networking. The Internet has had its name since the early 1980s, when it evolved from the ARPAnet. However, "intranet" and "extranet" came into use during the late 1990s. We define the concepts that underlie these buzzwords in terms of network services.

Internet

Every modern organization needs to be connected to the Internet, because email and web access are well on their way to replacing voice mail and facsimile. Most organizations will want to manage Internet access with a firewall. A firewall is a special-purpose computer dedicated to permitting use of the Internet from the inside and preventing abuse from the outside.

Most organizations will also want to maintain a web site on the Internet. Increasingly, ISPs and integration companies are offering secure Internet access and web hosting, which are attractive to companies that do not have the requisite expertise to maintain these services themselves.

Intranet

This term has become the popular way to describe the use of web servers to publish data internally. It also implies having the low-level services in place required for any system to connect to any other. It may be hard to imagine this as a feat, but firm-wide access to data is a milestone in the evolution of many companies.

A more sophisticated definition of intranet also includes the ability to deliver standardized access to all internal data, enabling drastic improvements in the ability to deliver ad hoc reports, and to share data among departments.

Extranet

This term was coined to reflect the business practice of establishing dedicated connections to key partners, allowing direct access to each other's applications. For example, a manufacturer implements direct links to its suppliers to automate ordering and billing. The manufacturer is then free to implement just-in-time inventory management, directly generating requests to suppliers based on product orders.

The term "extranet" will most likely die out in the next few years. Companies are already beginning to replace dedicated connections with Virtual Private Networks (VPNs). The perceived need for an extranet will wane as Internet commerce and encryption standards stabilize.

Linux and Network Technologies

LINUX supports all of the services mentioned in the previous section. Additionally, LINUX supports almost every network protocol needed to integrate these services into existing PC computing environments. LINUX can be integrated into Macintosh, Microsoft WINDOWS, NetWare, and of course commercial UNIX environments. Many system administrators who administer Microsoft WINDOWS networks prefer to use LINUX rather than native servers to provide file and print services.

LINUX is also prepared for the emergence of the IPv6 protocol, which in upcoming years will replace IPv4, today's standard networking protocol. IPv6 offers the same basic services as IPv4, but it supports a greatly expanded address space, is streamlined for more efficient processing, and has improved security.

In addition to the variety of higher-layer protocols, LINUX supports a variety of physical network types. Ethernet, Token Ring, and FDDI interfaces are supported, as well as a variety of high-speed serial interfaces.

More technical discussions of networking may be found in Chapter 13, "Network Technologies" and Chapter 17, "Network Services."

In most IT bureaucracies, security is the most important consideration—except for every other consideration.

7

Security Policy

To UNDERSTAND SECURITY in the context of system administration, let us recall that our Prime Directive concerns the provision of services. Security also concerns the corollary: the denial of service. Services are to be denied both in order to protect data from inappropriate disclosure and to ensure the provision of services to those legitimately requiring them. Because the services provided must rest upon correct data, security is also concerned with data integrity.

Policies follow from requirements analysis. Security requirements will often conflict with other requirements. In most organizations, everyone will say that security is paramount. Usually, getting the job done in a manner that is comfortable and familiar and that protects against blame takes precedence over security. The senior system administrator generally must keep this in mind as security requirements are translated into policies, and measures are chosen to achieve the policy aims.

As with other policies, an organization's security policy must be disseminated to those whom it concerns. The intranet is generally the best way to do this. A security policy that is secret will only breed dissension as users will demand services that are prohibited, without knowing that they are prohibited.

The policy questions of what services are to be provided and denied—and to whom and under what circumstances—should precede all other security considerations. Only then should the mechanics of enforcing policies, which is the day-to-day task of security, come into play.

The aims of security policy are to preserve data integrity, ensure availability, and protect the confidentiality of data. The measures for achieving these aims are prevention, detection, and recovery. We consider how each measure applies to each aim.

This chapter is concerned with security policy, rather than the enforcement of that policy. The latter is covered in the following chapter, "Enforcing Security."

Data Integrity

The value of any data is contingent upon its integrity. Data that has been corrupted, either accidentally or deliberately, is rarely useful and is often dangerous. For example, a doctor may rely on corrupted medical data to prescribe medication or plan a surgical procedure.

System administrators must take measures to preserve data integrity by preventing its corruption, to detect data corruption when it occurs, and to recover from corruption by restoring the data. The difficulty of preserving data integrity varies. However, detection of and recovery from data corruption are easy if proper preparations have been made.

Preventing Corruption

The obvious defense against the corruption of data is to restrict write access to only those who really need it. Ideally, all accesses would be logged, recording who changed the data and when.

Most databases allow highly granular control of who may access what. Most databases also provide effective logging, so system administrators must work with database administrators to ensure that write access to databases is restricted to those who need it, and that logs are maintained. It is generally appropriate for system administrators to maintain copies of the database logs to which the DBAs have read but not write access.

Most filesystems, on the other hand, are more limited in offering granular control over access. Generally, the only available access option that doesn't grant write permission to the whole world yet permits write access to more than a single user is group access. Files and directories may then have read, write, and execute attributes granted to a group.

Data may be corrupted by someone who has gained access by posing as an authorized user. The use of strong authentication and encryption often defeats such attacks. For example, protocols that send passwords (even encrypted passwords) over the network (even an internal network) should never be used. Consider two hypothetical authentication protocols:

```
Server:  What's your name?
Client:  Fred
Server:  What's your password, Fred?
```

```
Client:   7Xa!r5,h
[Server compares 7Xa!r5,h with the password on file for Fred.  If it
is the same, Fred is authenticated.]

Server:   What's your name?
Client:   Fred
[Server generates a random bit sequence.]
Server:   Use your passphrase to encrypt this, Fred: 4B04F81C9A37D5B6
[The client software Fred is using then prompts Fred for his passphrase
and uses it to encrypt the random bit sequence sent by the server.]
Client:   A59E15F048DA491C
[Server looks up Fred's passphrase on file and uses it as the key to
encrypt 4B04F81C9A37D5B6.  If the result is the same as the string
Fred sent, Fred is authenticated.]
```

Note that, in the first example, anyone sniffing packets on the network will see Fred's password and will be able to use it in the future. Automated tools for doing exactly this are widespread. In the second example, the passphrase is never sent over the network—not even in encrypted form. Someone sniffing the network could watch millions of such exchanges and never have enough information to gain access. Protocols of the former type are, lamentably, the default on most systems. They should be disabled and replaced by secure protocols, such as ssh or Kerberos, which are both more secure and more complex than those in our second example.

Some organizations have a policy that their website must be accurate, but not necessarily available. At the first hint that it might be under attack, they shut it off from the Internet. The decision to accept denial of service rather than risk corruption of data is purely in the realm of policy.

Detecting Corruption

Corrupt data are often obviously corrupt—but not always. While the corruption of data most often perpetrated by crackers is cyber-graffiti, the purpose of which is to be ostentatious, subtle corruption is most often perpetrated by insiders. Checksums are the method by which corruption is most often detected when it is not otherwise obvious. Note that the traditional checksum algorithm is not secure; MD5 checksums should be used instead.

Verifying checksums is arduous. Therefore, it should always be done by one or more scripts. Having two or more different servers independently verifying checksums each night makes it much more difficult for anyone to surreptitiously insert corrupt data. The attacker would need to know that scripts running on these servers would discover his attack and be able to subvert these scripts. See Chapter 11, "Scripting," for more about script writing.

Recovering from Corruption

Once data has been found to be corrupt, recovery entails replacing the corrupt data with a copy that is still intact. Typically, this is done by restoring the data from an archive, by getting another copy from its original (possibly external) source, or by regenerating it from source data. Any data of value that cannot be regenerated from source data should, of course, be backed up or archived. See Chapter 12, "Backups," for details on various backup methodologies.

Ensure Availability

Denial of service attacks are commonly attempted by both crackers and disgruntled employees. They range from outsiders bombarding gateway machines with carefully crafted ping packets to insiders deliberately unplugging networks to (usually insiders) planting Trojan horses and logic bombs.

These types of attack involve a trusted user maliciously emplacing software where it will be executed. Such software may shutdown systems or services (often intermittently), corrupt data, or destroy data. These are most often placed by disgruntled software developers and system administrators. The best defense against these is the maintenance of good morale.

Denial of service attacks are generally difficult to prevent, usually but not always easy to detect, and pose varying recovery challenges.

Preventing Denial of Service

Ensuring the physical security of servers helps to defend against some types of denial of service attacks. Servers should be located in a suitable data center. In addition to providing adequate cooling and redundant power, the data center should provide physical security for the servers. At a minimum, access to the data center should be controlled by card keys or a similar system that logs the entry (and preferably also the exit)[1] of each user. Obviously, only system administrators, network engineers, and wiring technicians should have access. The locks that come with the cabinets should be used.

Some services such as anonymous ftp and public WWW service are inherently unrestricted. But most servers in most organizations are meant to serve a limited set of clients. The limit may be enforced by either restricting the set of client machines to which the service will be provided or by restricting service to a set of uids. Which restriction is better for a particular server will depend on the nature of the service being provided. Occasionally, it will be appropriate to check both the client host and the uid before

---

1. It is essential that controlled exits have emergency overrides. As in other cases, overriding an emergency exit should sound an alarm and alert security.

providing service. Logs should be kept in all cases where authentication is required to use a service.

The final defense against denial of service attacks is to keep software up-to-date. Most denial of service attacks that don't involve physical access to the server are exploitations of newly discovered vulnerabilities in software. In the OPEN SOURCE community, patches for such vulnerabilities are usually available hours after the first attack, so it is important to keep up-to-date with security-related patches. At least one system administrator in each organization should be responsible for keeping up with security patches on a daily basis and for notifying all the other system administrators when a relevant patch becomes available.

Detecting Denial of Service

It is usually easy to detect that a denial of service attack is under way. Such attackers are rarely subtle, and their aim is most often to deny service as completely as they are able.

The detection effort is usually focused on who perpetrated the attack. Good logging is important, but realize that crackers generally both forge addresses and attack from systems where they have gained unauthorized access.

Recovering Availability

Attacks mounted from within the organization are defeated by shutting down the software used to perpetrate them.

Attacks mounted from without are usually short-lived because the person responsible doesn't want to be traced. The longer the attack continues, the more time available to track down the initiator.

Protect Confidentiality

Most data on corporate fileservers are confidential. Some data are trade secrets, some are marketing or other business plans, and some are personnel records. Furthermore, the dissemination of some data may be subject to legal limitations.

System administrators should treat all data as confidential unless its publication has been approved. Recovery from the loss of confidentiality is usually difficult, and often expensive, even in the rare cases where the loss is somehow detected. Therefore, prevention is critical.

Preventing Disclosure

The loss of confidentiality may happen in many ways. For example, a cracker may gain access to file services, an employee may mistype an email address, or an employee may deliberately hunt for valuable data that can be sold to the competition.

Unencrypted data is as secure as a message posted publicly. Weak encryption is comparable to placing documents in a paper envelope—it will protect them against casual snooping. Strong encryption is more like a vault—it might be possible for a determined expert to gain access, but it will take time if it is possible at all.

Strong encryption is not a panacea. It is a necessary but not sufficient measure for preserving confidentiality of data. Strong encryption will usually preserve confidentiality against the various losses noted previously. Strong encryption, however, is a more robust defense than nondisclosure agreements, which should be used anyway when appropriate.

If a cracker does gain access to file services, whether from within the organization or from without, well-encrypted files will not be decipherable to him, and the confidentiality of the data therein will be preserved. Any accidental recipient of email will be most unlikely to have the key needed to decipher an encrypted message intended for other eyes. Employees who hunt for data to sell (or publish free for spite) will be limited to data for which they have been granted keys.

Another approach is to employ firewalls within a corporate network, separating departments from each other. For example, it is essential that stock traders not know the business of their Mergers and Acquisitions department. A firewall separating Mergers and Acquisitions from the rest of an investment bank might be justified. However, it should not be a substitute for the general use of strong encryption and authentication within the organization.

Detecting Loss of Confidentiality

Most losses of confidentiality probably go undetected. Sometimes an intrusion and transfer of one or more files to the outside may be logged. However, most breaches of confidentiality are effected by insiders. Employees may take data with them to a new employer, or may even sell data to the competition on an ongoing basis.

Short of draconian physical security, little can be done to detect such losses. This is why prevention is so important with respect to confidentiality.

Recovering from Loss of Confidentiality

Once a loss of confidentiality has been detected, recovery is usually impossible, or costly. If the data have not been distributed widely, it may be possible to secure from a court and enforce an injunction ordering all copies not belonging to the legitimate owners to be destroyed. This will rarely be the case.

Sometimes the cost of recovery will be very high, but nevertheless justified. In some cases, this may mean taking drastic measures. In other cases, only passwords will need to be changed. For example, if you learn that the competition has a copy of your business plans, it may be best to change the plans if this can be done unbeknownst to the competition. Note that this means the business chooses to take a course of action that was judged not to be optimal.

Enforcement

Unenforced policies may be of academic interest, but they rarely provide value to the shareholders who paid for them to be written. This is particularly true with regard to security policies. They must be enforced, and the enforcement techniques are neither as obvious as they may seem nor as glamorous as Hollywood would have us believe.

The next chapter comprises tools, techniques, and methodologies for the enforcement of security policy. It is required reading for any system administrator who has hands-on responsibility for systems connected to a network.

II

Practicum

8

Enforcing Security

THE ENFORCEMENT OF SECURITY is the sexiest part of system administration. Hollywood does not depict the drama of moving an operational network from one place to another, the excitement of installing the latest hardware, the comedy of user questions, or the tragedy of failed restore operations. However, the intrigue of computer security has been the subject of numerous films.

The mystique that surrounds computer security derives from the seemingly magical ability of crackers to gain unauthorized access. This magical similitude follows, like any artful trickery, from a lack of understanding about the methods involved. Deep understanding of computer security is rare—even among experienced system administrators. This lack of understanding is manifested in the widespread absence of security policy, which was discussed in Chapter 7, "Security Policy."

The enforcement of security always follows from a security policy. Every security measure enforces a policy, whether explicit or implicit. The crafting of an explicit policy enforces deliberate consideration of threats and promotes preparedness for security breaches.

Securing the Organization

Most security efforts, at both the policy and enforcement level, are aimed at denying access to unauthorized users. While this is a sensible objective, most security breaches are perpetrated by authorized users. A firewall is a useful adjunct to securing an organization, but it provides no security whatsoever against the principal threat. This section takes a broad view and provides measures for securing the organization from both the Internet and internal users while providing the services required to conduct business.

The Internet

Nearly every organization operating LINUX systems has a business reason to connect to the Internet. Because the Internet includes potentially hostile adversaries, such as unscrupulous competitors, crackers, and spammers, most organizations enforce a policy specifying the sorts of traffic that may come in from and go out to the Internet.

The basic mechanism for enforcing an Internet security policy is packet filtering. External routers are configured to let packets matching an acceptable profile pass and to reject other packets. For example, packets to initiate a telnet session from an unknown system outside the company to a system inside would be rejected at most sites.

Packet filtering alone would suffice to provide security against threats from the Internet if there were not a requirement for services. Services that are too dangerous to allow in and out freely are often provided indirectly, via a firewall.

The firewall is located outside the packet filtering router and is configured to act as an intermediary between internal systems and the Internet. The firewall is trusted by internal systems, even though it is expected to come under attack. Therefore, the firewall should be configured to provide only a limited set of services. Only required software should be installed on a firewall. Its log files must be examined carefully every day, and it should never store sensitive data. A firewall should be configured to accept logins only on the console or only from trusted hosts via secure protocols such as ssh. Ideally, most system partitions are on a disk that is write-protected by a hardware jumper. /tmp and /var need to be mounted read-write. The /etc directory includes some files that must be read-write, but most of /etc should be write-protected. This can be done by placing the files that must be read-write in a directory on the read-write disk where /tmp and /var reside, with links from the /etc directory to the files.

The packet filtering software that may be compiled into the LINUX kernel is called ipchains.[1] Note that ipchains simply updates the kernel's packet filtering tables—it does not require that the interface be configured.

Virtual private networks (VPNs) may be set up over ordinary Internet connections by configuring FreeS/WAN[2] into the kernel. When two hosts both have FreeS/WAN enabled, all IP packets sent between them will be strongly encrypted. This is highly

---

1. This is true for 2.2 and later kernels. 2.0 kernels used a different packet filter called ipfw.

2. http://xs4all.nl/~freeswan

recommended for all Internet gateways. The use of FreeS/WAN internally presents an additional challenge to any cracker who may compromise one machine, as well as to employees attempting to access data or systems for which they are not authorized.

Remote Access

Before home Internet access was common, remote access was provided via direct dial-up. When most home Internet connections were made via analog modems, this continued to be a sensible approach. However, as employees increasingly acquired dedicated Internet access at speeds beyond the 128kbs offered by the fastest dial-up ISDN services, demand increased for remote access via the Internet.

Many IT departments have resisted the demand for remote access via the Internet due to security concerns. The concerns are reasonable because it is easier to eavesdrop on Internet traffic than on most telephone system traffic. However, these concerns can be overcome. Strong cryptographic authentication and encryption offer secure mechanisms for remote access via the Internet.

Access should be provided to employees via ssh and FreeS/WAN. This reduces the support and other costs of maintaining a large dial-in pool.

Internal Security

Most security breaches are committed by authorized users. There are two problems here— one is misuse of data to which a user has authorization, and the other problem is users gaining access to data for which they are not authorized. The former is a management problem. The latter is the subject of this section.

In most jurisdictions, every organization is obliged by law to keep certain information, such as personnel records, from access by unauthorized users. Public corporations are required to protect financial information until it is disclosed publicly. Investment banks are required to keep merger and acquisition information from the sales force.

Even data that are not subject to legal proscriptions must often be protected from internal users. In many firms, engineering data must be kept from the sales force lest they disclose information to customers in an effort to pre-sell products.

Therefore, internal systems should be crafted as if no external firewall were in place. It should be assumed that crackers are already inside the firewall. Strong encryption and authentication protocols such as ssh and Kerberos should be employed. Protocols such as rsh and telnet should be disabled. Consideration should be given to using IPsec to encrypt all internal IP traffic.

Firewalls may be erected to separate departments within an organization. Each department that is restricted should have its own NIS domain and its own servers. Only members of the department should have entries in the passwd map for the domain. The file servers should not export filesystems to machines outside the domain.

The Data Center

Data centers are built to ensure the reliable operation of servers by providing ease of networking, more reliable power and cooling, and physical security. Access should be granted only to persons with an essential business need.

Access to the data center should be controlled by a card key entry system. This provides a log of when each person entered. It also provides a mechanism for canceling access without changing locks and reissuing keys.

The cabinets used in data centers typically have low-security locks. In large data centers where many persons have access, these may be used to keep system administrators, network administrators, and electricians out of cabinets to which they should not have access.

Securing Systems

Securing the computing resources of an organization depends not only on arranging systems to provide security. Each system, individually, must also be secure. This section offers guidelines for securing individual systems.

Configuration

The first security system that each desktop needs is a screenlock program that cannot be disabled by the user. The idle interval is a matter of policy. In some environments, five minutes might be reasonable. In other environments, fifteen seconds might be justified.

The general configuration strategy for enforcing the security of a system is to disable all unneeded services. Check the /etc/inetd.conf file for services that are not needed. Also use /etc/inetd.conf to limit services to those that are needed. Make sure the appropriately secure /etc/inetd.conf file is part of each system profile. See Chapter 14, "System Profiles."

The services that are provided should be protected by means of TCP wrappers. To begin with minimal security, create the file /etc/hosts.allow containing

```
ALL: LOCAL
```

and create the file /etc/hosts.deny containing

```
ALL: ALL
```

Most sites will need more complex /etc/hosts.allow and /etc/hosts.deny files in order to limit particular services to specific hosts or domains within the organization. Unless the system is located outside the firewall and intended to provide external services, such as WWW or ftp, services should not be provided to hosts outside the organization. Consult the man pages for detailed information on other options.

Use the command netstat -na to list the TCP ports that are accepting connections. Each is followed by the word LISTEN. Look up the port numbers in /etc/services to see which service is using each port.

Passwords and Passphrases

The traditional UNIX password hashing algorithm is no longer secure because the computing power available to generate valid hashes has rendered it obsolete. In fact, the very concept of the password has been rendered obsolete. One should think in terms of passphrases of at least 12 to 20 characters. The MD5 hashing algorithm should be used for every computing environment that contains any valuable or sensitive data. To enable MD5 passphrases, use the pwconv command.

A good passphrase must satisfy two criteria: It must be unfeasible to guess (even with the aid of powerful cryptanalysis tools), and it must be easy for the user to remember. Prior to MD5 passphrases, this was difficult to achieve because of the eight-character length limitation. To be difficult to guess, an eight-character password had to include lowercase letters, uppercase letters, numerals, and punctuation marks. Such passwords are rarely easy to remember. One trick for composing easy-to-remember passwords or passphrases that meet this criteria is to condense an easy to remember phrase. For example, "Mary had a little lamb" could be condensed to "Mhad1ll." without making it too difficult to remember. Reversing it to ".ll1dahM" makes it even a bit more difficult to guess, at the expense of being a bit more difficult to remember. Of course, one should never use this particular example.

Each time a new user is added, an initial passphrase must be set. In cases such as schools, where many new accounts must be created at the same time and there is little at risk, it may suffice to set something like each user's date of birth as the initial passphrase. If this is done, the authentication mechanism must be configured to require the passphrase to be changed the first time each user logs in. In other cases, a system administrator could generate a random passphrase that is then securely conveyed to the user. This also requires that the user be forced to change the passphrase the first time he logs in. The only case that does not require the passphrase to be changed immediately is when a system administrator can sit down with the user and let the user type the passphrase in directly as the new account is created.

Regardless of how initial passphrases are chosen, they must be tested regularly or continuously. The system administrators should attempt to crack all the passphrases in the NIS maps. In large organizations, it may be appropriate to dedicate one system to this task. Typically, the system used might be one that has been recently retired from other duties. In some environments, it might be reasonable to require the department of any user whose password is cracked to pay a penalty to be used for improved security. Such incentives are often effective enforcement mechanisms.

File Permissions

The security of a LINUX system depends on the correctness and security of the file permissions and ownership present on the system. When configuring systems and defining system profiles, it is essential that the file system security is not compromised. For instance, the /tmp directory is compromised if the sticky bit is lost. In general, most files and directory permissions are set correctly upon installation, so it is a matter of not corrupting them during file maintenance or as part of the build process.

Certain programs have the set user id bit set. This means that the program will begin running with the effective user id specified by its file ownership. This is an important mechanism for allowing restricted access to secure resources, but it is also exploited as a means to gain unauthorized privileges. It is considered unsafe to mount filesystems from remote hosts allowing the set user id execution; therefore, use of the `nosuid` mount option is recommended.

In addition to the set user id option, NFS filesystems also should not be exported without restriction. Always specify a list of hosts or use wildcarding to restrict the hosts being exported to. If the environment is running NIS, then restricting exports to specific netgroups is appropriate. More information about NFS access control can be found in Chapter 20, "Working with NFS."

Special Accounts and Environments

Frequently, special accounts need to be created. Some are created because they are exposed to the public and must be secured to prevent intrusion. Others are pseudo–logins set up for the purpose of creating a uid to own a particular data set and are not intended for interactive use. Another special account type is one granted limited access to privileged commands (for example, an operator account).

The best way to secure a user account is to create a `chroot`'ed account. By specifying the `chroot` command as the login shell, system administrators can create an account that does not have access to the normal file hierarchy. The first argument should be a directory that contains the `chroot` environment. This is a minimal version of the normal Unix filesystem hierarchy, populated with the minimum number of utilities, shared libraries, and devices to perform the job at hand. This often requires experimentation because it is difficult to guess what may be required by `libc`, the C runtime library. The `strace` utility may be helpful in identifying the needed components. The third argument to `chroot` must be the command interpreter or the utility to be executed.

An account may be created solely to provide shared access to a data set or a binary distribution. Such an account needs the functionality of a normal user account, but with restricted access to the account itself. By specifying `/bin/false` as the shell, one can limit access to this account to those who know the password and already have another account on the system. Users may use the `su` command to access the account, an event which is reported to `syslog`. Note that this type of account is more of an administrative convenience than a security measure, but it does control access to the account. However, once a user gains access to the account, no audit trail exists. It will be impossible to determine what commands were issued by which user with access to the account. Most auditors hate this sort of thing, but they are generally unable to come up with a workable alternative.

The third type of account grants to the user special privileges beyond those normally permitted for a user-level account. The `sudo` utility can be used for this purpose. The `sudo` utility is configured via the /etc/sudoers file. This file allows the system administrator to define a command or set of commands that are available to users, groups, or netgroups (in an NIS environment). Users with sudo privileges are prompted for their own passwords when they invoke the sudo command. The argument to the sudo command is the utility to be executed with root privileges.

Tools

Several toolkits are available to assist with securing a system and for detecting potential security breaches. Many of the packages provided with LINUX already have security features—we encourage their use.

The highest degree of authentication security can be obtained by utilizing hardware tokens, such as products manufactured by SecureNet or Secure-ID. These require physical possession of a small device to authenticate. Several security software packages contain support for these products.

We suggest reviewing the following tools with an eye toward further enhancing the security of exposed systems or systems containing highly sensitive data. These tools improve access security by implementing stronger authentication mechanisms:

- PAM (Pluggable Authentication Modules). This is the LINUX authentication framework. There is currently no support for one-time passwords or hardware tokens, but the PAM framework should allow support for these technologies to be integrated into the LINUX operating system.

- s-key. This is a package for creating and processing one-time passwords.

- opie. This is another one-time password package.

- ssh (The Secure Shell). ssh can be configured to use public key passphrases and perform encryption.

These tools are intended be used for checking password strength and examining network services and filesystems for known weaknesses:

- COPS. Detects system and password security problems.
- Crack. This program checks for weak passwords.
- Tiger. Detects system and password security problems.
- SATAN. Detects network security holes.

These tools are for performing advanced diagnostics and logging:

- tripwire. This program detects files that have been altered.
- swatch. A utility for monitoring log files. This is a useful general-purpose tool.
- netcat. This utility can be used for low-level port scanning for TCP and UDP sockets.
- tcpdump. This is a general-purpose packet sniffer.

Exposed Systems

We define exposed systems as those that are exposed directly to the Internet or that reside in the DMZ of the firewall. The DMZ (or Red Net) of a firewall is the network segment on which the external interface of the firewall resides; it is normally connected to an Internet service provider via a filtering router.

Systems deployed in this environment should be configured with the minimum functionality needed to perform their tasks. NIS and NFS should not be used in this environment, and the RPC portmapper should be disabled. Entries in the `inetd.conf` file should be trimmed to a bare minimum. Only a minimum number of user-level accounts should be in the `passwd` file. The `passwd` file entries themselves should be tested periodically with `crack` or some other password checking utility. If the system is based on a distribution that uses a package manager, periodically verify the packages to check the integrity of the system. Also, the syslog service should forward events to a host on the inside, as well as retain logs locally. This makes it more difficult for an intruder to erase evidence of his presence. Finally, full backups of the system's data must be available along with an image on the build server (see Chapter 15, "Automated Installation and Upgrade") so that the system may be rebuilt rapidly from scratch if compromised.

Exploits and Consequences

The state of the art of enforcement of security policy responds to the state of the art of the exploits. Each time a new exploit is developed, system administrators and security specialists create a response. The response may be a bug fix, a change in configuration, or even a revised protocol.

To enforce security effectively, a system administrator needs some familiarity with the exploits of crackers and the consequences of those exploits. Then an effective strategy can be developed to enforce the organization's security policies. Studying the history of computer security exploits helps to put everything in perspective.[3]

User Exploits

Anyone who gains access to the system at the user level may steal any data readable by the user. Any files writable by that user id should be considered compromised. Most experienced intruders will not do much with a user-level account, because it is not possible to cover one's tracks. Instead, he will leverage the user-level access in an effort to gain `root` access.

---

3. See `http://www.rootshell.com` and `http://www.insecure.org` for examples of current exploits.

root Exploits

Once an intruder gains root access to a system, he will have the ability to remove or alter evidence of the break-in. The intruder will also have the ability to install back doors into the system so that he may come and go unnoticed at a later date.

By monitoring the system and the normal activities associated with a system, it may be possible to correlate unusual activities to an actual break-in. This is one reason why reviewing the log files is such an important component of security enforcement. Remote logging via syslog helps ensure the integrity of log information during attacks.

Trap Doors and Trojan Horses

A number of publicly available software packages were written to raise user consciousness about the possibilities for installing back doors into systems. The best known is rootkit, of which there are many variants. Search the Internet to find the latest versions, and experiment with them on your own systems to gain an understanding of what is possible and how to thwart and detect them.

It is wise to assume that privately held software packages have more advanced capabilities than those that can be found on the Internet. Do not assume that measures to detect the public versions will detect all versions.

Denial of Service

Denial of service attacks attempt to shut down or render useless a computing service. Some denial of service attacks crash a system, whereas others overload it such that it cannot provide service to legitimate users. Some attacks affect only one service; others affect an entire system or network.

Most denial of service attacks fall into two classes: those that exploit a bug in the network stack and those that exploit a weakness in the protocols. Other attacks include fork bombs, which consume all the available memory or file descriptors, and attacks on particular network applications, such as the X WINDOW system.

The only defense against denial of service attacks that exploit bugs in the network stack is to stay abreast of full-disclosure security mailing lists, such as BugTraq.[4] CERT should not be exclusively relied upon because they do not disclose many of the exploits reported to them. Once a bug has been reported and a patch posted, the patch should be applied, starting with exposed systems such as firewalls.

Typical attacks that exploit weaknesses in a protocol involve packets sent with forged destination and return addresses. Often one of these is a broadcast address. Thus, a small number of packets sent by an attacker results in a large number of packets bouncing back and forth between the two forged networks.

---

4. The home of BugTraq is http://www.SecurityFocus.com/

The defense is to filter at the external gateway all packets addressed to either the broadcast address of the network or the broadcast address of any subnet. Using `ipchains`, the command

```
ipchains -A input -l -d xxx.xxx.xxx.xxx -j DENY
```

will drop any packets with *xxx.xxx.xxx.xxx* in the destination field.

Because there is never a friendly reason to send packets addressed to another network's broadcast address, any such packets received at the gateway should be presumed hostile. Use DENY rather than REJECT to avoid sending ICMP `host unreachable` messages back to the alleged source of these hostile packets.

Breach Procedures

When an intrusion has been detected, tread softly until a decision has been made as to whether or not evidence will be gathered. If it will, take the affected systems offline and place clean spares into production.

Next, assess the nature of the exploit and the damage caused. In cases of user-level exploits, finding and closing the hole, changing the password, and restoring any lost or corrupted data may suffice. In cases of root-level exploits, a complete reinstallation is the only way to ensure that the system has no backdoors. Of course, after a reinstallation, the original security hole will still exist. It must be found and closed.

Unless it is a home system, never discount the possibility that the breach could have been committed or facilitated by an insider. Investigate logs on seemingly unaffected machines because they may hold clues, as well as possible backdoors.

After service has been restored, initiate a review of the security policies and procedures. If in-house expertise is lacking, consider retaining a qualified consultant. Ask whether a different policy or more rigorous enforcement would have prevented the breach without impeding business operations. Update the security policy if necessary.

Current Information

Current information on security tools and exploits may be found at the following sites:

- `http://www.SecurityFocus.com/`
- `ftp://coast.cs.purdue.edu/pub/tools/unix`

Further Reading

- *Firewalls and Internet Security,* William R. Cheswick and Steven M. Bellovin, 1994
- *Building Internet Firewalls,* D. Brent Chapman and Elizabeth D. Zwicky, 1995
- *Practical UNIX and Internet Security,* Simson Garfinkel and Gene Spafford, 1996
- *Applied Cryptography,* 2nd ed., Bruce Schneier, 1995
- Firewall HOWTO, by Mark Grennan
- IPCHAINS HOWTO, by Paul Russell
- Security HOWTO, by Kevin Fenzi
- Cipe+Masquerading mini-HOWTO, by Anthony Ciaravalo
- Firewall Piercing mini-HOWTO, by François-René Rideau

*In order to make an apple pie
from scratch, you must first create
the universe.*

~Carl Sagan (1934–1996)

9

Booting and Shutdown

LINUX BOOTING AND SHUTDOWN PROCEDURES are powerful, flexible, and complex. System administrators should be familiar with the software components involved in booting and shutdown, the role each component performs, and how each may be configured.

Machines will occasionally fail to boot. This may happen for a variety of reasons, including hardware failures, network failures (including server processes that are not running), and software configuration errors. An intimate understanding of the system startup procedure is needed to isolate the cause of a boot failure.

Lesser problems may also strike during booting. For example, a machine may complete the boot sequence without starting an essential service. This machine will be running, but it will not be doing its job. Familiarity with the boot sequence will be needed to solve the problem.

Finally, the system administrator may be required to start a new server on a system. Software packaged with `rpm` may insert the files needed to start and stop the server automatically, while other software distributions may require the system administrator to write custom scripts to integrate a new server into the system startup process.

Booting

All contemporary computers use the same general components and the same general sequence for booting an operating system. The CPU initializes itself internally and then begins to fetch instructions, starting at a fixed address of physical memory.[1] Hardware engineers arrange for firmware programmed into an EPROM or flash EPROM to map to these addresses. These instructions typically initialize the hardware, then load the next level of software to be executed (usually from hard disk, but sometimes from a floppy disk, CD-ROM, or the network), and finally pass control to this software. This next level of software is known as a bootstrap loader. If the computer architecture imposes severe-enough limitations on the size of the bootstrap loader, sometimes a secondary bootstrap program is used. The bootstrap program then loads the operating system proper.

The LINUX operating system is no exception to this model. LINUX differs from most other operating systems in that the initialization process varies based on the hardware architecture used. This permits LINUX to coexist with other operating systems. It also permits the same device drivers to be used in the boot loaders as in LINUX itself. Users of other PC operating systems will be surprised by the large number of boot configuration options available to the system administrator.

On Intel-based PCs running LINUX, the software loaded by the firmware is a package called LILO, the LInux LOader. For the Alpha architecture, one of two mechanisms is used—MILO or aboot. For the SPARC architecture, SILO is used. On Macintosh hardware, BootX is used.

PC Firmware and Loaders

Unfortunately, as of this writing, most firmware for Intel-based PCs is bug-ridden and not well-suited for LINUX. Because the source code is not widely available, it does not get fixed. The good news is that an OpenBIOS project is underway. It is possible that most PC motherboards will ship with an Open Source BIOS within a few years, and that system administrators with a good reason to configure and compile their own firmware will be able to do so sooner than that.

One good reason for system administrators to replace proprietary BIOSes with OpenBIOS, when it stabilizes, is that the former do not provide for booting over the network, while the latter will. This will facilitate the installation and upgrade of large numbers of PCs.

LILO is a small piece of software that exists to control which kernel will be loaded and booted. The system administrator determines the choices LILO will present to the user at the console during booting. The choices may include one or more LINUX kernels and one or more other operating systems. LILO also provides the system administrator

---

1. The Compaq Alpha Microprocessor is an exception. It fetches the first few instructions from a serial ROM (SROM), through a dedicated interface, before transferring control to conventional ROMs.

the opportunity to pass parameters to the kernel via the /etc/lilo.conf file. Options may also be set interactively at the console.

LILO is instantiated by running /sbin/lilo, which reads /etc/lilo.conf to determine the intentions of the system administrator. This creates the map file /boot/map, which records the locations of the kernels and all other files that the boot loader may need to reference. This is critical, because the boot loader does not understand filesystems; it must reference files by their location on the disk. Thus, it is imperative to run /sbin/lilo before rebooting whenever there has been a change to the kernel. Failure to do so is likely to render the system unbootable.

lilo can also be run in multi-user mode with either the -t (test) or -q (query) options to show what LILO would do during an actual boot. See the lilo(8) man page for more detail.

Some of the interesting options that may be configured in /etc/lilo.conf include whether or not to present a console prompt before uncompressing and loading the kernel, a list of up to 16 kernels that may be loaded and the parameters to be passed to each, and the timeout for the prompt, if present. Many other configuration options are possible. They are documented in the *LILO User's Guide*, distributed with the LILO source code.

LILO is sometimes also configured to uncompress and load a ramdisk image into memory, as well as a kernel. This is used by the LINUX kernel to load modules into the kernel needed to support the boot media. The most common case is SCSI support, where the SCSI adapter driver is specified as a kernel module. The filesystem is then deallocated when the driver(s) are loaded into the kernel.

Normally, /etc/lilo.conf is configured such that /sbin/lilo installs the first part of LILO's boot loader (along with the partition table) in the Master Boot Record (MBR) of the hard disk from which the system is to be booted. The first part of LILO's boot loader loads the second part, which is normally /boot/boot.b. However, /etc/lilo.conf may be configured to install LILO other places, such as a floppy disk, or in the first sector of a boot partition. The latter allows for the option of leaving management of the MBR to the software of another operating system also installed on the system.

In addition to passing parameters to the kernel, LILO is capable of passing parameters to init. These have the effect of defining environment variables. See the BootPrompt HOWTO for more information on passing parameters at the Boot: prompt.

Another mechanism for booting LINUX on PCs is Loadlin, which boots LINUX from within a Microsoft WINDOWS operating system.

Alpha Firmware and Loaders

Workstations with Compaq Alpha microprocessors were originally built to support the Digital UNIX, OpenVMS, and WINDOWS NT operating systems. The firmware comes in different flavors based on the operating system to be installed. Systems manufactured for use with Digital UNIX or OpenVMS were supplied with SRM firmware, which resembles the monitors associated with minicomputers and traditional UNIX workstations. These provide hardware diagnostics and an ability to boot from disks, CD-ROMs, floppy disks, and network adapters. SRM systems normally use aboot to load the kernel. Systems shipped with WINDOWS NT were supplied with the ARC or AlphaBIOS firmware. These are somewhat less-capable monitor ROMs, but some models running this firmware can load MILO into the flash-PROM, providing an elegant mechanism for booting the LINUX kernel on these models.

System administrators can install either of the firmware choices on most Alphas. Therefore, it is recommended to upgrade an Alpha with the ARC or AlphaBIOS firmware to the SRM firmware, if possible. Images are available to download.[2]

SPARC Firmware and SILO

SILO is the SPARC Improved boot LOader. Like LILO, it is a two-stage boot loader. The first stage loads the second stage, and then the second stage loads the kernel. The first stage is written to the PROM of the SPARC machine, and the second stage is stored on the hard disk.

The command /sbin/silo reads the configuration file /etc/silo.conf and writes the primary loader to PROM and the secondary loader to /boot/second.b—unless another location is specified in the silo.conf file.

Information on dual-booting a SPARC system is available from Sun.[3] SILO is also capable of writing bootable ufs CD-ROM images. This is useful because the SPARC PROM code is not capable of booting from an ISO9660 CD-ROM.

Macintosh Firmware and BootX

The firmware found in current Macintosh computers is called Open Firmware.[4] It is possible to configure Open Firmware to load a LINUX kernel and to boot LINUX directly. With Open Firmware versions 2.xx, this works reasonably well. However, because the NVRAM settings of Open Firmware versions 1.xx are overwritten by MacOS, the more common method is to boot LINUX from within MacOS.

The BootX[5] utility is analogous to Loadlin and provides an easy-to-use mechanism for booting LINUX from within MacOS. This method requires that a LINUX kernel and a compressed ramdisk image be available in the MacOS System Folder.

---

2. ftp://ftp.digital.com/pub/Digital/Alpha/firmware/ or
http://www.service.digital.com/alpha/server/firmware/

3. http://www.sun.com/software/linux/docs/dual_boot.html

4. Despite the name, source code for Open Firmware is not publicly available.

5. For more on BootX, see http://www.linuxppc.org/bootx.shtml

Kernel Boot Actions

Once an image of the kernel has been loaded into memory, execution is passed to the kernel.

The kernel begins by initializing the virtual memory subsystem and the task scheduler. Next, it initializes the timer subsystem and parses command-line options. The module system and various kernel buffers and caches are then initialized. If a ramdisk for loading modules has been specified, LILO has already loaded it into memory. The kernel will verify that it hasn't overwritten the image and will then copy it to a ramdisk (/dev/ram0). The ramdisk will be mounted as the root filesystem. Later in the boot sequence this will be replaced by the real root device. The new root filesystem is then examined for a /linuxrc file, and this is executed. The /linuxrc file is normally a shell script that runs insmod to load device drivers needed to mount the root filesystem.

Finally, the last step of the kernel boot sequence is to create the process context for init and begin execution.

init

init is the ancestor of all other processes. Its purpose is to spawn the core processes needed by the system. There are two flavors of init: BSD and System V.[6] Most LINUX distributions use the System V version of init, which parses the /etc/inittab file. inittab contains one entry per line, each with four colon-delimited fields. The first field is a tag of one to four characters that uniquely identifies the entry. The second field lists the runlevels associated with this inittab entry. The third field specifies an action keyword that controls the behavior of the entry. The fourth field is the process—the commands to be executed for this inittab entry along with their parameters. This is a typical inittab entry:

```
l3:3:wait:/etc/rc.d/rc 3
```

The action (third) field may contain any of the following values:

boot. The process will be executed once at system boot. The runlevel field is ignored.

bootwait. The process will be executed while the init process waits for processing of the initial runlevel to complete. The runlevel field is ignored.

ctrlaltdel. The process will be executed when the init process receives the INT signal. This is typically when the Ctrl-Alt-Delete key combination is pressed at the system console.

---

6. The BSD-style init invokes a central initialization script /etc/rc. The runlevel is passed as an argument.

Table 9.1 **Run levels**

0	Used to halt the system
1	Single-user mode
2	Multiple-user mode, but no server processes
3	Multiple-user mode, with server processes
4	Unused
5	Multiple-user mode, with server processes and X11
6	System reboot
7–9	Unused

initdefault. This entry determines which runlevel should be started. The runlevels are defined in Table 9.1. The process field of the initdefault entry is ignored. Never specify runlevels 0 or 6 in initdefault, because this will render the system useless. Supplying no value in the runlevel field will cause the system to prompt for the runlevel at the console during boot.

kbrequest. The process will be executed when a special key sequence is pressed. The keyboard map must have a definition for the KeyboardSignal key, which is used to define the key sequence used for this feature.

once. The indicated process will be executed once when the specified runlevel is entered. Used to start update, the LINUX process that periodically flushes disk buffers.

ondemand. This entry allows the indicated process to be executed when the associated runlevel is entered. The ondemand runlevels are a, b, and c. No actual change in runlevel occurs. The process is simply run when the ondemand runlevel is selected via init.

off. This action disables the current entry. The entry is a no-op.

powerfail. This action is called when init receives the SIGPWR signal. This indicates that the system is about to lose power. The indicated process is launched, and init returns immediately. The process should shut down the system gracefully.

powerokwait. This action is also associated with the SIGPWR signal. In this case, init also checks for the file /etc/powerstatus and expects the contents to be the word OK. This means that the power has returned to normal. This action is used along with the powerfail or powerwait actions to implement support for Uninterruptible Power Supplies (UPSes). init waits for the process to complete before continuing.

powerwait. Similar to powerfail, except that init waits for the completion of the process before it continues.

respawn. The respawn action starts the process associated with this entry when the indicated runlevel is entered. If the process exits, init will restart it. respawn entries are traditionally used to manage getty processes.

sysinit. The process will be run at system boot time, before any boot or bootwait actions. The runlevel field is ignored.

wait. The wait action starts the process associated with this entry when the indicated runlevel is entered. init waits for the completion of the process before continuing.

Specifying no runlevel in the runlevel field equates to specifying all runlevels. The exceptions are actions that ignore the runlevel field altogether and the initdefault action.

The superuser can use the init command to reboot or halt a running system. Runlevel 6 reboots a system, and runlevel 0 shuts down a system in an orderly fashion. System administrators should boot a system one runlevel at a time to become familiar with the processes that run at each level.

The rc Scripts

The runlevels specified by the /etc/inittab file correspond to directories beneath the /etc/rc.d directory.[7] When a new runlevel is invoked, the scripts in the corresponding directory are executed. The files in the rc directories are symbolic links to shell scripts in the /etc/rc.d/init.d directory (see Figure 9.1).

These symbolic links have an orderly naming convention: The first character is either the letter S or K, indicating whether the subsystem controlled by that script should be started (S) or stopped (K) at that runlevel. Then there are two numeric digits, followed by the script name as it appears in /etc/rc.d/init.d. The numeric values indicate the order of invocation. The scripts start and stop subsystems that comprise one or more related processes that provide a specific operating system service.[8]

When the runlevel changes, init invokes the /etc/rc.d/rc script that processes all of the K files and then the S files for that runlevel. The rc script first checks the /var/lock/subsys directory to verify that a subsystem is running before taking any action. This prevents subsystems from being stopped or started more than once.

Any service without a shutdown script in runlevels 0 and 6 won't be killed before a halt. Therefore, any service needing special handling during shutdown needs a K script, and a symlink to it from the rc0.d and rc6.d directories. Existing scripts can be used as examples.

The rc scripts are invoked each time the runlevel changes, as well as at boot time. For example, when a system administrator boots into single-user mode to perform some

---

7. These directory paths are those found on RedHat and derivative distributions. SuSE uses /sbin/init.d and /sbin/init.d/rcN.d while Debian places rc scripts in the /etc/init.d and /etc/rcN.d directories. Other distributions may place the rc scripts elsewhere. Note also that /etc/sysconfig contains many script fragments used during startup.

8. A nice way to disable a service is to create a directory named disabled under the rcN.d directory for the runlevel and move the symlinks for the service into the disabled directory. Note that this technique is self-documenting.

actions and then invokes `init` 3 to enter multi-user mode, the scripts in `/etc/rc.d./rc1.d` are run to establish single-user mode, and then the scripts in `/etc/rc.d/rc3.d` are run to start multi-user and server processes. They are also invoked during shutdown to kill processes in an orderly manner.

Because scripts are started and stopped in numerical order, system administrators should be careful when writing their own `rc` scripts to number them such that required services are already running.

The `chkconfig` command can be used to modify the startup and shutdown of subsystems. `chkconfig --list` lists all subsystems and whether they are on or off at each runlevel.

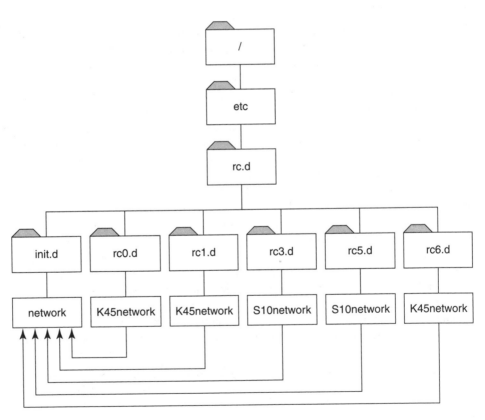

Figure 9.1 Startup scripts

Shutdown

It is important that LINUX systems be shut down correctly. Simply turning off the power will leave a LINUX system in an "unclean" state. In other words, disk buffers will not be flushed, files will not be closed, and filesystems will not be unmounted. Use the shutdown or reboot command to cleanly shut down a LINUX system. The shutdown command is the preferred mechanism.

The shutdown command calls init to change the runlevel to 0, 1, or 6, depending on the options with which shutdown was invoked. See the shutdown man page for option details.

When init is called to change the runlevel to a more quiescent state—typically single-user mode or a shutdown—init invokes rc, which executes the scripts in /etc/rc.d/rcN.d (where N is the new runlevel). In the case of a shutdown or reboot, most of these scripts will begin with a K, indicating that they kill a subsystem's process or processes. They will be executed in numeric order, shutting down the processes in the prescribed order.

Systems may optionally be powered off when halted. Intel systems may be powered off when halted if both the hardware and the kernel support Advanced Power Management (APM).

Further Reading

There are several LINUX HOWTOs and mini-HOWTOs pertinent to booting—in particular, to various boot loaders. Among them are

- BootPrompt HOWTO
- Bootdisk HOWTO
- LILO mini-HOWTO
- Linux+NT-Loader mini-HOWTO
- Loadlin+Win95 mini-HOWTO
- MILO HOWTO
- Multiboot using LILO mini-HOWTO
- Remote Boot mini-HOWTO
- SRM HOWTO

That we are not much sicker and much madder than we are is due exclusively to that most blessed and blessing of all natural graces, sleep.

~Aldous Huxley (1894–1963)

10

Configuring and Building Kernels

L INUX IS BEST DESCRIBED AS A MULTITASKING, multiuser operating system. This means that the LINUX operating system can create the illusion of many programs running simultaneously on behalf of several different users. This is true even on a personal computer, which is typically used by one person at a time.

This concept of a multiuser operating system allows LINUX a higher level of system integrity and reliability than would otherwise be possible. All of the basic facilities necessary to provide this multitasking, multiuser environment are encapsulated within the LINUX kernel.

While the kernel is often thought of as a monolithic executable, it is really more a collection of privileged system calls (see Figure 10.1). The kernel's privileges are enforced by the CPU, ensuring that processes in user space cannot interfere with each other.

This chapter is concerned with configuring the appropriate collection of system calls into the kernel, compiling it, and preparing it for installation on a large number of systems.

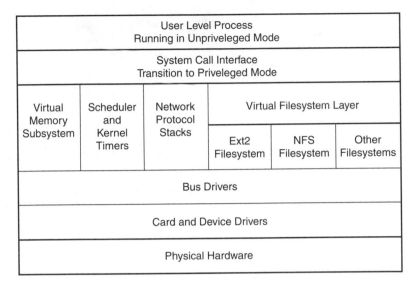

Figure 10.1   Kernel processes

Kernel Basics

The kernel is loaded at system boot time. Once loaded, it initializes the computer's hardware resources and begins the LINUX startup sequence. It is the only software component allowed complete access to the entire computer's resources. The kernel schedules CPU time among the running processes, manages memory, and controls I/O.

The kernel is said to run in *privileged mode*. All microprocessors on which LINUX runs contain support for privileged (kernel) and unprivileged (user) modes. All user processes run in unprivileged mode. They are constrained by the hardware from directly accessing any physical component in the system, or each other.

The upper half of the kernel provides a carefully designed set of subroutines that transfer data between a process and the kernel. Only through the system calls can a process interact with the outside world.

The lower half of the kernel interacts with the physical hardware, as shown in Figure 10.1. This is done in a consistent modular fashion via *device drivers*. Device drivers have a common interface to the upper layers of the kernel. This enables the kernel to treat functionally equivalent devices in an identical fashion, despite differences in the hardware implementation.

The lower half of the kernel also has to contend with asynchronous hardware events known as interrupts. Device drivers must supply interrupt handlers and arrange with the kernel to have them called when the computer hardware signals an interrupt.

The kernel provides three basic abstractions to user programs:

- A virtual computer, also known as *virtual machine*
- Filesystems for persistent storage
- Mechanisms for communicating with other programs

Virtual Machine

A program written to run on LINUX does not have to do anything special to share the system with other processes. It happens automatically, because the kernel supports preemptive multitasking. The kernel scheduler is responsible for switching processes in and out of context as they contend for available CPU time.

Persistent Storage

The kernel provides access to persistent storage, such as disk and tape drives. It interacts with storage devices via direct hardware addresses and provides this service to user processes. However, the kernel also provides filesystems that permit user processes to address persistent storage at a higher level of abstraction.

Interprocess Communication

The kernel supplies mechanisms for user-level processes to exchange data with one another and to synchronize access to shared resources. The System V IPC module provides shared memory, semaphores, and message queues for this purpose. The addition of network protocols allows interactions between processes on different systems.

Kernel Structure

Kernels fall roughly into two types: monolithic kernels and microkernels. Monolithic kernels include all kernel functionality in one large package. Microkernels include only that which absolutely must be part of the kernel, leaving ancillary functionality to be loaded as modules when required.

The advantage of the microkernel is that the smaller set of software changes less and hence is more stable. Most revisions to kernel code are to ancillary functions, such as device drivers, which must change as new hardware is released. The microkernel makes it possible to update a driver without having to replace the microkernel itself.

The disadvantages of the microkernel system include the performance hit taken when module loads occur, as well as the security risks of reading code from a file and loading it into the kernel. Microkernels also suffer from the overhead of copying messages, which is expensive compared to passing pointers to static buffers in a common kernel-wide address space. So, the principal advantage of a monolithic kernel is performance.

Starting with version 1.3, it became possible to compile the Linux kernel either as a monolith or a hybrid. By compiling some features as loadable modules, the kernel gains some of the size and flexibility advantages of a microkernel. Because loadable modules run in kernel space, Linux kernels are not microkernels even if every possible feature is compiled as a loadable module.[1]

Linux Kernel Versions

LINUX kernels have a three-part version number. The first part is the major version number, the second part is the minor version number, and the third part is the revision number. Kernels with even minor version numbers are officially stable and suitable for production use. Kernels with odd minor version numbers are experimental and likely to cause serious problems in production environments. So, while development progresses with an odd-numbered kernel series that incorporates new features, the even-numbered series is updated to fix bugs and support new hardware.

When a developmental kernel series attains the goals set for it, a feature freeze is declared, and it is revised as bugs are fixed, much like with a stable kernel series. When the kernel appears to be stable, its minor version number is increased by one (or set to zero when the major version number is increased by one), and it becomes the first of a new stable kernel series. Shortly afterwards, a new experimental kernel series begins.

This chapter covers the 2.2.x series of kernels, because it is the current stable series as of this writing. Millions of computers are still running 2.0.x kernels, but most are being upgraded. The 2.1.x series is not in use, because it evolved into 2.2.x. The 2.3.x series kernels are of great interest to kernel developers, but not yet to system administrators. Eventually, the 2.3.x kernels will evolve into 2.4.x, at which time system administrators will need to learn about them.

Virtual Memory

The LINUX virtual memory manager provides traditional UNIX virtual memory. Although implementations vary considerably, they all provide common functionality. The virtual memory manager maps virtual addresses generated by the kernel and user programs into physical memory addresses. The virtual memory manager manages the allocation of virtual memory, assigning locations in physical memory or secondary storage (swap) as needed.

At the same time, user programs are presented with a simple flat address space model that is not limited by the size of physical memory, as shown in Figure 10.2.

When the virtual memory manager detects that the system is running low on physical memory, it initiates the swapping process. Initially, small blocks of pages from programs are swapped out in an attempt to free sufficient memory. Eventually, entire processes will

---

1. There is a microkernel version of LINUX called mklinux, which is based on the Mach microkernel. Development of mklinux was funded in part by Apple Computer. As of this writing, development of mklinux has languished.

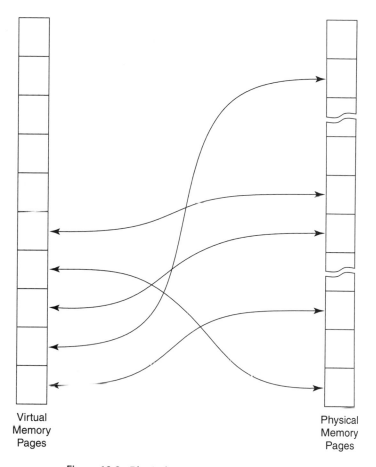

Figure 10.2 Physical to virtual memory mapping

be swapped out if the demands for memory remain high. Finally, processes that attempt to allocate memory will be killed if all virtual memory is exhausted.

The Process Scheduler

The scheduler is a central feature of a multitasking operating system. The role of the scheduler is to determine which processes are available to run and to select the next one to run from that set. The LINUX scheduler design is simple and robust. It performs well in a wide number of circumstances and has few degenerate cases.

Processes can be in one of four states at any given time. The process may be runnable (or running), waiting, stopped, or in a zombie state. Runnable processes are the only processes dealt with by the scheduler. Tasks in the wait state are waiting for external events, like disk data to be returned or a timer interval to expire. When the event occurs, the process is awakened, and it becomes runnable. A stopped process is suspended due to job control or is being run under a debugger. A stopped process must receive a continue signal to become runnable. Zombie processes occur when a process has completed but the parent process has not yet checked its exit status. They consume process resources until either the parent checks the exit status or the system is rebooted.

Initially, a process runs until it has consumed its allotted slice of time or it sleeps on an event. Processes that consume their entire time slice are the least eligible to run again. Processes that were sleeping on an event and have awakened tend to have a greater chance of being selected to run next. This tends to cause I/O-bound processes to run quickly and go back to sleep. Meanwhile, CPU-bound tasks continue to get rescheduled with a low priority.

The Linux 2.2.x kernel implements POSIX 1b real-time extensions. This permits real-time scheduling algorithms and real-time priorities to be selected by root-level processes. See the sched_setscheduler(2) man page for the API.

The final wrinkle in the scheduler is the introduction of symmetric multiprocessing (SMP). This introduces several interesting conditions that the scheduler must deal with. The most basic difference is that more than one runnable process may be active at the same time. Then things get complicated. On an SMP system it is quite possible that the scheduler may be running in parallel on several CPUs at once, so the algorithm must be written to consider this possibility.

There is a non-trivial cost to migrate a process from one CPU to another, due to the overhead involved in reprogramming memory management hardware and flushing caches. The scheduler attempts to avoid this overhead by rescheduling a process on the CPU on which it last ran. Also, the scheduler checks for a common case that results in poor utilization. The SMP version of the scheduler keeps the average amount of CPU time consumed by each process in the Proc structure and compares it to the cost of migrating a process to another CPU. The SMP scheduler also checks to see if both the current process and the process about to be scheduled hold locks in the kernel. If both conditions are true, the process will not be migrated, even if it means leaving a CPU idle! This is done to avoid wasting time migrating a process that is most likely destined to spin on a kernel lock.

Network Support

The Linux kernel can be configured with every major networking protocol in use, as well as a few that are less well-known. In addition, the support for TCP/IP is extremely feature-rich. Here we list some of the more popular networking features that may be compiled into the kernel:

- TCP/IP (version 4) is the standard Internet and LINUX networking protocol. This protocol should always be enabled.

- IPv6 is the next generation of the TCP/IP protocol. As of this writing, the IPv6 stack is complete and has growing application support.

- IP firewall support is provided by several options that allow a host to function as a firewall. Note that the system administrators responsible for these hosts will want to review the IPCHAINS-HOWTO, which discusses these capabilities in great detail. Also note that ipchains replaced the earlier ipfw code.

- PPP is the Point to Point Protocol. It is used to encapsulate other protocols (such as TCP/IP) over serial (usually modem) connections.

- IPX is the native protocol for Novell NetWare. Novell-centric sites should include this protocol.

- AppleTalk or DDP is a Macintosh-specific network protocol. Macintosh-centric sites should include this protocol.

Filesystem Support

Another major subsystem of the LINUX kernel supports the various filesystems available. As is almost always the case with UNIX operating systems, access to the filesystems is through an abstraction layer. The abstraction layer makes it possible to add support for new filesystem types as they become available.

LINUX has changed its primary filesystem twice over the last few years and is preparing to do so again. Originally LINUX was brought up using the minix filesystem. Later it migrated to the ext filesystem. More recently, the ext2 filesystem was developed, and now it's the primary disk filesystem used by systems based on LINUX kernels in the 2.0.x and 2.2.x series. Now under development as part of the 2.3.x experimental kernel series, the ext3 filesystem will be standard for stable kernels from 2.4.0. ext and ext2 will continue to be supported.

- ext2 is the second extended filesystem. It is the primary disk filesystem for LINUX kernels in the 2.0 and 2.2 series, and it should always be enabled.

- ISO 9660 support is available for reading and writing ISO 9660 CD-ROMs.

- HFS Macintosh filesystem support. It is still experimental as of this writing.

- MS-DOS filesystem support, which is useful primarily for reading and writing floppy disks.

- NTFS support for the WINDOWS NT filesystem is read-only as of this writing.

- VFAT support for the WINDOWS 95 or 98 filesystem.

- /proc virtual filesystem support provides access to kernel configuration information and should be included under most circumstances.

- devfs provides a virtual /dev filesystem (similar to /proc) as a replacement for the traditional character and block device entries on disk. It is available as a patch[2] to the 2.2 kernels and will be a standard feature of the 2.4 kernels.

- Quota support provides functionality for imposing per-user limits on disk space.

Support for several different network filesystems may be compiled into the LINUX kernel. Here we list some of the more commonly used network filesystems:

- NFS support includes both client and server NFS functionality, limited at the time of this writing to NFSv2 over UDP. NFSv3 and TCP support are in development.

- Auto FS is the implementation of the automounter, which manages NFS mounts dynamically.

- SMB support is provided for LINUX clients that need to mount filesystems from WINDOWS NT servers.

- NCP support enables the mounting of NetWare volumes.

- Coda is an advanced network filesystem.

Ext2 Filesystem Support

The second extended filesystem is the primary disk filesystem for LINUX. This should always be configured into the kernel.

Microsoft Windows Filesystem Support

LINUX allows local disks with FAT filesystems to be mounted. Support for long filenames is included. Additionally, NTFS and HPFS filesystems can be mounted in a read-only mode. As of this writing, there is experimental support for mounting NTFS in a read-write mode.

NFS

LINUX supports the Network File System, with both client and server functionality. The 2.2.x kernel now supports the option to use a kernel-level implementation, known as knfsd. Previous versions of LINUX only supported a user-level implementation. The kernel-level implementation provides higher performance due to the faster response times due to the shortened code path, as well as the reduction of context switching overhead under heavy loads. Also, an NFS lock manager has been implemented.

Work is currently under way for NFSv3 support for both the client and server. Finally, kernel support for NFS over TCP will also be implemented.

---

2. http://www.atnf.csiro.au/~rgooch/linux/kernel-patches.html

Auto FS

The autofs filesystem type is designed specifically to implement the automounter. The autofs filesystem manages NFS mounts dynamically.

SMB Support

The Microsoft WINDOWS network filesystem SMB (Server Message Block) is also supported. The kernel support is for mounting SMB-based filesystems, not exporting filesystems to SMB. Run samba to serve local files to Microsoft WINDOWS clients. A special user-level command is needed to mount SMB filesystems. See the fs(4) man page.

NCP Support

Novell filesystem support is available as well. The system administrator should have also enabled IPX networking support if this option is to be used.

Coda FS

The coda filesystem is a new network filesystem. Coda is implemented as a user-level process on the server side.

Proc FS

The Proc filesystem, /proc, is a special type of filesystem. It is not actually used to store and retrieve data. Instead, /proc is a method to access and modify parameters of running processes and the kernel. Each virtual file within the /proc directory has unique semantics based on the data it represents. Some of the virtual files are read–only, others can be written. For example, issuing the following command enables ipv4 packet forwarding:

```
echo 1 > /proc/sys/net/ipv4/ip_forward
```

The best approach to take with /procfs is to read the proc(5) man page and then dedicate short periods of time to it a few times a week. It contains an incredible amount of useful information and one will glean more each time it is visited.

Capabilities

The security of any system is determined by its weakest link. But the material from which those links are forged is provided by the kernel. Every kernel provides a model or schema of how it will determine the privileges or capabilities any given process will have. These models may consider things inherent to the process; things inherited from the parent process, such as the uid of the user who spawned it; or things about the data files it would read or write.

The security model employed by LINUX is the traditional UNIX model, which is rather simple. A process either has the unlimited powers of root, or it has the powers of a user or predefined group of users. Any process needing just a portion of root's powers must be granted all of them. Clearly, this is not optimal.

To improve the security model of the LINUX kernel, its developers are undertaking to implement the Capabilities Model, as defined by the POSIX standards. This development effort is part of the 2.3.x developmental kernel series and is expected to be a feature of production kernels numbered 2.4.0 and higher.

In the academic definition used by computer scientists, capabilities are intangible tokens that are passed among processes and are used to mediate all accesses. Under this model, no privileges are implicit or derived from the uid. Every privilege is explicit. This is an elegant model. The implementation, however, would require rewriting not only the kernel, but the APIs and every utility and application. Someday an operating system may be developed in accordance with this model, but it will not be LINUX.

The Capabilities Model under development for LINUX does require making changes to the filesystem. The ext3 filesystem is planned to provide the necessary features. Changes will also have to be made to programs such as tar that need to record the filesystem's meta-data. But other software will continue to work as is.

Hardware Support

Rapid tracking of emerging personal computer hardware standards has allowed LINUX to be deployed on the latest generations of personal computers. This section is biased toward the Intel port, but this is justified, since the PC world is driving these advancements.

Perhaps the biggest contribution to overall processing capability has been the drastic improvement of SMP support available in the 2.2.x series of kernels. Dual CPU motherboards are common now, four-way systems are available from systems vendors, and eight-way systems are just now becoming available. The current implementation of LINUX supports SMP systems with up to sixteen processors. Spin locks have been added to manage critical sections that could be entered by multiple processors. Note that this is in addition to the traditional code to make sure that sections did not get reentered due to interrupts. As of this writing, SMP on non-Intel architectures is still experimental.

PCMCIA support in LINUX has been stable since the 2.0.x series of kernels. PCMCIA is noteworthy because it is a key feature for enabling LINUX on laptops. It is also significant because it demonstrates the power and flexibility of the module system. PCMCIA specifies that devices must be hot-pluggable. The PCMCIA module detects the removal and addition of PCMCIA cards and cardmgr loads or unloads the appropriate driver module as needed. Note that the PCMCIA source is distributed independently of the kernel, so to build a kernel with PCMCIA support, it is necessary to download and install the latest PCMCIA sources in addition to the kernel.

Advanced Power Management allows systems to transition to power-saving modes of operation without halting the LINUX operating system. Used mostly with laptops, APM support can monitor battery levels and handle suspend and resume APM events. APM does not currently manage spinning disks up and down, although this may be done with `hdparm(8)`. Most APM functionality is incompatible with SMP support, although the code is modified to provide software power-down capabilities to SMP machines.

The LINUX kernel can be configured to support many popular sound cards and chipsets. Sound card support falls into two categories: those provided as part of the free version of the Open Sound System (OSS), and a number of discrete drivers. In addition, there are both graphical and command-line utilities that utilize kernel sound support. Both the Gnome and KDE desktop environments can be configured to use sound.

Unfortunately, support for sound on laptop computers is lagging, due to proprietary implementations and a lack of documentation.

Configuring the Kernel

System administrators will generally want to use the latest stable kernel. Up-to-date sources are available from `ftp://ftp.xx.kernel.org/pub/kernel/linux/` where *xx* is the two-letter ISO code for the country from which it is to be downloaded. For example, a system administrator in the United States would use `http://ftp.us.kernel.org/` while a system administrator in Germany would use `http://ftp.de.kernel.org/`. If no mirror exists in a particular country, choose a nearby country to which there is good Internet connectivity.

After acquiring the kernel sources, apply any patches that are needed, using the `patch` command. See the `README` file included with the kernel sources. Once the sources are as desired, the `.config` file must be prepared. This file directs which features are to be compiled directly into the kernel, as modules, or not at all.

There are three tools for preparing the `.config` file: `make config`, which is a command-line utility; `make menuconfig`, which offers text-based menus, radio lists, and dialogs; and `make xconfig`, which is an X WINDOW-based configuration tool. In the experience of the authors, `make config` is kept up-to-date better than the graphical tools, though this is not likely to be a problem with stable kernels. However, `make config` lacks any facility for returning to a previously chosen option, so a typo requires running `make config` again. Defaults are taken from an existing `.config` file, if present.

Additionally, `make oldconfig` is similar to `make config`, except that it asks questions only for new configuration options, setting all other options to the `./.config` file from the last time a kernel was configured. If configuring a new kernel revision using `make oldconfig`, be sure to move the previous `.config` file into the new directory if the previously chosen options are desired.

System administrators with experience compiling LINUX kernels may prefer to edit `.config` directly. This may not work if the kernel revision to be compiled has configuration options that were added since the `.config` file was originally generated. Also note that just commenting out lines in `.config` may not have the desired result. If at all unsure, use one of the configuration tools.

Regardless of the tool used to generate the `.config` file, be sure to compare it with the previous `.config` file, and understand all the differences. In rare cases it may be necessary to reference the source code, but the documentation should suffice. If the previous `.config` file is unavailable, have a good look at the new one before compiling the kernel. The options should all make sense. Consult the documentation if they don't.

Note that once a kernel that includes Proc filesystem support has been compiled, many kernel features can be reconfigured without recompiling. As described above, LINUX provides a pseudo filesystem located at `/proc` that provides the means to view and change many parameters of a running kernel as though they were entries in ASCII files.

Modules

Determining whether or not particular features may be needed by the kernel is a straightforward requirements analysis task. However, LINUX provides two different methods for including kernel features. A feature may be either statically compiled into the kernel or compiled as a loadable module.

The advantages of statically compiling functionality into the kernel are simplicity and speed of execution. The advantage of compiling a loadable module is that the base kernel remains smaller, using less memory when the module is not needed. Of course, when the module is loaded, a bit more memory is used than the static kernel would have, and loading imposes a small execution delay.

The two questions to ask before deciding whether to compile something statically into the kernel or as a loadable module are How many of the systems will require this? and How often will they require it? The former question is the more important of the two. Functionality that will be used frequently by a small minority of systems should be compiled as a loadable module.

For example, someone may have a business justification for a particular printer that is not available with a network interface. This will require a print host, with kernel support for printing. Compiling a nonstandard kernel for this machine would make support and upgrading unnecessarily difficult. So, it would be better to compile print support as a loadable module available to all machines, though few if any would ever need it.

Compiling the Kernel

Once the `.config` file has been prepared, it is time to compile the kernel. Follow the instructions in the README file included with the kernel sources. These evolve as the kernel does, so it is not appropriate to reproduce them here.

Pay attention to dependencies, because a new kernel often requires one or more updated packages, such as `binutils` or `net-tools`. The Changes in the Documentation directory of the kernel source should provide a complete list.

Organizations that employ a kernel developer may be tempted to make him responsible for compiling kernels that are to be used in production. This would be unwise. Developers do not normally have the mindset of extreme caution needed for the task. A system administrator should compile kernels and ask the in-house kernel developer questions if technical difficulties arise that are not explained in the documentation.

Installing the Kernel

There is, of course, some quality assurance work to be done before installing a newly compiled kernel on a production machine, and even more before installing on a thousand or ten thousand machines. The instructions for installing a kernel that appear in the documentation are appropriate for installing a kernel on one or a few machines. For testing the new kernel, this might suffice.

Some caveats should be kept in mind whenever a new kernel is installed. It is critical to run /sbin/lilo after any new kernel is added and before the machine is rebooted. It is also important to ensure that the System.map file to which /etc/lilo.conf points matches the kernel version. If multiple kernel version are located in /boot, corresponding System.map files (with distinct names) should also be there with /etc/lilo.conf reflecting the correspondence.

However, since the kernel should be packaged for mass installation anyway, it would be propitious to do so from the beginning. This approach has the advantage of testing the package as well as its contents—the kernel. Deploying a perfect kernel in a flawed package can be just as disastrous as deploying a flawed kernel.

Once the new kernel has been packaged, installation is simply a matter of installing a package. This should be done first on a test machine. When all appears to be well with the test machine, the new kernel package should be installed in a staging environment. Finally, when correct functionality has been verified in the staging environment, the new kernel can be deployed into production. We provide suggestions on how to deploy new software in Chapter 15, "Automated Installation and Upgrade."

Never send a man to do a script's job.

11

Scripting

ONE OF THE GREATEST STRENGTHS OF LINUX is the ease with which it can be configured or modified. Two features of the operating system make this possible— nearly all configuration and system data files use plain ASCII text, and much of the system initialization code exists as executable shell scripts. Shell scripts are stored in files as human-readable instructions that are executed by one of the many command interpreters[1] available on a LINUX system.

This chapter describes many of the interpreted languages used by the LINUX system itself, as well as those used to build system administration tools. Examples are provided in a variety of scripting languages. This is done not to suggest that particular tasks must be scripted in a particular language, but rather to show that a variety of choices are available. Of course, some languages are better suited to particular tasks than others, but nearly any scripting language can be used. The best choice often depends as much on the skills of the system administrator as on the nature of the task.

---

1. Command interpreters are programs that implement a programming language by interpreting a series of commands as they are executed. This contrasts with a compiler, which translates the entire program into machine instructions for later execution.

The Shells

Shells are command interpreters that are intended primarily to be used interactively by users and system administrators. The basic shells provide a small set of built-in commands that are implemented within the shell itself. The rest of the commands used by the shell are actually programs stored in the /bin and /usr/bin directories or others in $PATH.

The bash, ash, and tcsh shells are present on most systems. Many other shells may be installed as well, such as pdksh or zsh. The default shell on most LINUX systems is bash.

Shells can be used interactively or can execute stored programs called shell scripts. Shell scripts can be written using any text editor, such as vi or emacs. The real power of the shell programming environment is not the capability of any single tool (in fact, most are fairly simple) but the ability to combine simple commands into powerful constructs. Commands can be combined using pipes and I/O redirection. For example, to find processes that are owned by user root, one can enter the following:

```
ps aux | awk '$1 == "root" { print }'
```

The pipe operator (represented by the | character) redirects the output of the ps command to the input of the awk command. Now, to look at user root's processes sorted by memory size, we add sort to the pipeline:

```
ps aux | awk '$1 == "root" { print }' | sort +3n
```

Of course, we missed the first few processes because they scrolled past the top of the terminal window. We add the more command to the end of the pipeline to display one screen of output at a time:

```
ps aux | awk '$1 == "root" { print }' | sort +3n | more
```

In this manner, very powerful expressions can be created from the simple utilities provided with LINUX.

Common Utilities

A number of intrinsic UNIX utilities are always available within shell scripts. The expr command is used for simple math and pattern matching. The test command is used for conditional evaluation; it can be used to determine information about files and to compare strings or numbers. The stream editor sed is used to edit streams in an automated fashion. The grep utility prints lines that match a pattern. The awk programming language is used for basic data processing, such as summing fields of input or extracting fields from lines of tabular data. The sort utility can be used to sort lines of data. Typically, these and dozens of other utilities are invoked by a shell interpreter to perform most of a shell program's work.

Table 11.1 **Some Tcl extensions**

Tk	A set of widgets for the X WINDOW system.
Expect	A set of extensions for automating programs that normally require interactive sessions, like telnet or ftp. This extension is a necessity for system administrators.
Itcl or incr Tcl	Object-oriented extensions for the Tcl language.
Tcl-DP	Tcl Distributed Programming. This is a set of extensions providing network programming features.
Oratcl	Tcl extensions for accessing Oracle databases.
Sybtcl	Tcl extensions for accessing Sybase databases.

Other Programming Languages

Several new interpreted programming languages have become popular within the last few years. These offer a richer command syntax than the shells and are usually not used interactively.

Tcl, the Tool Command Language, was originally developed to assist in the rapid prototyping of applications. It was designed to be embedded within C or C++ programs, giving them access to a simple language for configuration and scripting. There are many extensions to Tcl, a few of which are listed in Table 11.1.

The Perl programming language has become a mainstay for both system administrators and programmers, fitting a niche between small shell scripts and larger applications. Many people find they do much less C or C++ programming once they have been introduced to Perl. Perl has an elegant extension mechanism called the module system. The Comprehensive Perl Archive Network (CPAN) at http://www.cpan.org/ provides access to the currently available set of modules, as well as to the Perl language itself.

Recently, a newer language called Python has been gaining popularity. It is useful for the same kinds of tasks as Perl. System administrators who work in an organization with many existing Perl scripts may find it important to learn Perl, even if they choose Python for new scripts.

Motivations for Scripting

Frequently, scripts must be written or adapted for specific situations. Perhaps the most common usage is to create *application wrappers*, which are shell scripts that define environment variables needed for an application and then launch the application. The other common case is to modify an aspect of system startup, usually to add a service to the system boot and shutdown sequence.

Many monitoring tools, like Watcher and Big Brother, are built around shell scripts and are extended and configured by writing or modifying shell, awk, and/or Perl scripts. Other tools, like cfengine and scotty, have their own scripting languages or dialects.

While most shell scripts are quite short (fewer than 100 lines), some can be quite complex. There is an ambiguous area beyond which scripting becomes "real" programming. This is appropriate for those system administrators who are interested in programming. In other cases, it may be necessary to negotiate the assignment of some scripting projects to a programming team or to outsource further development and enhancements.

It is useful to ask, "What does a script *do* for us?" System administrators often answer, "Saves time," "Makes things easier," or "Makes things less error-prone." One may also think in terms of the "-ates"—abbreviate, automate, regulate, and delegate.

Abbreviate

System administrators often repeat a sequence of commands. Enclosing them in a script provides an abbreviated way to invoke that command sequence. This is the simplest sort of script.

After typing a long, complex command, or a sequence of shell commands that will be needed again, one can make them into a script by using a command like this:

```
history > ~/bin/newscript
```

and then editing that file, cutting out the unnecessary portions, adding the appropriate header at the top, and setting execute permissions.

Here is a sample expect script for abbreviating a telnet session:

```
#!/usr/bin/expect -f
# Sample telnet automation
## call with autotel host
## --- expects a directory named ~/.autotel and
## a file corresponding to a nickname for the host thereunder.
## reads the true hostname, username and password therefrom

set nick [lindex $argv 0]
set rcfile [open ~/.autotel/$nick  r ]
gets $rcfile host
gets $rcfile user
gets $rcfile pass
spawn telnet  "$host"
expect "login:"
send "$user\r"
expect "word:"
send "$pass\r"
interact
```

This script reads the hostname, login name, and password from the "nick" file (a user's nickname for the remote system) under ~/.autotel/ that corresponds to the hostname.

It then attempts to open a telnet session to that host using that username and then "interact"—leave the user running interactively with the resulting session.

This is just the barest hint of the power offered by the expect scripting language and the Tcl library around which it is built.

Most distributions of LINUX and expect ship with a few sample expect scripts. Two scripts that are particularly useful to many system administrators are autopasswd and kibitz. autopasswd automates the setting of new user passwords, such as for new school terms. kibitz enables two or more users to collaborate on a single shell session—each can see the screen and type commands on a shared shell session. kibitz can even support curses/ncurses programs, such as vi and xemacs.

There are also modules for Perl and Python that implement the core features of expect, allowing one to use these languages to spawn programs, expect output from them, send input to them, interact with them, and generally automate one's way around those unavoidably interactive programs.

Automate

Many system administration tasks must be performed on a regular basis—mundane tasks like trimming log files, cleaning up /tmp directories, and performing nightly backups. By automating these tasks, system administrators free themselves to do other work. So, it is typical for system administrators to script these tasks and have them scheduled by cron. The cron facility provides the ability to run programs automatically on a specified schedule, relieving system administrators of having to remember to perform these tasks. Typically, maintenance jobs are run at night by cron, and scripts mail the output of the jobs to the system administrators.

Regulate

Abbreviating a list of commands does more than save typing time. It regulates the procedure, ensuring that the commands will be run in the same sequence every time the script is invoked and that no steps are overlooked.

As system administrators gain experience with particular scripts, they add various sorts of sanity checks, tests, and options—particularly in cases where other users and operators may be using them. Such a script regulates the operation, ensuring that there is enough disk space for a build, or that temporary files are properly removed, and so on.

In some cases, it may not be clear exactly how to script a particular operation—one can just prompt skilled users/operators with reminders of what to do, and they will know what commands and parameters to provide. For these cases, and for the early prototyping stages of any script, just use simple sequences of echo, read, and eval commands to step a user through a process.

For example:

```
echo "Enter the directory to use"
read dirname
[ -d "$dirname" ] && cd "$dirname" || {
    while [ ! -d "$dirname" ] do
        echo "This must be an existing directory: Try again: "
        read dirname
        done
    cd "$dirname"
    }
echo "Issue your build command here ('make' ?)"
read cmd
eval $cmd
# etc
```

Obviously, this script could be improved further. For example, it could test to make sure that the directory is accessible and display an appropriate error message if, for example, the permissions are wrong or the filesystem is unmounted.

Delegate

Many system administration tasks involve a long sequence of commands. These sequences often vary, depending on the result of intermediate commands. Sometimes an error in the sequence has disastrous results, such as lost or corrupted data. Entrusting such tasks to junior or mid-level system administrators is ordinarily dangerous.

Scripting provides a mechanism for delegating complex and difficult tasks to more junior system administrators. A senior system administrator begins by writing a script that automates and regulates a process. After a little more work to check things as the script progresses, and perhaps some improved diagnostics, the script can enable delegation of the task to a more junior system administrator.

Instead of having to understand all the details of each step in the task, the junior system administrator can simply run the script. The script should echo each step so that the junior system administrator can better understand the overall process of the particular task and also better get an idea of how commands may be used together in sequence. Eventually, the junior system administrator can begin modifying existing scripts and writing new ones.

Log File Filtering and Aging

Linux offers excellent system logging facilities. These provide a wealth of data that can be used to track and troubleshoot problems and to warn of impending failures.

The problem with the default configuration of the logging settings on typical Linux systems is that too many innocuous messages are logged, and the logs grow interminably.

Thus, most system administrators write scripts or install packages to manage their log files. Log file scripts are easy to write and offer a relatively safe way for junior system administrators to learn scripting, since the loss of some log files is usually not a catastrophe.

Here is one such script (written in awk):

```
#!/usr/bin/gawk -f
        # filter.log
        # by James T. Dennis

        # syntax filter.log patternfile  datafile [datafile2 .....]

        # purpose -- trim patterns, listed in the first filename
        # from a series of data files (such as /var/adm/messages)
        # the patterns in the patternfile should take the form
        # of undelimited (no '/foo/' slashes and no "foo" quotes)

        # Note:  you must use a '-' as the data file parameter if
        # you want to process stdin (use this as a filter in a pipe
        # otherwise this script will not see any input from it!

ARGIND == 1 {
                # ugly hack.
        # allows first parameter to be specially used as the
        # pattern file and all others to be used as data to
        # be filtered: avoids need to use
        # gawk -v patterns=$filename ....  syntax.
        if ( $0 ~ /^[ \t]*$/ ) { next }  # skip blank lines
                # also skip lines that start with hash
                # to allow comments in the patterns file.
        if ( $0 !~ /^\#/ ) { killpat[++i]=$0 }}

ARGIND > 1 {
        for( i in killpat ) {
                if($0 ~ killpat[i]) { next }}}

ARGIND > 1 {
        print FNR ": " $0 }
```

This script contains only eight lines of code. The first block, executed only when this script processes its first argument/filename, loads a "pattern file," a list of regular expressions (regexes) that describe all the innocuous messages. The second and third blocks are active for all arguments/filenames *after* the first. The second block compares the current record/line to each pattern and, if a match is found, skips all further processing of that line and skips to the next record (without printing anything). This effectively filters those records. The last block simply prints anything that is left.

Obviously, most of the real work is in maintaining the list of patterns. An overly general pattern like .* will filter out *everything*. Therefore, the system administrator must have a good understanding of awk regular expressions to use this script and to maintain pattern files for each type of log to be filtered.

This example is suitable for a typical /var/log/messages file on a host named antares:

```
# Patterns for a /var/log/messages file
# the pattern ... .. ..:..:.. antares should match the
# date and time that leads each line.
... ..? ..:..:.. antares kernel:[ \t]*
... ..? ..:..:.. antares kernel:   Type: .*
... ..? ..:..:.. antares kernel:   Vendor: .*
... ..? ..:..:.. antares kernel: aha1542.c: Using extended bios translation
... ..? ..:..:.. antares login\[[0-9]+\]: ROOT LOGIN on 'tty[0-9]+'
... ..? ..:..:.. antares innd: .*
... ..? ..:..:.. antares nnrpd\[[0-9]+\]: localhost.starshine.org .*
... ..? ..:..:.. antares rnews: offered .*
... ..? ..:..:.. antares rnews: rejected 4.*
... ..? ..:..:.. antares named.[0-9]+.: NSTATS .*
... ..? ..:..:.. antares named\[[0-9]+\]: XSTATS .*
... ..? ..:..:.. antares pppd\[[0-9]+\]: Connect script failed
... ..? ..:..:.. antares pppd\[[0-9]+\]: Hangup \(SIGHUP\)
... ..? ..:..:.. antares pppd\[[0-9]+\]: Modem hangup
... ..? ..:..:.. antares pppd\[[0-9]+\]: local  IP address 10.45.123.[0-9]+
... ..? ..:..:.. antares pppd\[[0-9]+\]: Connect: ppp0 .... /dev/modem
... ..? ..:..:.. antares pppd\[[0-9]+\]: local  IP address 206.61.225.[0-9]+
... ..? ..:..:.. antares pppd\[[0-9]+\]: pppd 2.2.0 started by root, uid 0
... ..? ..:..:.. antares pppd\[[0-9]+\]: remote IP address 192.160.13.[0-9]+
... ..? ..:..:.. antares chat\[[0-9]+\]: abort on \(NO CARRIER\)
... ..? ..:..:.. antares diald\[[0-9]+\]: Delaying [0-9]+ seconds .*
... ..? ..:..:.. antares diald\[[0-9]+\]: Closing down idle link.
... ..? ..:..:.. antares diald\[[0-9]+\]: Link died on remote end.
... ..? ..:..:.. antares diald\[[0-9]+\]: Running .*
... ..? ..:..:.. antares su\[[0-9]+\]: \+ ttyp?[0-9]+ jimd-root
```

This script is updated by taking the results from earlier runs (sent to a system administrator nightly) and pasting them into the pattern file. They are then made into regexes by replacing the date elements (MMM DD HH:MM:SS) with single-character wildcards (dots)—adding a question mark to the optional second date digit—and replacing other variable data (such as the PID numbers that are commonly found in this example) with regex descriptions like [0-9]+, which signifies a string of digits.

These patterns filter most of the kernel boot-time messages, most messages from diald (a program that opens a PPP connection whenever traffic is destined for an outside network), and the pppd, innd, and named dæmons. This host is a gateway to the Internet (performing dial-on-demand routing over a modem), as well as a news and DNS name server. (Not shown are rules to ignore local messages from the POP server, and so on.)

The script filters out everything that is expected to happen every day (or that is unremarkable) and mails the remainder to the system administrator.

Here is one way to call this script from another script that rotates daily logs:

```
#! /bin/bash
# jtd: Rotate logs

# This is intended to run as a cron job, once per day
# it renames a variety of log files and filters/summarizes
# them

cd /var/log
TODAY=$(date +%Y%m%d)    # YYYYMMDD convenient for sorting

function rotate {
        cp $1 OLD/${1}.$TODAY
        cp /dev/null $1
        }

rotate maillog
rotate messages
rotate secure
rotate cron

(
   echo "To: jimd"
   echo -n "Subject: Filtered Logs for:  " ; date "+%a %m/%d/%Y"
   echo; echo; echo;
   echo "Security:"
   /root/bin/filter.log /root/lib/security.filter  OLD/messages.$TODAY
   echo; echo; echo;
   echo "Messages:"
   /root/bin/filter.log /root/lib/messages.filter  OLD/messages.$TODAY
   echo; echo; echo "Cron:"
   /root/bin/filter.log /root/lib/cron.filter OLD/cron.$TODAY
   echo -e "\n\n\n--\nYour Log Messaging System\n\n"
   ) | /usr/lib/sendmail -oi -oe  -t
```

The rotate shell function copies the specified log file to a subdirectory and appends the name in a format that is suitable for simple sorting—the files are thus all listed in proper order by the ls command. cp /dev/null is used to overwrite the log file to avoid creating an anonymous file handle. Otherwise, it would be necessary to signal the syslogd dæmon that its file has been removed and force it to restart.

The other part of the script uses a subshell with a few `echo` commands. It invokes our log-filtering script with the names of our pattern files and newly copied logs.

The same script could be used (with a different pattern file) to filter or summarize the /var/log/maillog file, which is found on systems running either sendmail or qmail. Note that sendmail includes a mailstats program that provides useful summaries. Writing pattern files for /var/log/maillog and /var/log/secure is left as an exercise for the reader.

The output from all commands in this subshell is piped into sendmail -t for delivery to the appropriate system administrators. This option is the safest way for a script to mail messages using sendmail. It feeds the header into sendmail's standard input rather than trying to supply the address and other header information on the command line (with all the subtleties of shell syntax and quoting). This technique is not necessary for security in this case (no "tainted" variables are present). It's a convenient example of how to safely pass other messages to sendmail in CGI scripts and the like.

Perl

The Perl language provides the system administrator who understands computer programming with a complete language with which utilities can be rapidly developed. It allows lower-level access to the UNIX C library and system call interface than shells, while sparing the programmer the details of memory management, which is a constant issue with C and C++ programming. Here is a sample utility that can be used to merge the group(5) files from several NIS domains. This script assumes that NIS domains use the same group names for the same functions.

```
#!/apps/exe/perl52
#   $Id$
#   Created Tue Oct 25 11:08:17 1994 by Stephen Degler
#   Description:
#
# this program merges several group(5) files
# together. It will not deal with group passwords
# in a sophisticated fashion, but it will output the
# logical union of all the input groups.
#

%group_db;

# process cmd line args

for(;;)
{
  if ( $ARGV[0] eq "-log" )
  {
```

```perl
      # reopen stderr to logfile
      open(STDERR, ">>$logfile") || warn("open of logfile failed!");
      shift;
    }
    elsif ( $ARGV[0] eq "-debug" )
    {
      shift;
      $debugLevel = $ARGV[0];
      shift;
    }
    else
    {
      last;
    }
  }

while($#ARGV)
{
  &get_groups($ARGV[0],
        *group_db);
  shift;
}

#
# now splatter out all that group trash
#

foreach $key (sort(keys(%group_db)))
{
  printf("$key:%s:%d:%s\n",
  $group_db{$key}->{"password"},
  $group_db{$key}->{"gid"},
  join(',',@{ $group_db{$key}->{"users"}}));
}

# end of sequential program flow
#------------------------------------------------------------------------
# get_groups
#
#

sub get_groups
{
  my($file , $groups ) = @_;
  my($user,@k1,@k2,%mergetemp);
```

```
if ( $debugLevel >= 1 )
{
  print( "entering subroutine get_groups\n");
  print( "file = $file\n");
}
open(GROUPFILE,"<$file") || die("could not open $file");

while(<GROUPFILE>)
{
  if ( /([^:]+):([^:]*):([0-9]+):([^:]+)/ )
  {
    my($key,$passwd,$gid,$users) = ( $1, $2, $3, $4 );
    $users =~ s/\n//g;
    # here is the core logic of the program
    if ( !defined($groups{$key}))
    {
$groups{$key}->{"password"} = $passwd;
$groups{$key}->{"gid"} = $gid;
@{ $groups{$key}->{"users"}} = sort(split(',',$users));
    }
    else
    {
if ( $groups{$key}->{"password"} ne $passwd )
{
  print( STDERR "$file: line $., passwd for group $key changes from
    $groups{$key}->{password} to $passwd\n");
  $groups{$key}->{"password"} = $passwd;
}
if ( $groups{$key}->{"gid"} ne $gid )
{
  print( STDERR "$file: line $., gid for group $key changes from
    $groups{$key}->{gid} to $gid\n");
  $groups{$key}->{"gid"} = $gid;
}
# merge in group users
@k1 = @{ $groups{$key}->{"users"}};
@k2 = split(',',$users);
foreach $user (@k1)
{
  $mergetemp{$user} = 1;
}
foreach $user (@k2)
{
  $mergetemp{$user} = 1;
}
```

```
@{ $groups{$key}->{"users"}} = sort(keys(%mergetemp));
undef(%mergetemp);
      }
    }
    else
    {
      warn("$file: line $., syntax error" );
    }
  }
}
```

This program is far from a perfect Perl programming example. However, it does utilize nested data structures and is simple enough to read through.

The program begins by gathering the command-line arguments that are needed to send diagnostic output to a log file and to turn on some program debugging. The rest of the arguments are assumed to be files to be merged. The subroutine get_groups is then called for each remaining argument. The get_groups routine performs the logical union of the group files. Once all the group files have been processed, the resulting groups are printed on standard output.

expect

As mentioned in the "Abbreviate" section of this chapter, the expect variant of the Tcl language is invaluable for the system administrator, who often is faced with either automating a task or performing it repetitively. The expect command offers the system administrator an opportunity to automate functions that normally must be interactive. expect does this by opening a pseudo terminal (pty) device and presenting the application the slave side of the pty as if it were an interactive terminal.[2] The automated program never knows the difference.

Security

Users of scripts have occasionally been able to exploit them in ways not intended by their authors. When writing scripts, one should be conscious of security considerations. A good place to start is the CERT advisory on removing meta-characters from user-supplied data in CGI scripts.[3]

Possible exploits include the following:

- Smashing the stack. The cracker places malicious code somewhere in memory where it will be executed. This is usually accomplished by overflowing a buffer.

---

2. For an explanation of pseudo terminals, see *Unix Network Programming* by W. Richard Stevens.
3. http://www.cert.org/tech_tips/cgi_metacharacters.html

- Forcing a core dump. The cracker either dissects the core for confidential information or makes use of the now-free port that is trusted by the firewall or packet-filtering software, or both.

- Poor permissions may allow a carefully crafted request to retrieve a file that had not been intended to be available. chroot is a good defense against such an exploit, as is avoiding unnecessary use of symlinks.

Running Perl with the -T option places it in taint mode, where Perl distinguishes between trusted data and data that were supplied by the user or that might be under the control of the user (tainted data). When Perl detects that an unsafe operation is to be performed using tainted data, it aborts.

Further Reading

- *Exploring Expect*, Don Libes, 1994
- *Advanced Programming in the Unix Environment*, W. Richard Stevens, 1992
- *The UNIX Programming Environment*, Brian W. Kernighan, et al., 1984
- Tcl information available from http://www.scriptics.com/software/
- *Special Edition Using Perl for Web Programming*, http://www.pbs.mcp.com/ebooks/0789706598/index.htm
- *The Awk Programming Language*, Alfred V. Aho et al., 1988
- *Learning Perl*, 2nd ed., Randal L Schwartz and Tom Christiansen, 1997
- *Programming Perl*, 2nd ed., Larry Wall et al., 1996
- *Programming Python*, Mark Lutz, 1996
- *Learning Python*, Mark Lutz and David Ascher, 1999
- *Tcl and the Tk Toolkit*, John K. Ousterhout, 1994
- *Learning the bash Shell*, 2nd ed., Cameron Newham et al., 1998

I don't believe in learning from my mistakes. I prefer to learn from the mistakes of others.

~Otto von Bismarck (1815–1898)

12

Backups

Backups are copies of data held in reserve against loss or corruption. These copies are made periodically, according to a predetermined schedule. Backup solutions vary greatly with the size and scope of their environments, depending on the organization's requirements. The elements of a backup system are the hardware, the backup media, and the software. The hardware can range from a single SCSI tape drive to a tape librarian the size of a living room. The media required is a function of the hardware, the amount of data maintained, and the retention policy for the data. Typically, backups reside on magnetic tape because it is an affordable medium. Finally, the software can range from free utilities like `tar` and `cpio` to distributed, cross-platform storage management systems costing tens of thousands of dollars.

Backups generally provide three distinct services:

- They allow for the recovery of files that have been accidentally deleted or lost because disk hardware has failed.

- They provide regular snapshots of the state of the organization's data. The organization may use this service extensively for a variety of technical and business purposes. Financial and budgetary data can be recovered to assist in audits. Data may also be used to assist in litigation.

- They provide a data source for disaster recovery. The backup system must play a role in any comprehensive recovery planning. In a large-scale disaster, data will be retrieved from tape archived at an off-site storage facility. The backup system itself must be in place and working at a disaster recovery site.

Some of the terms used in relation to backup and restore planning are confusing and are often used inconsistently. The terms archive, backup, data set, differential, full, incremental, level zero, and media set are defined in the Glossary.

It's possible to build a backup plan out of just full (level zero) backups or combinations of full with incrementals or differentials. It is even possible to build a complex plan involving all three. For example, one might do a level zero backup followed by a series of differentials (cycling among several media sets).

Assumptions

The assumptions one makes about backups and the implications gathered from them are primarily based on previous experience. However, risk assessment and disaster planning should not be based only on first-hand experience. System administrators generally hope to avoid personal experience with most types of disasters. Therefore, we recommend a more comprehensive look at a site's needs as part of the process of developing a restore strategy. This process is discussed in detail in Chapter 3, "Recovery Planning."

It is worth noting that these same issues are involved in developing security policies and procedures. This is handy because there are many security/integrity concerns that should be addressed concurrently with recovery strategy. For example, discarding old tapes may inadvertently release confidential data, even if the tapes have been erased—or corrupted data might be backed up and result in the restoration of bad data.

Requirements and Policies

When designing a backup system, the first task is to obtain an accurate set of requirements. The second task is to reconcile these requirements against the available budget for a backup system. This may require several design iterations because some individuals—particularly those in management—have unrealistic expectations. Once the initial design phase is complete, all interested parties should be aware of the costs and capabilities of the system and should use these to establish policies.

Estimating Costs

Key factors that determine the cost of a backup system are the amount of data that must be backed up and the time available to do it. The higher the quantity of data per hour, the more expensive the backup solution will be. Environments that have narrow maintenance windows or that require 24x7 operation must consider the backup solution as part of the design of the systems and applications to ensure that the backups represent a valid system snapshot. If key data change while backups are taking place, inconsistencies may render the backup process worthless. On the other hand, an organization running a 9 a.m. to 5 p.m. operation can employ a simpler and less expensive solution.

Scheduling

Daily backups should normally be done at a time when the data are in a well-defined state, such as the end of the business day. If the backup system runs while nightly batch processing is taking place, data restored from the tapes may be inconsistent and incapable of re-creating the state of the organization at any one point. If it is not possible to get the organization into a quiescent state, management must be made aware of the implications. In some cases, it won't matter, because the environment as a whole is not likely to run in lockstep. However, it is clear that processes with data sets that change during the backup operation may not have valid backups.

Most backup systems are driven by either cron or their own internal scheduler. Typically, these permit a moderately complex schedule to be developed and maintained. The backup system may also need to interact directly with applications, such as databases. In this case it is usually desirable to have an application or script initiate its own backups.

Retention

Because tapes are expensive, another important factor affecting the cost of backup systems is data retention policy. The retention policy reflects the nature of the organization, its work flow, and the regulatory requirements imposed by external interests, like governments and auditors. Disaster recovery plays a part in retention policy as well, and for this reason many organizations will contract a vendor to store data off-site.

Most backup systems support efficient tape utilization by offering at least two relative levels of data storage. A full or level zero backup will archive all files unconditionally. An incremental backup will archive only those files that have changed since the previous full or incremental backup. Some systems also provide intermediate levels. By combining the levels, the system administrator can develop a backup strategy that balances efficiency and reliability.

Here, as an example, is the backup policy of a firm known to the authors. All data are dumped on Saturday. Sunday through Friday, incremental backups are performed. All tapes are kept forever. Once tapes are two months old, they are shipped off-site for storage.

Here is another example: All data are dumped on Saturday. Sunday through Friday, incremental backups are performed. A special set of tapes is set aside for month-end backups. Month-end tapes are sent off-site for storage. Weekly and nightly tapes are reused after six weeks. Here, a policy decision was made that files not on disk at the end of a month are lost forever.

System Features

Although the functionality of a complete backup system has been discussed, there are specific features that merit explanation. These include archive formats, cataloging, and robotics.

Archive Formats

There is a great deal of debate on archive formats. Many system administrators think that a backup product must write a standard UNIX format (dump, tar, or cpio). Meanwhile, several vendors have developed proprietary tape formats. In an effort to win support for their decision to use proprietary formats, vendors have provided format specifications and have released open source stand-alone restore utilities. These actions have had limited impact on their detractors.

The real concern underlying this discussion is the ability to recover data several years after it is written, even if the vendor no longer supports the backup software or if the vendor is no longer in business.

Cataloging

Backups are exercised when a request to restore data comes in. In most cases, the previous night's tapes are retrieved—a simple matter. It is quite another matter to find the correct media for a backup of a server that has been retired, or to locate database dumps made two years earlier.

In these circumstances we look to the cataloging capabilities of the backup system— or the system administrators. Many of the more sophisticated backup software systems maintain a catalog of all media in use, including the volumes written on those media. For large environments, this catalog may require considerable disk space.

Basic utilities such as tar and cpio do not offer such catalogs.[1] If these are to be used, either additional software must be written to support them, or manual procedures must be implemented so that tapes may be recovered. Also, many systems that do have a catalog do not have a mechanism to convey that a tape has been moved to off-site storage. This may have to be implemented by labeling and keeping good records.

Tape Robots and Jukeboxes

Robotic tape changers reduce the demands on operations staff and automate the backup process as much as possible. This is good for two reasons: first, the reduction of computer operator time saves the organization money; second, taking the operator out of the loop reduces the possibility of human error. Larger tape robots support multiple tape drives and utilize bar code readers to manage the tapes, resulting in far more reliable operation.

---

1. The -t option to tar could be used with some scripts to form the basis of a primitive cataloging system.

Application Considerations

Some applications absolutely require a consistent set of data in order to function usefully. Database management systems are the most common example, although Enterprise Resource Planning (ERP) systems have similar requirements. These applications require their own backup procedures.

Because the data belonging to such systems are often in flux, the task of capturing a consistent state is beyond the capabilities of software such as `tar`, `cpio`, and `dump`. For example, data referenced early in the process may be deleted or changed before the backup system gets to it.

To accommodate this problem, vendors of systems that have such needs usually include backup software for capturing a consistent state. They may include hooks provided in an API, or simple shell scripts called by the application, which can be modified or replaced. If these applications and the backup system do not have a common interface, a glue layer will have to be developed.

In cases where the business processes allow the database applications to be offline and the databases themselves to be closed periodically, a simple backup scheme might work, but it should be thoroughly tested.

Database systems that support replication still require backups. Replication does not protect against accidental or intentional deletion of needed data. Also, the network connection between the replicated systems may fail, resulting in inconsistencies. Other types of failure tend to happen during such conditions.

The backup strategy for databases should be worked out in cooperation with the database administrators (DBAs). It may be acceptable to permit the DBAs to manually initiate backups and restores, or it may be necessary to involve system administrators. This depends largely on the skill sets of the personnel at hand.

Systems Versus Data

In this section, we discuss some of the problems that may arise when attempting to restore a complete system. We do this to underscore the recommendation we made in Chapter 3, "Recovery Planning," that the recovery plan for systems should be to rebuild them from a well-developed template. We urge system administrators not to rely on backups for anything but data. Rather, we suggest that systems be recovered by rebuilding them as described in Chapter 15, "Automated Installation and Upgrade."

Conceptually, doing backups is pretty simple—just make a copy of everything you might want to restore later. However, there are complications with that. Let's consider the following scenario:

A full system is backed up to a SCSI tape with the following command:

```
tar cf /dev/st0 /
```

Let's assume that all went well and the whole system fit on a single tape. The tape is verified to be readable using

```
tar tf /dev/st0
```

or perhaps it is checked even more thoroughly with

```
tar df /dev/st0
```

In the former case, it is assured that the tape can be read from that tape drive, though all we get is a list of the filenames on the backup tape. In the latter case, we get a list of differences between the data on the tape and the current state of the system.

How to do a full restore? If a root filesystem is trashed tonight, what is the exact procedure to bring the full system back into operation by morning?

Let's assume that you've created and tested a rescue floppy, and that it has all the modules, drivers, and utilities needed to

- Boot the system
- Access the tape drive
- Partition the (replacement) drive
- Make new filesystems in those partitions
- Extract the files from the tape archive

That sounds simple enough. However, there are a few more issues to consider. One issue is that the entire /proc hierarchy of pseudo-files will be restored as regular files and directories in the process. The normal boot process will mount a copy of the /proc filesystem right over a non-empty directory without complaint, so it may be some time before anyone realizes where the extra space on the root filesystem went. This is easily remedied with an rm command. The only harm done is the waste of a bit more disk space than there is RAM in the system.

Sparse Files

Another relatively minor issue is a bit more difficult to understand and explain. It has to do with sparse files (that is, files with "holes"). Under the ext2 and other UNIX filesystems, a file can be created in such a way that regions of the file do not have data blocks allocated. Programs typically create these files by using the lseek system call to skip over portions of a file. Blocks within the skipped portion are not allocated. If an application later writes to the "hole," then filesystem blocks will be allocated for that region of the file.

Any normal operations on these files (such as using the cat, grep, or other commands on them) will behave as though these regions of the file are filled with NULs. This applies to the default behavior of the cp, tar, and cpio commands (dump works on filesystems at a lower level such that this consideration doesn't apply to it). When restoring files, it is preferable to preserve this sparse allocation wherever possible. For this to work with GNU tar, the -S (--sparse) switch must be used when the archive is created. If the sparse file has been stored without the -S option, the restored file will take up significantly more space than it did at the time of the backup.

Ownership

Another problem with restoring systems from backups concerns the ownership of the files. When items are extracted from a `tar` file as `root`, the GNU `tar` utility attempts to restore the ownership (user and group) of each file, if the `-p` (`--preserve-permission`) switch is specified. Otherwise, `tar` will use the settings of the current `UMASK`. However, if the users and groups listed in the `tar` file don't exist, then the ownership will not be set properly![2]

Thus, either NIS service or the `/etc/passwd` and `/etc/group` files must be restored before any non-root system files.

As we've seen, a number of factors about the restore process must be considered prior to implementing a backup process. Under multi-user operating systems, the meta-data (information *about* the file) is often as important as the data (information *in* the file). Even when LINUX is used as a workstation, with only a single user on the system, the proper functioning of many programs and subsystems depends upon the ownership and permissions of the system files.

Media

The tape systems used by LINUX system administrators today typically connect to their host via a SCSI interface and have one or more drives to handle one or more tapes of either 4mm DAT, 8mm Exabyte, 8mm AIT, or DLT form factor. The number and type of tape will be chosen after determining the quantity of data to be backed up, keeping in mind the data transfer rate. Always assume that capacity requirements will at least double during the life of the tape system.

Tapes have a life span of several years. When data must be preserved for longer periods, another medium must be chosen. Media with a life span of ten years or more include CD-R, CD-RW, DVD-R, and magneto-optical. Cost considerations preclude the use of magneto-optical as an archive medium. CD-R has been the medium of choice, but the increased capacity and declining costs of DVD-R presage its widespread use for archiving.

Testing

In the experience of the authors, most backups that are untested turn out to be unrecoverable. Going to the effort of backing up data and then not verifying that it can be restored is probably worse than not doing backups at all. It is likely to provide a false sense of security while wasting time and money. Therefore, we recommend testing the restore procedure prior to relying on backups.

Consider an experiment you might run on one of your systems. *Don't really do this! Just think about it!*

```
cd / ; chown -R nobody *
```

---

2. This might be dependent on the version of tar being used.

This command line will neither destroy any files nor change their contents. However, there will be quite a bit of damage to the system. The system as a whole will be almost as dysfunctional as if you'd used `rm -fr`. However, the problems won't be nearly as easy to diagnose.

Obviously, we will have destroyed some important meta-data—information that is about the files rather than in them. How then do we know that our restore utilities actually restored everything including the meta-data, and how do we know that it was all restored correctly?

We could simply take it on faith—these tools were designed to do this job, and many people use them, so they must be working. However, we really don't know that the situations for which these tools were written match our own. We also don't know what assumptions the authors and other users of `tar`, `cpio`, and `dump` make about their use. They may assume that you restore the base operating system from CD-ROM and that you manually restore your `/etc/passwd` and `/etc/group` files prior to attempting a restore of the rest of the system.

We also don't know that our hardware will work correctly under the conditions from which we might be working when we need to do a full system restoration. For example, we may find that a special driver, configuration file, or program is needed to access the tape drive, WORM drive, or other backup device.

Thus, it makes sense that we should test the recovery procedure. We should do this for the same reason that most large organizations should conduct periodic fire drills. Note that even in small organizations, the person responsible for testing backups should never be the same person who performs them.

Many changes may affect a backup procedure. Often the implications are not obvious, so the backup procedure does not get updated to accommodate the change. Therefore, testing should be performed at regular intervals.

Risks of Testing

Testing recovery procedures has its own risks. It's possible to accidentally overwrite, even corrupt, files that are in use while attempting to restore files belonging to a different application.

The safest way to perform recovery drills is on a spare workstation rather than on a production server. Setting aside an extra disk or an extra partition may be a more reasonable precaution. Negotiating to have "extra" equipment for this purpose can be stressful—but consider the stress of losing files to inadequate backup procedures or misunderstandings of the restore process.

Basic Utilities

This section provides examples of preparing full, selective, differential, and incremental backup sets; restoring full systems and file sets; extracting selected files and indices; and verifying archives using the simple utilities: `tar`, `cpio`, and the `dump`/`restore` pair.

For comparison, we also describe AMANDA (the Advanced Maryland Automatic Network Disk Archiver), a freeware client/server backup and volume-management package.

System-Specific Extensions

As of this writing, GNU tar and cpio don't store "non-standard" meta-data specific to the ext2 filesystem. System-specific features like the ext2 attributes (immutable, dumpable, compressed, and bits) and the BSD UFS flags are neither stored in nor restored from standard tar and cpio files.

As support for more of these features (access control lists or ACLs, privilege bits or capability sets, and others) is added to LINUX (and other UNIX implementations), tools will have to be enhanced to address these issues.

Using tar

tar is one of the oldest and most commonly used UNIX archiving tools. It's the most common file format for distributing files on FTP sites and the like. Because most UNIX users are familiar with tar, we'll compare all of the others to it.

Old versions of tar had limitations regarding maximum filename length (typically 100 characters) and device nodes (special files). Most of these have been eliminated in the GNU version. However, it is best to test your assumptions before relying on these features. One version of GNU tar within the last couple of years restored incorrect permissions on empty directories.

We're not picking on tar here. Similar problems might apply to any utility you may use (including commercial packages). Testing is the only way to be sure.

Backups: Local Tape Drives

Assuming that you have a tape drive installed on a given system, the simplest invocation of tar to back up is just

```
tar c /
```

This assumes a version of tar that defaults to creating archives on the tape drive (/dev/rmt0 on some versions). However, there are several problems with this example. First, it might not default to the same type of tape drive that is installed, or it might not default to a tape drive at all. Some versions of tar are compiled to write to stdout if no f option is specified. Also, this example will traverse the entire filesystem tree. That would include the /proc filesystem and any mounted CD-ROMs, NFS, Samba, or other network shared filesystems.

There are a couple of other potential problems with this example. With this command, GNU tar neither preserves "allocation holes" in sparse files nor performs any compression.

Here is a better example:

```
tar cSlzf - $(bakdirs) | buffer -o /dev/st0
```

This example creates (c) an archive that preserves file sparsity (S), keeps to "local" filesystems (1), compresses the data (z), and writes the archive to the file (f) stdout (denoted using the - (dash) convention).

This archive is then piped to Lee McLoughlin's buffer program, which writes it out (-o) to the first SCSI tape device. This should be used whenever piping the backup through a compression program or over a network.

We reference a bakdirs command using the preferred form of the command substitution operator.[3] The more commonly used backticks (`) are easier to type and harder to read—and they can't be nested. This is a hypothetical script that lists the directories and files that you want included in your backup. bakdirs could be as simple as an echo command that lists all of the local filesystem mount points (not including /proc, any /tmp directories, CD-ROM mount points, or NFS and other network directories). Basically, bakdirs parses and filters the output of the mount command to dynamically include only the appropriate filesystems. The risk of using a static list is that it may not be updated when additional filesystems are added—and it might go unnoticed that the backups aren't getting all of the desired files until it is too late.

Be careful about duplicate references on the tar command line. If /some/mountpoint and /some/mountpoint/somedir are listed and they are on the same filesystem, then tar will archive everything under /some/mountpoint/somedir twice (unless the -1 option is specified). There is no real harm in this—except that it might unnecessarily fill a whole tape and slow the process and possibly the network, which is harm enough.

Backups: Selective

Here are examples of scripts that use tar for differential and/or incremental backups. Both use GNU tar's -T ("take list") option. The filename argument that corresponds to this option is read by tar as a list of filenames and directories to include in the backup. We use - as the filename to represent stdin (a common UNIX idiom), just as we use the - name for stdout in the argument that corresponds to tar's -f parameter.

```
#!/bin/sh
# Differential Backup Script
# this uses the timestamp of the ~root/backup/last-full
# --- so that file must be touched by our level-zero
# backup scheme (and nothing else).
touch $HOME/backup/last-backup
# this is to allow us to use this script in a
# hybrid of differential and incremental scripts
find $(bakdirs) -mount -not -type d \
-newer $HOME/backup/last-full -print \
| tar cS1zTf - - | buffer -o /dev/nst0
```

---

3. Note that not all shells support this command substitution operator.

In this example, we find all of the links that

- Are below one of the directories listed by our bakdirs script
- Are on the same filesystem (-mount)
- Are not directories (-not -type d)
- Have an mtime value (last-modified time stamp) that is more recent than that of our sentinel file (-newer)

This is fed (-print) to tar's stdin. Although the -print option isn't required for GNU find, we add it here for portability in case this script is ever copied to a system not using GNU find—although the requirement that it use GNU tar is not addressed.

In this case we direct our backup to /dev/nst0, the node for the non-rewinding tape driver. Because differentials and incrementals are typically small, multiple data sets are often placed on the same tape. This can be done by using the mt command to position the non-rewinding drive at the tape EOD (end of data), using a command like

```
mt -f /dev/nst0 eod
```

The script could be improved by including this command. If the script is executed after a reboot, data could be lost because most tape drivers rewind the tape at reboot. We describe the mt command on page 142.

As the comments point out, the touch command is not required for cases where no incrementals are ever intended. However, it is a trivial matter. If we're concerned about the use of the timestamp on our sentinel files, then we can use a relatively simple shell scripting trick to store the date in a file and some date arithmetic to calculate the number of days since that date. Here's an example:

We prepare the date file with

```
date > $HOME/backup/last-full
```

and we calculate the number of days from then to now using the following:

```
echo $(( $(( $(date +%s) - $(date -d "$(cat $1)" +%s) )) / 86400 ))
```

This is the current time (in seconds since the epoch) minus the time stored in the specified file (assuming we call this script or shell function with the name of the file that contains our timestamp) and then divided by 86400 (the number of seconds in a day).

We could simplify the expression a bit by storing the date in the file in the "seconds since the epoch" format using just

```
echo $(( $(( $(date +%s) - $(cat $1) )) / 86400 ))
```

However, that wouldn't save much, and it would leave backup/last-full in a format unsuitable for human reading.

In either case, we can use these date arithmetic tricks to make the script more robust. We can save the date stamp in a shell variable before starting the backup and only write the new date into the file *after* successfully performing and testing the backup. If we were to try that using just touch, we'd have a small problem—files modified while this script was running would not be backed up in the next incremental. We could play games with other options to touch, but they are unnecessary when the GNU date command and our shell arithmetic (or the expr command) are used to calculate these dates. Another method would be to touch temporary files before executing tar and then using mv to change the names of the temporary files after tar has completed, like this:

```
touch filename.NEW
tar
mv filename.NEW filename
```

So, here are improved versions of the script. The first does differential backups and the second does incremental backups:

```
#!/bin/sh
# Differential Backup Script (with date arithmetic)
# this uses the timestamp of the ~root/backup/last-full
# --- so that file must be touched by our level-zero
# backup scheme (and nothing else).
START_TIME=$(date)
DAYS_SINCE="$(( $(( $(date +%s) - \
$(date -d "$(cat $HOME)" +%s) )) / 86400 ))"
 find $(bakdirs) -mount -not -type d \
-ctime "+$DAYS_SINCE" -print \
| tar cSlzTf - - | buffer -o /dev/nst0

#!/bin/sh
# Incremental Backup Script
# this uses the timestamp of the ~root/backup/last-backup
# --- so that file must be touched by our level-zero
# backup scheme, by this script *and by nothing else*.
 touch $HOME/backup/last-backup.new
 find $(bakdirs) -mount -not -type d \
-newer $HOME/backup/last-backup -print0 \
| tar cSlz --null -T - -f - | buffer -o /dev/nst0
 mv $HOME/backup/last-backup.new $HOME/backup/last-backup
```

The primary difference here, as you might expect, is which sentinel file (or date stamp) is used. In the latter case, we touch a "new" file before starting our backup and then use that file's timestamp as a "reference" to set the timestamp on the sentinel file.

If there were any chance of these backup scripts or any other programs using the tape drive being executed concurrently, then it would be wise to set lock files. The lockfile program included with procmail[4] should suffice.

Note: We also included another enhancement to this example—using the -print0 directive on find and the corresponding --null tar option. This find command generates

---

4. http://www.procmail.org/

a list of NUL-terminated links (also known as ASCIIZ strings), and the -0 flag on this cpio example corresponds to that -print0 directive from find. Therefore, this command will properly handle degenerate filenames.

Using cpio

cpio is the other traditional backup and filesystem archiving tool. It works very differently from tar. Early versions had major advantages over older versions of tar. Current GNU versions of tar and cpio have fairly comparable features, though they are still much different to use.

In many ways, the cpio approach seems opposite to the tar approach for specifying files and directories to back up and/or restore. When creating an archive, tar takes a list of file and directory names as command-line arguments. Each directory named is traversed recursively. To create an archive under cpio, it must be provided with a list of objects (file and directory names, the names of any device nodes, UNIX domain sockets, named pipes, and so on). This list is normally fed into cpio's stdin through a pipe and is usually generated with a find command.

A simple command to back up an entire file tree looks like this:

```
find / -print0 | cpio -oOB > /dev/st0
```

This is a more elaborate example than is minimally needed because the -print0 directive and cpio's -0 ("zero") option are again used to make the script more robust in the face of "weird" filenames.

Of course, this example suffers one of the same problems as our first tar command— find includes links under /proc and so on. We fix that by adjusting the parameters to find:

```
find /* -fstype ext2 -print0 | cpio -oOB > /dev/st0
```

In this example, we limit our backup to just ext2 filesystems. Hidden files and directories (those beginning with a period) are skipped.

Backups: Remote Tape Drives

Tape drives are expensive. One of the nice features of UNIX is the ease with which we can access remote devices. It's almost as easy to access remote tape drives as it is to access those locally connected.

```
find /* -fstype ext2 -print0 |
    ssh $TAPEHOST ''cpio -oOB
| buffer -o /dev/st0''
```

In this example we use ssh, the popular secure replacement for rsh. rsh would work equally well, though allowing the traditional BSD r* commands to be used is generally a bad security policy. There are also Kerberos-enhanced versions of rsh, rlogin, and rcp that provide reasonable security and encryption.

Note that we always use `buffer` when using remote tape drives. See page 143 for more on `buffer`.

Also, `buffer` can be used in the other direction to pull files from a remote system and write them to the local tape drive:

```
ssh $OTHERHOST
'find /* -fstype ext2 -print0
    | cpio -oOB '
    | buffer -o /dev/st0
```

Backups: Locally Mounted Filesystems

The only trick to making backups on locally mounted, removable filesystems is to ensure that you don't recurse down into the target directory tree.

Consider a backup to a removable drive mounted on `/mnt/more` (a magneto-optical drive, perhaps) and started at the root directory. It would end up making a copy of `/mnt/more/mnt/more`! This is usually not infinitely recursive; however, it's still a bad idea.

We use the same options to our backup software that we've been using to prevent traversing over the `/proc` filesystem. When using `tar`, we include the `-l` option, and when using `cpio` we include the `-mount` option on the `find` command that feeds it its file list. This is not a problem using the `dump` command, since `dump` always operates on individual filesystems.

One advantage of `dump` over `cpio` and `tar` is that the system administrator can set permissions such that a non-root user or pseudo-user can perform backups without relying on any SUID programs. Make the `/dev/` nodes for the raw disk partitions group-writable, and make `dump` SGID.

Restore: Local Tape Drives

Another directory difference between GNU `tar` and GNU `cpio` is in the storage and restoration of absolute paths. Under GNU `tar`, the leading slash for absolute filenames is removed as the backup is made. This can be a problem when restoring `.tar` files made by other versions of `tar`. Under `cpio`, the paths must be forced to be relative during the restore process.

Usually, files should be restored to paths that are relative to the current directory (or rooted in some other place). By default, `cpio` will not restore directories, so we must add the `-d` switch:

```
cpio -ivd --no-absolute-filenames < /tmp/tst.cpio
```

Restore: Remote Tape Drives

Restoring from remote tape drives is simply a matter of "reversing" what we did to send the archive over there. For example:

```
ssh $OTHERHOST 'buffer -i /dev/st0'
| 'find /* -fstype ext2 -print0 | cpio -id'
```

If the desire is to restore only select files, append a list of glob patterns to the end of the cpio command, which may have to be quoted in some cases.

This highlights another difference between cpio and tar related to selective restores. You can list file and directory names on tar's command line—it will restore any of the files and recurse down through any of the named directories. However, tar will not allow glob patterns here.

The usual way to cope with this limitation of tar—particularly for large numbers of files—is to extract an index (using the tar -x switch) into a file (using simple redirection). Then we can filter that file (using grep and grep -v) and pass the resulting list of files to the tar extract command using the -T ("take list") option, like:

```
ssh $OTHERHOST 'buffer -i /dev/st0'
| 'tar xTf /tmp/restorelist.txt - '
```

after preparing a restorelist.txt with filenames and directories on separate lines or even space-delimited.

NFS

You might note that we've avoided examples of performing backups over NFS. There are a number of reasons for this. Passing data archives through TCP pipes is usually more reliable than NFS. Also, most installations of NFS perform root squashing and have other limitations.

The foregoing scripts should demonstrate that we can do just about any sort of copying, archiving, and file restoration operations over TCP sockets about as easily as via NFS.

Using AMANDA

Many system administrators write their own scripts and do most of their volume management and tape handling manually. Others use large commercial packages like Legato Networker and Cheyenne/CA ARCServe.

A happy medium between these is AMANDA, the Advanced Maryland Automatic Network Disk Archiver,[5] developed at the University of Maryland and maintained by the Open Source community at large. Although it has some limitations, AMANDA is continuing to improve.

AMANDA manages the process of spooling a combination of full and incremental backups from sets of network clients (servers and workstations) to a holding disk on a tape host. These data sets are then written to tapes. Once it's installed properly, AMANDA

---

5. For more information, see: http://www.amanda.org/

is completely automatic. One cron job (on each tape host) checks to ensure that the correct tape is loaded in each tape drive, that all clients are accessible, and that there is sufficient space available on the holding disks. This is normally done during the day so that any errors can be mailed to a list of backup operators and system administrators in time for tapes to be changed and other errors to be corrected. Another cron job, usually late at night, actually performs the backups—connecting from the tape host to each of the clients. It has features to perform these connections in parallel and to monitor and throttle its own bandwidth utilization. A module (the planner) determines which levels of incrementals to perform on each filesystem on each host.

Under the hood, AMANDA uses dump or (optionally) tar for the archiving. Thus it's possible (with a bit of dd and mt scripting) to extract AMANDA archives using conventional tools. Normally, AMANDA's amrecover command is used.

Supporting Commands

Notice that many examples in this chapter rely on a supporting cast of commands like find, buffer, and mt.

find

find is a powerful command. It searches a specified directory structure and evaluates all files according to specified expressions. Each match is processed in accordance with specified actions. The default action is to print the name of the file. See the man page for complete information.

mt and mtx

The mt and mtx commands provide magnetic tape control. mt can be used to report the status of the tape drive, report or set the absolute and/or logical position of the tape head, rewind the drive, eject tapes (on some drives), and seek forward to the end of the last block of recorded data (allowing the next command to add new data sets to a given tape).

This aspect of tape handling under Unix is often confusing to new system administrators. A tape can hold multiple data sets—each of these is treated as a separate, nameless file on the tape. Using ioctl(), it's possible to sequentially access these separate tape members. The mt and mtx commands make use of the ioctl() function.

The contents of an unlabeled tape can be identified by means of the following steps:

1. mt -f /dev/nst0 eod

2. mt -f /dev/nst0 stat

3. Read the output—the file number (of the last file on the tape) indicates how many members are stored on the tape.

4. mt -f /dev/nst0 rewind

5. For each of the members:
  (a) `cat /dev/nst0 | file -`
  (b) `mt -f /dev/nst0 fsf` (file seek forward).

After this, rewind the tape and issue the appropriate command to extract archive indicies or files from the members on the tape. Notably, it's possible to use UNIX tape drives in applications. Thus, one might find a system where applications are storing large data sets on tapes, spooling portions of the tape into memory or a temporary directory, working on it, and writing it out to another drive. This is rarely necessary given today's huge hard drives and relatively expensive tape drives, but it can be done under UNIX or LINUX just as it was on mainframes for decades.

Leonard Zubkoff's `mtx` command has extensions for the most common tape changers. One can issue commands like

```
mtx -f /dev/st0 next
```

to load the next tape. There are other options to load specific tapes by their slot number, for example.

buffer

The `buffer` command keeps data streaming to the tape drive (or another device) even when the command that's supplying it is being bursty—which is common with compression, networking communications, and even normal archiving operations on busy multitasking systems.

bakdirs

This script tests all the filesystem mountpoints to see which are mounted locally and which are mounted via the network or from a removable medium. It is used to limit backups to appropriate filesystems.

```
 mount | while read dev x mpoint x type options
do
[ "$type" == NFS ] && continue
[ "$mpoint" == /mnt/cdrom ] && continue
[ "$mpoint" == /proc ] && continue
.
.
.
echo $mpoint
done
```

In this example, the output of the `mount` command is piped into a `while`/read loop. Every output line of the `mount` command is like this:

```
/dev/hda5 on /usr type ext2 (rw)
```

It's of the form *device* on *mountpoint* type *fstype (options)*. We read in values using `$x` as a placeholder to gobble up the words on and type. We also grab `$opts`, although it is not used in this example. Parsing out the option strings would require some fussing with $IFS and other work that is not necessary in this case. However, if we wanted to automatically exclude filesystems that were mounted read-only, we could implement the extra scripting code (or call sed, tr, or awk to do the parsing) or rewrite the script in Perl, Tcl, or such.

For each line of input, the script performs a series of tests that check for characteristics of the filesystems that should be skipped. The script outputs the mountpoint of each filesystem that passes the tests.

This script or simple variations of it can also be used with find in other cases to limit traversal to locally mounted filesystems.

Multi-Volume Backups

These examples make no provisions for backups that span multiple tapes, because it is preferable to avoid them. Gnu tar and cpio have switches to support spanning any archive across multiple volumes (media), but the man pages for the Linux dump and restore currently note that they do not yet implement multi-volume support.

Spanning multiple tapes increases risk, because a failure of any tape may render all the tapes in the set useless. Experiment with these features with caution if they are necessary for your site, but it's best to avoid them if possible.

Sites with simple-enough requirements to use these utilities generally can structure filesystem sizes and backup scripts to fit media constraints. If not, consider recommending the purchase of higher-capacity tape drives. Using tar, cpio, or pax provides for the backup of selected subsets of data regardless of filesystem boundaries.

Other Backup/Restore Packages

There are many other packages (free and commercial) for performing file backups. Most of the popular packages for other forms of Unix have been ported (such as Legato Networker, Cheyenne Arcserve, and so on). Coverage of these is beyond the scope of this book. The key principles are the same regardless of which package you use—and the necessity for *testing* is just as relevant.

*Anyone who considers protocol
unimportant has never dealt with a cat.*

~R. Heinlein

13

Network Technologies

THE PROTOCOL SUITE KNOWN AS TCP/IP has achieved world domination. There are several reasons for its success. First, it has scaled to meet the explosive growth of the Internet, the world's largest network. Second, it is an open standard and has been successfully implemented in systems ranging from IBM mainframes running MVS to palmtop computers and personal organizers. Finally, TCP/IP has been successfully adapted to every variety of networking hardware developed since its inception in the 1970s.

Ironically, the current TCP/IP protocol suite is doomed to be a victim of its own success. The exponential growth of the Internet has nearly exhausted the 32-bit address space defined in IP (Internet Protocol). This prompted the development of IPv6, which was first published in 1995. The major improvements include a 128-bit address space, a streamlined packet header structure, a new header extension mechanism for optional header fields, and extensions to support authentication and encryption. Eventually, all networked devices will transition to IPv6 from the current TCP/IP protocol, which we refer to as IPv4.

This chapter examines the IPv4 and IPv6 protocols in detail, as well as LINUX support for specific features they provide. Although LINUX supports many proprietary network

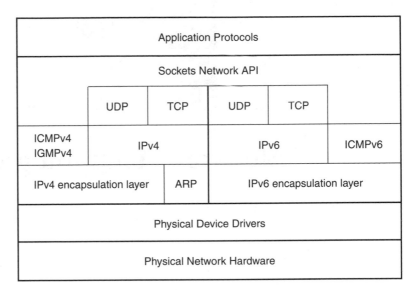

Figure 13.1   Network layer implementation

protocols that enable Linux systems to participate in older networks, their use is dwindling. Therefore, this chapter focuses exclusively on the IPv4 and IPv6 suites.

The IP Protocol Stack

The objective of computer networking is to enable communication among applications running on separate computers. During its design, the creators of IPv4 decided to insulate computer applications from the different types of network hardware that existed and would exist in the future. They also foresaw that the best way to encourage reliable communications was to integrate a reliable communications layer within the IP suite. With this in mind, they crafted a conceptually layered[1] approach we refer to as the IP protocol stack or IP protocol suite.

Protocols are layered in order to facilitate the sharing of network hardware among applications with divergent requirements. This permits application-level protocols to differ while relying on common lower-level protocols. Figure 13.1 shows the layered protocols of the IP stack.

The physical layer underlies all the others. It could be fiber, coaxial, shielded or unshielded twisted pair, or, in theory, a taut piece of string. The data link layer provides some abstraction, presenting higher-level protocols a unified network view. For example,

---

1. For the sake of performance, the boundaries between layers are not as clear in most IP implementations as they are in theory.

Ethernet, which is a data link layer protocol, runs on many different physical layer technologies—even mixed together in a network. This enables IP, which is a network layer protocol, to see a network comprised of both fiber and twisted pair as a uniform Ethernet network. Similarly, an IP network can span different data link protocols, presenting the transport layer with a unified view of a network that spans Ethernet, Token Ring, and serial links.

Just as one layer in the network stack can span different implementations of the layer below it, each layer can support multiple simultaneous implementations of the layer above it. For example, Ethernet supports IP, IPv6, IPX, and Appletalk all running at the same time. This is not a problem from the perspective of the protocols, but reliability tends to suffer from the added implementation complexity. Similarly, IP supports the simultaneous use of multiple layer protocols, such as TCP, UDP, ICMP, and ARP.

To communicate freely, LINUX applications have a simple API known as the sockets interface. This API dates back to the first BSD network implementations and has required only small amounts of work to meet the needs of network programmers for the last two decades. Other APIs have been written, the two most prominent being the TLI and the Streams APIs. Neither has provided a compelling reason to port existing applications from the Sockets API. Both the TCP and UDP protocols may be used with the Sockets API. Additionally, specialized interfaces allow specific programs to obtain and manipulate low-level network information.

IP Version 4

Internet standards are defined in documents known as RFCs (Request For Comments). These are available from many sources on the Internet. The RFCs document the protocols, the numbering assignments on which the protocols depend, the standards process itself, and much of the history behind the RFCs.

IPv4 Address Architecture

IPv4 addresses are 32-bit values, typically expressed as four decimal numbers from 0 to 255, separated by periods (for example, 127.0.0.1). IPv4 addresses are segregated into classes. Within each class, addresses have two distinct parts, the network address and the host address. The classes are outlined in Table 13.1.

At the time of IPv4's inception, it was completely unclear what network technologies would exist in large internetworks. Consequently, the original address class assignments did not match the networking topologies. The solution developed was called *subnetting*, which allowed an organization to choose an arbitrary boundary between the host and network components of addresses within a particular network. A subnet is expressed as a subnet mask and is usually written in a dotted quad address format. The one bits indicate the network portion of an address, and zeroes indicate the host portion. Therefore, if Class A network 10 were subnetted with a mask of 255.255.255.0, the network would

Table 13.1 **IPv4 address classes**

Class	Address Range	Networks	Hosts
Class A	1 to 126	126	16777214
Loopback (a reserved class A)	127	NA	NA
Class B	128.0 to 191.255	16384	65534
Class C	192.0.0 to 223.255.255	2097152	254
Class D (Multicast Addresses)	224.0.0.0 to 239.255.255.255	NA	NA
Class E (Reserved)	240.0.0.0 to 247.255.255.255	NA	NA

appear internally as having 65,534 (sub)networks of 254 hosts each. Hosts and gateways external to the network do recognize the subnet mask applied within the network. This contrasts with CIDR (Classless Inter-Domain Routing), where networks are aggregated in a fashion that is visible to external gateways.

Network 127 is reserved for the *loopback interface*, which always has the address 127.0.0.1. A loopback interface is used in every IP implementation. IP datagrams transmitted to the loopback address are received by the transmitting host and never appear on the physical network.

IP supports several forms of *broadcasting*, a technique for sending a single packet to multiple hosts. There are three forms of the broadcast mechanism: local, subnet wide, and network wide. The local broadcast address is all ones, that is 255.255.255.255. This address is guaranteed not to be forwarded by routers. This broadcast is used in conjunction with maintenance and utility protocols such as BOOTP, DHCP, and RARP to find a host that supports those services on a local network segment. Subnet broadcasts address all hosts within the subnet and are formed by substituting all ones for the host portion of the subnetted network address. Finally, an entire network can be addressed by setting the host portion of the IP address to all ones, ignoring any subnet mask. Note that this reserves the all ones subnet address for broadcasting.

A family of addresses related to the broadcast address is the *unspecified address*. It was originally intended for use strictly as the source addresses of some ICMP packets and RARP packets. However, confusion has ensued because most routers treat addresses of all zeroes or all ones like broadcast addresses, and most hosts are allowed to specify broadcast addresses based on either zeroes or ones. This confusion results from proprietary software vendors having knowingly done the wrong thing, as the RFCs are clear on this issue.

There is no form of broadcasting that spans multiple networks. However, a host is permitted to send a *directed broadcast* packet to another network, by using either the network or subnetwork broadcast address of the intended destination.

Using the network 10 example, consider a host on the 10.0.1 subnet. The examples in Table 13.2 demonstrate the various broadcast types.

Broadcasting places a load on hosts that are not interested in the broadcast data because they must receive and decode each packet before discarding it. Also, the sender must

Table 13.2 **Broadcast types**

Host	Destination Address	Hosts Seen
10.0.1.1	255.255.255.255	All hosts on physical network
10.0.1.1	10.0.1.255	All hosts on same subnet, probably same set as above
10.0.1.1	10.255.255.255	All hosts on net 10, possibly 16 million hosts!
10.0.1.1	8.255.255.255	All hosts on net 8, as a directed broadcast
10.0.1.1	8.0.1.255	All hosts on subnet 0.1 of network 8, assuming a 24-bit subnet mask

know the networks where all of the clients reside, which requires manual configuration or some form of registration. Finally, broadcasting has the potential for abuse, so most organizations do not accept broadcasts from external networks.

To offer a better mechanism for providing data to multiple hosts, the IP multicasting extensions to IP were developed. Multicast addresses are termed "groups," and packets reach only hosts that have been configured to participate in the corresponding multicast group. This is achieved by configuring IGMP, the Internet Group Management Protocol. Analogous to ICMP, IGMP is a simple, low-level protocol that allows hosts to register and deregister group memberships with a multicast router. Multicast routers run DVMRP (Distance Vector Multicast Routing Protocol) to forward multicast packets over internets. The Mbone[2] or the Multicast Internet is a set of organizations that participate in multicasting over the Internet. The primary use of the Mbone is to experiment with IP multicasting and to distribute audio and video. IP Multicasting is also used by market data vendors in the development of data distribution engines.

The explosive growth of the Internet caused the size of routing tables on the Internet backbone routers to became a major problem. Most class A and B networks had already been used, and large numbers of class C networks were being assigned. In an effort to reduce the number of routes necessary to maintain the Internet, Classless Inter-Domain Routing was developed. This allowed the Internet backbone routers to address blocks of contiguously assigned addresses as a single route in order to keep the size of the routing tables manageable.

RFC 1918 Addressing

RFC 1918 provides another solution for the shortage of address space available under IPv4. The RFC reserves three network addresses: 10.0.0.0 is a 24-bit block, 72.16.0.0 is a 20-bit block, and 192.168.0.0 is a 16-bit block. These addresses may be used by networks that masquerade as a single IP address (that is not part of one of these reserved network addresses). In other words, an organization that needs a large address space can

2. See http://www.mbone.com/ for information about the Mbone.

use one of these reserved network addresses *internally* while pretending to the rest of the Internet that it is a single (non-reserved) IP address.

The Address Resolution Protocol

The Address Resolution protocol, or ARP, is a co-requisite protocol for IPv4. Although IP does not include ARP in its protocol suite, the ARP protocol is a requirement for IP on most network types. ARP provides the mapping from IP addresses to physical layer addresses, using a broadcast-based mechanism. Hosts and routers utilize an ARP table to store translations from IP address to physical layer address. When a system has a packet to transmit, the ARP table is consulted. If the appropriate translation exists in the ARP table, no extra work is required. If the data is not found in the table, then the system broadcasts an ARP request packet. If a system replies with an ARP response, the table is updated and the IP packet is transmitted. The ARP table can be viewed and manipulated with the arp command.

Reverse ARP (RARP) is a protocol that supplies IP addresses when given physical layer addresses. RARP is used to support diskless booting.

IPv4 Data Transmission

The IPv4 protocol suite transmits data grouped in units called *packets* or *datagrams*. A datagram is the fundamental unit of data transmission for the IP layer. Datagrams can be from 20 to 65536 bytes long, including both the data and the IP header. The packet header has a minimum length of 20 bytes but can vary based on the inclusion of optional fields. A checksum exists for the header portion of the packet. If a host or router finds a packet with a bad header checksum, it will simply drop it. This is why the IP layer is said to be unreliable. Ensuring end-to-end integrity of transmitted data is left for the higher layer protocols like TCP.

The IP protocol governs itself by generating and processing various Internet Control Message Protocol (ICMP) messages. ICMP is used to notify the sender of a number of error conditions, to manage the flow and routing of data, and to provide diagnostic information.

One of the fields of the IP header is the time to live field. Originally, this was specified as the maximum lifetime of the packet in seconds. Since all IP implementations just decrement this field by one, this has come to be understood as a hop count field. When a router decrements this counter to zero, the packet is dropped and a time-exceeded ICMP message is sent to the originating host. This is an important feature for packet-switched networks, because it removes datagrams misdirected by routing loops or other errors.

The IPv4 standard defines the term Maximum Transmission Unit (MTU) to describe the largest datagram size allowed for a particular network medium. IP is free to transmit packets of any size less than or equal to the MTU of the local network interface to any destination. If a datagram reaches a network with a smaller MTU, the packet is split into a number of smaller datagrams, a process termed *fragmentation*. The IP header utilizes two flag bits and a fragment offset field to support fragmentation. At the destination host, a buffer known as a fragment reassembly window and a timer are used to manage the reconstruction of fragmented packets. If the timer expires before the fragmented packet is reassembled, a fragment reassembly time exceeded ICMP message is sent back to the originating host.

Hosts may also indicate that fragmentation is unacceptable by setting the Don't Fragment bit in the IP header flags. In cases where fragmentation is required to send a datagram on its next hop, the router will drop the packet and send an ICMP message back to the originating host, reporting that the DF bit was set and fragmentation was needed. This functionality provides a mechanism for avoiding fragmentation entirely, called Path MTU Discovery.

Fragmentation has turned out to be an undesirable feature of IP, because the loss of a single fragment requires the retransmission of the entire original datagram. This has led to the adoption of Path MTU Discovery as the preferred mechanism for sizing IP datagrams.

IPv4 Routing

IP packets that travel over more than one network are said to be routed. Each system visited by the packet between the source and destination hosts are known as routers (or gateways, in the terminology of the older RFCs). Each router makes an independent decision about where to forward the packet next, according to its routing table. This is known as "hop-by-hop" routing. Routers execute one or more dynamic routing protocols. The purpose of the routing protocol is to arrange that the routing table is populated with a desired set of routes, and to update the table as quickly as possible to adapt to changes in the network.

There are two major classes of routing protocols. One set is designed to connect large sections of the Internet, which are themselves composed of many networks. These sections are known as Autonomous Systems (AS), and each registers a unique AS number. These autonomous systems are composed of Internet Service Providers (ISPs), universities, and some large corporations. The second class of protocols is designed to be used within an Autonomous System, and are known as Interior Gateway Protocols.

The protocols used to exchange data between Autonomous Systems are called Exterior Gateway Protocols (EGPs) or Inter Domain Routing Protocols (IDRPs). Confusingly enough, there are two routing protocols that go by these names. This family of protocols is oriented toward reducing the overall number of routes needed, and they enforce routing based on policy, not just simple reachability. These policies reflect the role of the Autonomous System in the Internet, as well as business relationships among them. An example policy might be "Large corporation X does not route traffic not destined for it" or "Carrier A is preferred to Carrier B for traffic destined to AS C." Examples of exterior gateway protocols are EGP, BGP3, BGP4, and IDRP.

Interior Gateway Protocols are concerned with creating an optimal set of routes and updating the routing table quickly. These protocols are generally based on two common routing algorithms known as "distance vector" and "link state." Distance vector algorithms are easier to implement but require more time to converge after a change in topology. Link state algorithms converge faster but require more computing resources. The RIP, RIPv2, and Cisco proprietary IGRP protocols are examples of protocols that use Distance Vector algorithms. OSPF and IS-IS are examples of protocols that use link state algorithms.

User Datagram Protocol

The User Datagram Protocol (UDP) provides simple low-level packet transmission and reception to applications. A UDP packet contains the IP header, a UDP header, and the packet data. The UDP header contains two fields known as ports and a checksum that includes the UDP header, packet data, and portions of the IP header. The ports serve to differentiate UDP conversations, so that multiple applications on a host can use the UDP protocol simultaneously. The most common applications register their port numbers with the Internet Assigned Numbers Authority (IANA) to avoid conflicts in port usage.

UDP is described as a connectionless protocol because there are no fixed relationships among hosts communicating via UDP. UDP is also a stateless protocol, because the protocol does not specify relationships among any packets transmitted or received. This does not mean that all UDP communication is stateless; it simply means that higher layer applications and protocols define the relationships. UDP does not provide end-to-end reliability, so applications that use UDP typically provide sequence numbers and retransmission algorithms.

Applications that need to use IP broadcasting or multicasting must use UDP. Broadcasting and multicasting are incompatible with TCP, which is strictly a connection-oriented protocol between two endpoints.

Many protocols are implemented on top of UDP and are available to programmers via a library. The Open Network Computing Remote Procedure Call (ONC RPC) protocol is an example. The RPC library includes all of the logic to create a reliable transport on top of UDP. This removes the burden of low-level network programming from the application programmer.

The following applications use UDP to communicate:

- The Domain Name System (DNS)
- The Network Time Protocol
- bootp
- The Network File System (via RPC)
- The Network Information System (via RPC)

Transmission Control Protocol

The Transmission Control Protocol (TCP) is a high-level protocol for the reliable communication of data between two endpoints. TCP is layered on top of IP, so a TCP packet contains the IP header, the TCP header, and the TCP data. Like UDP, TCP also uses the port concept to demultiplex communication sessions. TCP differs from UDP in that TCP connections are defined by two endpoints, so it is the combination of local port, remote port, local IP address, and remote IP address that distinguishes a unique TCP connection. Because TCP is connection oriented, it also contains state information. The state of a TCP connection can be viewed via the netstat command. Also, the TCP protocol contains flow control mechanisms, which allow it to deal transparently with variations in network throughput.

The design of TCP is robust and much research has gone into refining its retransmission and flow control algorithms. Therefore, TCP should be the protocol of choice for any application that does not require IP broadcasting or multicasting.

Here are just a few examples of popular protocols that use TCP to communicate:

- Telnet
- The File Transfer Protocol (FTP)
- The Hypertext Transfer Protocol (HTTP)
- The Network News Transfer Protocol (NNTP)
- The Post Office Protocol (POP)
- The Simple Mail Transfer Protocol (SMTP)

From this short list, it should be obvious that most of the Internet runs over TCP.

IP Version 6

Crisis loomed over the Internet in 1990. The 32-bit address space defined by IPv4 was running out. Even more pressing was the massive growth in the size of the routing tables of the core Internet routers. If the routing tables continued to grow, it did not seem that it would be possible to manufacture routers powerful enough to manage the burden. Development of IP version 6 began in 1992 as a response to this growing crisis.

Version 6 of the Internet Protocol was developed to address these problems. IPv6 uses 128-bit addresses, which create a vast new address space. In addition, IPv6 addresses the complexity of configuring hosts, which was hindering the rate at which IP could be deployed. Much to their credit, the designers of IPv6 did not improve parts of the protocol that already worked well. They strenuously avoided adding any complexity to the protocols that would impact the time needed to process a packet. The result is that the IPv6 packet structure has been simplified, and it is reasonable to expect an IPv6 protocol stack to perform as well or better than an IPv4 implementation on the same host.

While IPv6 was still in development, a solution was engineered to address the explosive growth of routing tables in IPv4. Classless Inter Domain Routing (CIDR) was developed and deployed via the BGP protocol. This significantly reduced the number of routes maintained in the core Internet routers.

Also, the wide adoption of private networks in accordance with RFC 1918 has somewhat reduced the pressure on address space. This comes as a relief, as it delays the inevitable: the world's largest and most complex network upgrade.

Given the current state of affairs, IP version 6 is now waiting for those who manage the Internet to have a sufficiently compelling reason to begin the transition. Considerable research and testing goes on over the 6bone, an IPv6 network that is tunneled over the existing IPv4 Internet.

IPv6 Addressing Architecture

IPv6 has been designed using 128-bit addresses. Of this address space, only 8 percent has been allocated to hosts, using the current addressing architecture. Of that 8 percent, it is reasonable to expect that IPv6 will also be limited to the 21 percent address space efficiency currently experienced on the Internet. This would limit the practical deployment of IPv6 to 5,716,743,764,271,766,186,184,693,404,853,705,952 hosts. This limit is not expected to hinder continued growth of the Internet.

IPv6 addressing differs significantly from IPv4, and this is reflected in the new terminology used to describe IPv6 addresses:

- Unicast. These addresses are analogous to traditional IP addresses. A unicast address refers to a single interface on an IPv6 host. Unicast addresses may be routed. There are no class distinctions for unicast addresses as there are in IPv4 addresses.

- Multicast. Approximately 0.4 percent of the available address space has been dedicated to multicast addresses. Multicasting is integral to the design of IPv6 and is used extensively. Host auto-address configuration is based on multicasting, as are the host and neighbor discovery procedures. Most routing protocols defined for IPv6 use multicasting as well.

- Anycast. Anycast addresses are a new concept not present with IPv4. A packet directed to an anycast address will be received by the closest host that has been programmed to receive this address. It is anticipated that anycasting will be hosted by the network routing infrastructure and used to locate network applications. Anycast addresses are allocated from the unicast address space. At this point only one anycast address has been defined. It is called the subnet-router anycast address and is formed by appending zeroes to a valid network prefix. Routers attached to the network segment having this assigned prefix must accept this address.

- Site-Local Unicast Addresses. A small portion of the address space has been reserved for private networks. These addresses do not route beyond the site in which they are deployed.

- Link-Local Unicast Addresses. Another small portion of addresses is dedicated to unicast addresses that do not route off of their immediate network segment. Hosts automatically configure themselves with link-local unicast addresses to use for auto-address configuration and neighbor discovery.

Choosing a successful addressing architecture has been a goal of IPv6 since its inception. The initial addressing schemes have been updated to reflect an allocation policy based on the network topology. There was much controversy surrounding this decision, because it means that an organization's IP addresses will change if the organization changes its network provider. The purpose in defining the "Aggregatable Global Unicast Address" architecture was to create an efficient routing infrastructure for IPv6. This addressing scheme allows efficient aggregation of addresses in a fashion similar to CIDR.

IPv6 Address Allocations

It should be noted that most of the protocol specifications for IPv6 were written long before the addressing architecture had stabilized. There was good reason for this. Most of the protocol mechanics are well understood, but the design of the addressing architecture underwent major revisions. This was possible because IPv6 hosts need to treat only a few addresses in a special fashion. The routing protocols are concerned with the structure of most addresses, but IPv6 itself is not.

The following special addresses have been defined for IPv6:

- The Unspecified Address. This is used to express the absence of an address. It may only be used as the source address, and is intended to be used only during auto-address configuration and duplicate address detection.

- The Loopback Address. The loopback address is used by systems to communicate within themselves. The address 1 is reserved for this purpose.

- Multicast Addresses. Multicast addresses begin with most significant 8 bits set to one. Applications can register multicast addresses with IANA for their use, in the same fashion that TCP and UDP ports are reserved.

Figure 13.2 details the structure of "Aggregatable Global Unicast Addresses."

The Top Level Aggregator identifies the major Internet backbone service providers. Also included in this level are exchanges, which are proposed interconnections for second tier providers.

The Next Level Aggregator field is used by first and second tier service providers to structure their networks. This may involve reserving some of the most significant bits to identify second and third tier providers. The remaining bits would then be used to identify the subscriber.

Site Level Aggregators are then allocated within organizations based on their physical network topology. They are used much as IPv4 subnets.

3	13	8	24	16	64 Bits
FP	TLA ID	RES	NLA ID	SLA ID	Interface ID

LEGEND

FP	The Format Prefix (3 bit) for Aggregatable Global Unicast Addresses, defined to be 001
TLA ID	Top-Level Aggregation Identifier
RES	Reserved for future use
NLA ID	Next-Level Aggregation Identifier
SLA ID	Site-Level Aggregation Identifier
INTERFACE	ID Interface Identifier

Figure 13.2 Aggregatable global unicast addresses

The Interface ID specifies a unique identifier for each network interface on a host or router. These are specified to be IEEE EUI-64 format global identifiers. For the Ethernet, Token Ring, and FDDI media types, EUI-64 identifiers are formed directly from the 48-bit MAC addresses. For example, if the MAC address assigned to an Ethernet controller has the following value:

```
00:00:F8:73:00:1D
```

then the interface identifier for this controller is

```
02:00:F8:FF:FE:73:00:1D
```

There is one final twist. Notice that in addition to FF:FE being inserted into the middle, a bit has been set. The seventh most significant bit of the IPv6 interface identifier is inverted to avoid generating a potental conflict with the unspecified address.

IPv6 Address Notation

The textual representation of IPv6 address is based on 16-bit groups of hex digits. Since much of the address space will be sparse, a few notational shortcuts can be used to reduce the number of zeroes written.

Here is the link local address for a workstation, the unspecified address, and the loopback address:

```
FE80:0000:0000:0000:0200:F8FF:FE73:001D
0000:0000:0000:0000:0000:0000:0000:0000
0000:0000:0000:0000:0000:0000:0000:0001
```

The first shortcut allows the leading zeroes to be removed from addresses, as long as at least one digit remains in each field:

```
FE80:0:0:0:200:F8FF:FE73:1D
0:0:0:0:0:0:0:0
0:0:0:0:0:0:0:1
```

The next shortcut is somewhat more complicated. Groups of 16-bit fields that contain all zeroes may be replaced with a single "::" sequence. This may appear only once, because the address might become ambiguous otherwise.

Here are the addresses again, presented in their most compact format.

```
FE80::200:F8FF:FE73:1D
::
::1
```

There is also a notation for prefixes, which are specified in the same manner as addresses except that they are terminated with a "/" character followed by the number of bits in the prefix. For example, the prefixes that specify link local and site local addresses can be written as:

```
FE80::/64
FEC0::/64
```

DNS Extensions for IPv6

These addresses are ugly enough that we hope not to have to type many of them. To resolve hosts to IPv6 addresses, a new resource record has been defined for DNS. This is the AAAA record. The format is as follows:

```
myhost.atmy.org          IN      AAAA    FEC0::200:F8FF:FE73:1D
```

PTR records are written differently, however. To overcome the problems with DNS reverse address delegation, the reverse address is specified as nibbles (4-bit units) separated by periods. The reverse address for this site local address is

```
D.1.0.0.3.7.E.F.F.F.8.F.0.0.2.0.0.0.0.0.0.0.0.0.0.0.0.0.C.E.F.IP6.INT.
```

This was difficult to type, and it certainly is difficult to read. Fortunately, DNS has a dynamic update facility. It is anticipated that dynamic updates will be integrated into the auto-address configuration methods for IPv6 so that system administrators can avoid entering any data manually.

Auto-Address Configuration

An IPv6 implementation can form a link local address without having to interact with any other hosts. It simply prefixes its interface identifier with the site local prefix (FE:80::/64), and it has a valid IPv6 address with which to communicate with the rest of the network segment. The host tests this address to ensure its uniqueness by transmitting a neighbor solicitation message with this address as the destination address. If no hosts respond, then the address is good. If any hosts do respond with a neighbor advertisement message, auto-address configuration halts, and manual intervention is required.

After obtaining a link local address, the next task is to obtain a global unicast address, and this begins by sending a router solicitation message to the *all routers'* multicast address. A router will respond with a router advertisement, which will also contain information indicating whether the host should begin stateless or stateful auto-address configuration procedures.

Stateless auto-address configuration is performed by examining the router adver-tisement messages for a subnet prefix option. If this option is included, the prefix is concatenated with the interface identifier to form a global unicast address. This address is also tested for uniqueness using the same procedure as the link local address.

Some sites will want to use a stateful address configuration process, using the Dynamic Host Configuration Protocol (DHCP). DHCP implementations in beta test at this time support dynamic DNS updates, which will be an important feature because manual assignment of DNS addresses defeats the advantages of auto-address configuration.

Neighbor Discovery

The IPv6 protocol does not use ARP to resolve hardware addresses. Instead it follows a procedure related to the auto-address configuration procedures defined above. Router Advertisement messages contain the set of prefixes that are associated with this link. The host records the prefixes in a table, which is then used to determine whether an IPv6 node is on the same link or needs to be routed to its destination. Packets addressed to IPv6 addresses on the same link send a Neighbor Solicitation message addressed to a special multicast address known as the solicited-node multicast address. This is a multicast address computed from the IPv6 address of the neighboring node. The neighbor returns a Neighbor Advertisement message which includes its link layer (or MAC) address. The transaction is then complete, and normal data transmission can begin.

IPv6 Security

The IPv6 specification mandates that all systems must be able to perform encryption and authentication of their data payloads. DES and HMAC encryption must be supported by every system, and many other encryption algorithms have been proposed. Hosts also need to know which set of keys to use for a particular conversation. Several key management protocols have been proposed.

The Linux IPv6 Implementation

An IPv6 protocol stack was integrated into the LINUX kernel during the 2.1 experimental kernel series. IPv6 is a standard option in the 2.2 kernel series. As of this writing, many of the user-level network applications and tools shipped with the major LINUX distributions are not compatible with IPv6. In the majority of cases, the incompatibilities are trivial, such as simply not recognizing IPv6 addresses nor allocating sufficient space to store the larger address structures.

Only a few programs actually need to be modified to understand IPv6-specific system features. Most of these programs are distributed together as the net-tools package. Current versions of net-tools are already IPv6-ready.

A comprehensive site for IPv6 on LINUX is located at http://www.bieringer.de/linux/ IPv6. It includes links to utilities ported to IPv6 and information on how to get connected to the 6bone, the experimental IPv6 network.

Linux Network Configuration

Configuring LINUX for IPv4 and/or IPv6 involves two general configuration steps. First, the kernel must be configured with the desired network options and device drivers. The second step is to modify the configuration files needed for the desired networking features. This is normally done as part of the installation process, but system administrators will need to understand what the components are and how they work. Additionally, there are many tools one can use to examine the networking software and troubleshoot problems.

Network Initialization

When a LINUX system boots to runlevel 3 or 5, the /etc/rc.d/init.d/network script is executed. This script first initializes the kernel variable which controls whether the system will forward packets. This is a security feature—doing this first ensures that the system will not forward packets during the boot process unless forwarding is intended. Next the script brings up the network interfaces one by one. This is done by running the /etc/sysconfig/network-scripts/ifup script on each interface. The configuration details for each interface are contained in the /etc/sysconfig/network-scripts/ifcfg-*xxx* scripts, where *xxx* is the name of the network interface (such as eth0). These files determine whether the interfaces are to be configured statically or dynamically, using either the bootp or dhcp protocols. Systems that have PCMCIA network interfaces, such as laptops, defer the initialization of PCMCIA devices to later in the boot sequence. In this case, their network interfaces will be initialized when the /etc/rc.d/init.d/pcmcia script is run. Finally, if a default gateway has been indicated, it will be set during this stage of initialization. This normally completes the network configuration for most home or office systems.

When a LINUX system is configured for a more complex network environment, such as a router or firewall system, additional configuration and initialization becomes necessary.

Dynamic Routing with Linux

To configure a LINUX system to act as a router, the ipforwarding kernel variable must be set to 1. This is done in the /etc/sysconfig/network file by setting the variable FORWARD_ IPV4 to true. Next, a routing protocol must be selected. Most LINUX systems are supplied with routed, which implements the RIP interior gateway protocol—this is useful in small- to medium-size organizations. For a larger site, one will want to implement a protocol that scales better, such as OSPF. Most versions of the gated dæmon include OSPF. Unfortunately, recent versions of the gated sources are not open, and what source code is publicly available does not implement the latest changes to the routing protocols. Nevertheless, gated is the best of what is available at this time.

It is also possible to configure a LINUX system to exchange routes with another autonomous system. Again, gated is the program of choice, but in this case, one will run BGP to peer with other Autonomous Systems.

Firewalling with Linux

Most organizations use a firewall to connect to the Internet. The LINUX kernel supports a number of firewall configurations. The 2.2 kernel contains a mechanism called IP chains, which allows almost arbitrarily complex packet filtering and forwarding rules to be created. As an additional security feature, the TCP wrappers program is integrated into most releases of LINUX. TCP wrappers allow network services to be granted or withheld based on host, domain, or network and includes identd support to guard against spoofing.

The 2.2 kernel series also supports Network Address Translation (NAT), which can circumvent many of the limitations of configuring an RFC 1918 network. NAT ensures that packets from machines on an interior network have their packets dynamically renumbered to the address of the host performing network address translation. The host also keeps track of which sessions have been renumbered, such that it is possible to match responses to these packets and map them appropriately. The result of NAT is that hosts on an interior network have nearly transparent access to external networks (usually the Internet). There are some problem protocols for which some special processing must take place. The LINUX kernel supplies special "helpers" for most of these. A properly configured firewall that supports NAT provides reasonable security while presenting the look and feel of being directly connected to the Internet.

Further Reading

- various RFCs
- *Internetworking with TCP/IP,* v1, 3rd ed., Douglas E. Comer, 1995
- *Unix Network Programming,* v1, 2nd ed., W. Richard Stevens, 1997
- *Unix Network Programming,* v2, 2nd ed., W. Richard Stevens, 1998
- *TCP/IP Illustrated,* v1, W. Richard Stevens, 1994
- *Power Programming with RPC,* John Bloomer, 1992
- *Firewalls and Internet Security,* William R. Cheswick et al., 1984
- *Building Internet Firewalls,* D. Brent Chapman et al., 1995

- *The Network Administrators' Guide,* Olaf Kirch, http://www.kernelnotes.org/guides/NAG/
- The Gate Daemon Documentation at http://www.gated.org/
- The IPv6 FAQ/HOWTO http://www.kernelnotes.org/IPv6/
- Ethernet HOWTO, by Paul Gortmaker
- IPCHAINS HOWTO, by Paul Russell
- IPX HOWTO, by Terry Dawson
- ISP Hookup HOWTO, by Egil Kvaleberg
- Intranet Server HOWTO, by Pramod Karnad
- Modem HOWTO, by David S. Lawyer
- Multicast HOWTO, by Juan-Mariano de Goyeneche
- NET-3 HOWTO, by Terry Dawson
- Networking Overview HOWTO, by Daniel López Ridruejo
- PPP HOWTO, by Robert Hart
- UUCP HOWTO, by Guylhem Aznar
- Unix and Internet Fundamentals HOWTO, by Eric S. Raymond
- Asymmetric Digital Subscriber Loop (ADSL) mini-HOWTO, by David Fannin
- Bridge mini-HOWTO, by Chris Cole
- Bridge+Firewall mini-HOWTO, by Peter Breuer
- Cable Modem mini-HOWTO, by Vladimir Vuksan
- Cipe+Masquerading mini-HOWTO, by Anthony Ciaravalo
- DHCP mini-HOWTO, by Vladimir Vuksan
- Firewall Piercing mini-HOWTO, by François-René Rideau
- IP Alias mini-HOWTO, by Harish Pillay
- IP Masquerade mini-HOWTO, by Ambrose Au
- IP Subnetworking mini-HOWTO, by Robert Hart
- ISP Connectivity mini-HOWTO, by Michael Strates
- Leased Line mini-HOWTO, by Rob van der Putten
- Proxy ARP Subnet mini-HOWTO, by Bob Edwards
- Token Ring mini-HOWTO, by Mike Eckhoff
- VPN mini-HOWTO, by Árpád Magosányi

That which comes after ever conforms to that which has gone before.

~Marcus Aurelius Antoninus. 121–180 A.D.

14

System Profiles

EVERY SYSTEM ON A NETWORK should have a profile; every organization should have a taxonomy of the systems it employs. Each system should fit into a category or class of machines. At the highest level, each machine should be categorized as either a client or a server. Most likely, servers will be further categorized into classes such as NFS servers, NIS servers, mail servers, DNS servers, database servers, and so on.

Standard profiles should be defined for each class of machine, based on the specific requirements of the organization. As we discuss in Chapter 15, "Automated Installation and Upgrade," each standard profile may be installed automatically from a build server using a set of packages prepared for that profile. This facilitates installation, upgrades, and disaster recovery.

It is not necessary that all existing machines exactly fit the profiles. The objective should be that each existing machine could be replaced with a machine built from one of the profiles. In other words, the profiles should be defined such that they can be used to build all the machines that the organization may need.

Clients

To the extent possible, the software configuration of all client machines should be the same. The only differences should be the configuration parameters that enable each machine to be a part of the network, such as hostname, IP address, broadcast address, default route, and so on. DHCP permits even these to be stored on a server.

Each user should find exactly the same environment on any machine to which he can log in. Everything specific to a user should be in his home directory mounted from an NFS server, not installed locally on a client machine. Similarly, application software should be mounted from a server, or kept under strict version control.

No permanent data should ever be stored on any client machine. All data should be stored on servers. Compliance with this principle obviates any need to back up clients. Servers should be the only machines that require backing up.

If a client machine suffers a failure, it can be replaced by a spare already built with the standard client profile, which needs only to have its network parameters set. Then the failed system may be diagnosed and corrected as the system administrators have time. Once corrected, it becomes a spare.

Servers

Many different services may be provided by server machines. Often, more than one service may be provided by a single host. Indeed, LINUX can reliably run almost any combination of services and applications on the same machine. For example, a strong case can be made for configuring a single host to provide (caching) DNS, NIS, and mail services to a department. Because mail hosts make frequent lookups in both DNS and NIS, providing all three services on the same machine eliminates some local network traffic.

Some servers will necessarily require a different configuration than others. For example, hosts that provide NFS or database services will require vastly more disk space (probably in a RAID configuration) than will hosts providing DNS, NIS, or mail services. In practice, it is rare to combine (on a single host) NFS service or database service with other services.

NFS servers and database servers require partitions not found on other types of servers, so they will clearly require their own profiles. Or will they? It is possible to define server profiles such that all the server software used by the enterprise is installed on every server, in a standard set of partitions. Obviously, NFS exported volumes would have to reside on a separate (probably external) drive array, as would database volumes. However, it is possible to install bind and ypserv on database servers. Ample disk space should be available. The problem is that most of the database software in use is still proprietary and subject to licensing restrictions. Depending on licensing terms, there may be a problem with installing Oracle, Sybase, or Informix on hundreds of servers without paying for it, even if the software is never run.

One strategy is to install all server software on every server, and enable only the required services. This permits an organization to have one server profile from which most or all servers can be built. The alternative strategy is to install on each server only the software that it needs to run. The former is more convenient, but the latter is more flexible and may be more secure. The revisions will also be less frequent.

Unique Machines

Unique machines are the bane of scalability, but sometimes there will be a business or technical requirement for a machine that deviates from the defined profiles. When this happens, the first question to consider is: Do we need to redefine an existing profile, or is this really a unique case requiring a new profile?

When the requirement really is for a unique machine, the task at hand will be to adapt a standard profile to meet the need, if possible. First, build the standard machine nearest to that which is required, and then add what is needed, carefully documenting all that is added. If anything must be removed, document that also.

Once the system works as desired, prepare a set of packages to install all that was needed to configure the system beyond the standard profile from which it was built. Then build a standard system again and install the packages to test that this procedure works. Finally, fold these packages back into the automated build server and test that the automated build works correctly. Now a recovery procedure is in place if anything happens to the machine. Of course, any transient data of value will have to backed up too.

Documentation

Profiles should be self-documenting. Each profile should include a README file in the and so on directory that identifies and describes the profile. If a unique machine cannot be built automatically from a profile, the README file should indicate on which profile the machine is based and all the steps needed to recreate the machine from the nearest profile. A copy of this README file should be printed and taped inside the case.

Partitioning Theory

Every LINUX system must have partitions. Selecting the number and size of the partitions and then distributing the filesystem over them must be done sensibly if the system is to be reliable. Partitions ensure that disk capacity needed by particular types of processes will not be consumed by others. This helps ensure that systems and processes continue running, even if some partitions are filled.

Every LINUX system must have a minimum of two partitions: at least one for the filesystem and at least one swap partition.[1] We strongly recommend at least two filesystem partitions: one for directories that tend to grow, and the other for directories that need to maintain free space for the system to function.

We also recommend an alternative root partition for rescuing the system in the event that the / partition becomes damaged. This is discussed in Chapter 3, "Recovery Planning."

There is not much controversy about how a filesystem should be divided into partitions, but neither is there universal agreement. The advantage of fewer partitions is that it makes more efficient use of the available disk capacity. By reducing the number of partitions on which free space and free inodes must be preserved, the total space that must be kept free is reduced. The advantage of more numerous partitions is a reduced impact of any one partition filling to capacity.

Rather than advocating a particular partitioning scheme, we explain the filesystem in terms of how various directories may fill to capacity, and the consequences when they do. This should help the reader determine which parts of the filesystem may safely be placed on the same partition, and which parts should be kept separate.

The / Directory

The / directory is the root of the hierarchical filesystem. All other directories are under the / directory (called the root directory), either directly or indirectly. Because the / directory can never be mounted under another directory, there must be a / partition.

Each directory that is immediately under the / directory and that does not have its own partition is necessarily a part of the / partition. The root directory itself is, of course, always located on the / partition.

Generally, directory structures placed on the / partition are small, are very unlikely ever to grow much during operations, and may require some free space in order for the system to run. Such directories typically reside together without doing each other harm.

The /bin Directory

A good example of a directory that is normally placed on the / partition is /bin. The /bin directory contains only executables, so it grows only when a system administrator adds to it. This means that operations in this directory are most unlikely to ever fill the partition on which it is stored.

Thus, the characteristics of the /bin directory are such that it could be placed on any partition of the filesystem. It doesn't harm others, nor does it need free space to execute its role in the system.

---

1. The 2.0 kernels constrained the useful size of swap partitions to no more than 128MB, so servers often employed multiple swap partitions. This limit has been removed with the 2.2 kernels, so rarely will there be a need for more than one swap partition on a machine.

The /boot Directory

The /boot directory is, by convention, the place where LILO finds everything it needs to boot the kernel. Specifically, one or more kernel images, module information, and maps that let LILO know where things are located may be found in /boot. None of these things are changed or added to during normal system operations. The need for free space arises when a new kernel needs to be installed.

If /boot were on a partition that had become full, that alone would not prevent the system from booting. However, it would be inconvenient to not have ample space on whatever partition includes the /boot directory. For these reasons and because there would be little advantage in having it on its own, it is usually included on the / partition.

The /dev Directory

Interfaces to hardware devices exist as pseudo-files in the /dev directory. They exist so that the stdin and stdout conventions may be employed when sending data to and receiving data from hardware devices.

The directory also contains one executable, /dev/MAKEDEV, which creates device entries in the directory.

Because devices are created during normal system operations, a full partition that included the /dev directory would crash the system. The directory uses very little space, but often more than a thousand inodes. So, normally, /dev is included on the / partition.

Note that, in the future, /dev will be a virtual filesystem, not actually resident on disk, as is the /proc filesystem.

The /etc Directory

Most system configuration information is stored in various files in the /etc directory. Some of these files contain transient configuration information that the system maintains on an ongoing basis, so it is important that /etc not be part of a partition subject to filling.

It is uncommon for the /etc directory to have its own partition. Because it tends not to grow much, it is usually included on the / partition. One exception is when, for security reasons, such as on a firewall, the / partition is placed on a drive which is write-protected by a physical jumper.

The /home Directory

Except on isolated systems, such as a home user might have, /home is typically an NFS mount. On systems that do have a local /home directory, it should be a symlink to a /usr/home directory on the /usr partition or have its own partition, because home directories tend to fill, and filling the / partition can cause serious problems.

The /lib Directory

The basic system libraries are found in /lib. These are usually updated only during system upgrades, so there is little danger of this directory causing a partition to fill. Also, normal operation of the system will not be impaired by a lack of free space in the /lib directory. Since /lib neither affects nor is affected by other directories on the same partition, there is no reason not to make it part of the / partition. The compelling reason why the /lib directory should be included on the / partition is that nearly every executable depends on the shared libraries therein.

The /lost+found Directory

Every filesystem has a /lost+found directory. This is where fsck places filesystem entries for files that are orphaned by a filesystem failure, such as when a system is shut down (perhaps due to a power failure) without a filesystem synchronization. These directories are not of concern in partitioning.

The /mnt Directory

This directory exists to provide mount points at which other filesystems may be mounted. Floppy disks and CD-ROMs are normally mounted here, and NFS filesystems may also be mounted here, so the /mnt directory should never consume disk space, and not a large number of inodes. However, if the partition on which the /etc directory is found becomes full, the mounting of any filesystems that should happen automatically will fail because /etc/mtab will not be writeable.

Typically, the /mnt directory is located on the / partition.

The /opt Directory

The /opt directory is one of the conventional places for third-party applications to be installed. If it is used for this purpose, it should probably have its own partition. Alternatively, if applications are to be stored under /usr/local, then /opt may be located on the / partition. In the latter case, we recommend that it be a link to /usr/local/opt, so that anything that may be installed in /opt is actually stored on the /usr or /usr/local partition.

The /proc Directory

The /proc directory is not a real directory. It is an interface to various configuration parameters belonging to the kernel. It does not take up any space on any disk, and it does not reside on any partition. Therefore, it is not of any concern in matters of partitioning, except that the mountpoint must exist.

The /root Directory

This is the home directory for the root user. It contains files such as .Xdefaults and .bashrc to provide defaults for the root user. Other sorts of files should not be located here, so this directory should never grow out of control, nor should a lack of space here impair the system. Therefore, the /root directory is normally located on the / partition. Applications, such as Netscape, that cache files should not be run as root.

The /sbin Directory

For the purposes of partitioning, this directory is very similar to the /bin directory. The difference is that /sbin contains executables used by the system at a lower level than those found in /bin, which are more typically user-level commands.

Thus, /sbin tends to change even less often than /bin. The /sbin directory is nearly always a part of the / partition.

The /tmp Directory

The /tmp directory is the conventional place for both users and applications to put files that need to be stored for a short but indeterminate time. Sometimes these files may be large, and an application may depend on space being available. Also, because some applications are not fastidious about cleaning up after themselves, /tmp can grow over time.

If /tmp fills, it is not likely to crash the system, but it will probably interrupt the process that caused it to fill and interfere with other processes trying to write to /tmp. Because it is subject to considerable growth, it is best kept separate from the / partition. Therefore, most systems have a /tmp partition. The alternative is a symlink to a /usr/tmp directory on the /usr partition.

The /usr Directory

Most application software is installed in the /usr directory. By convention, software that is site-specific is installed in either /opt or /usr/local. On many LINUX systems, the /usr directory occupies more than 500MB and grows each time a new application is installed or an updated application requires more space than an earlier version.

The /usr directory nearly always has its own partition. On some systems, /usr/local occupies yet another separate partition. Of course, /usr/local may be mounted from an NFS server, in which case an option would be to make /usr/local a very small separate partition to ensure that no one installs software in a directory over which NFS will mount the official /usr/local directory.

The /var Directory

Files that will be kept either for a determined period or until a particular event occurs are contained in subdirectories of the /var directory. In other words, /var is the canonical place for applications to keep their working data that can not be kept in memory. Examples include mail, news, and print spools, which are kept until they have been processed, as well as log files, which are usually rotated and then deleted after a fixed number of rotations.

Thus, the contents of the /var directory grow and shrink during normal system operations. If space is not available in the /var directory, a number of applications will be interrupted—some gracefully, others not. Therefore, the /var directory may be part of the / partition on client machines, but it nearly always resides on its own partition on server machines. In fact, on servers it is often sensible to install the subdirectories /var/log and /var/spool on their own partitions. As an alternative or adjunct to a distinct /var/log directory, it is possible to install a syslog server to accumulate the log files from multiple machines.

Partitioning Clients

The partitioning requirements on client workstations are simpler than on servers. This is because there are fewer processes running on clients that might fill a partition, and because the consequences of filling a partition on a client are less severe than on a server.

We recommend a minimum of three partitions for a LINUX client, including a swap partition. The only reasonable partition strategy for only two filesystem partitions (plus one swap partition) is to include all the directories the filling of which would interfere with system operations in the / partition, and all the directories that might tend to fill a partition in the other.

Fewer than five partitions should be employed only when disk space is at a premium, because the symlinks required to keep multiple top-level directories in the same (non-root) partition complicate matters. It is simpler to put /tmp and /var on their own partitions. Dispensing with the requirement for symlinks makes it easier for a system administrator who comes along later, because everything is exactly as it appears.

Partitioning Servers

Servers naturally justify more partitions than do clients because it is more important that servers be robust. We recommend that every server have separate partitions for /, a rescue root, /tmp, /usr, and /var, in addition to the swap partition(s). Many servers will need even more partitions, depending on the services to be provided. In this section, we examine various sorts of servers in detail.

A server that may be subject to heavy loads should either have the swap partition on its own disk or have one swap partition on each of two or more disks. Swap partitions on different disks should have equal priorities.[2]

DNS Server Partitions

DNS servers provide directory information to the other machines on the network. They are used redundantly so that if one fails, clients still get the information they need. This involves delays, so it is best to partition DNS servers to be robust.

Not much spooling takes place on DNS servers, so separate partitions for /var/log and /var/spool are not required. But /var should definitely have its own partition of at least 100MB, because DNS can generate significant log files and backup files if secondary.

NIS Server Partitions

The partitioning requirements of NIS slave servers are similar to those of DNS servers, except that the log files should be kept from filling the partition containing the YP maps (usually /var/yp/maps). Therefore, we recommend separate /var and /var/log partitions. The /var/log partition should be at least 50MB, and the /var partition should be considerably more than twice the maximum size to which the YP maps may be expected to grow.

NIS masters have the same needs as NIS slaves, but the /var and /var/log partitions should be even more generous. One cannot have too much space.

Mail Server Partitions

The concern with mail servers is to ensure that /var/log and /var/spool each have ample space and that neither impairs the other. Therefore, either or both should be on partitions separate from /var. The /var/log directory should be on a partition with at least 100MB of space. The space required is proportional to load. The /var/spool directory will require enough space to retain all the mail messages for all the users whose mail resides there. This could easily run into the gigabytes for machines serving mail for many users.

ftp and http Server Partitions

All ftp and http servers should have at least 100MB available on either the /var or a /var/log partition to accommodate log files. The space required is proportional to load.

Additionally, the directory structure made available by the ftp dæmon or the http dæmon should occupy its own partition(s). This permits it (or them) to be mounted with its (or their) own options, such as ro (read-only). If one server provides both ftp and http services, the partition on which the data are stored should be shared. This facilitates the configuration of a chrooted environment, and so on.

---

2. The exception is when not all disks with swap partitions are accessible during booting.

NFS Server Partitions

The directories to be served over NFS should be on partitions separate from the operating system. This makes backing them up simpler. Better yet, the exported directories and the operating system should be on separate disks. The use of RAID for the exported partitions is highly recommended—less so for the operating system.

Recent implementations of NFS permit the export of directories spanning multiple partitions, as well as the export of directories that are less than a complete partition. However, we recommend that directories belonging to distinct business units be kept to separate partitions. Doing so avoids contention and simplifies the issue of whom to bill for an upgrade.

Samba Server Partitions

As with NFS, directories that are to be exported using Samba should be kept on partitions separate from the operating system, and better yet on separate disks. The use of RAID for the exported partitions is recommended. Because the operating system should be quickly rebuildable from packages, it has less need for RAID.

Home directories and others that tend to grow and belong to particular departments or cost centers should be kept on separate partitions. When home directories fill, it is important to be able to tell the department that they need to either clean up their files or pay for more disk space. Do not give them the opportunity to blame another department sharing the partition.

News Server Partitions

News servers process much transient data of low-to-moderate value. The news spool can be very large, and access to it may need to be speedy. It generally is not backed up, but it should definitely be kept on its own partition, and it probably should be spread over several partitions.

The `/var/spool/news` partition(s) should, ideally, be kept on disks separate from the operating system. This will help performance and, if a disk for the news spool fails, the replacement will need only to be partitioned. Also, because news spools contain very large numbers of small files, the ratio of inodes to disk space should be three or four times that for typical filesystems.

Database Server Partitions

The partitioning of database servers should be planned in cooperation with the database administrators. Most large databases should be installed with several filesystem partitions spread over multiple disks and, often, with one or more raw partitions that host the databases.

Additionally, ample space should be reserved on either `/var` or `/var/log` for log files.

Application Server Partitions

Application servers run software that is usually mission-critical and often developed in-house. That is, this software performs core functions of the business. In many cases, if one of these servers stops working, part or all of the company stops doing business.

The application software that the server runs is normally located in either /opt or /usr/local. Whichever of these is chosen should be on its own partition, because the space required is likely to grow with each new revision. Also ensure that sufficient space is available to store multiple copies of the application to facilitate upgrades and rollbacks.

Generalizing Server Partitions

A generalized server partition layout should be developed, both to enable single machines to provide multiple services and to facilitate maintenance of the kickstart server.

The generalized server should have separate partitions, as shown in Table 14.1. The suggestions therein should be adapted in accordance with local requirements. Usually,

Table 14.1 **Possible partitions for a generalized server**

Partition	Minimum Size	Description
/	100MB	The / partition may contain the /bin, /boot, /dev, /etc, /lib, /mnt, /root, and /sbin directories. Any other directories, especially /tmp and /var, should be placed on separate partitions.
(altroot)	120MB	This partition should not be mounted during a normal boot. It should be a copy of the / partition, with some extra tools for repairing and restoring damaged partitions and filesystems.
/opt	500MB	Either this directory or /usr/local should exist on its own partition.
/tmp	200MB	This directory should have its own partition on every server. More space is better, especially on generalized servers.
/usr	1000MB	This directory contains a lot of software and tends to grow over the life of the server.
/usr/local	500MB	Either this directory or /opt should be used to store local applications. Whichever is employed should have its own partition.
/var	200MB	System administrators are frequently surprised by things found growing in /var.
/var/log	100MB	We recommend a separate partition just for log files, because it is possible for them to impact other directories in /var.
/var/spool	200MB	Any server that may be used to serve mail needs to have a large /var/spool partition, separate from the other directories in /var.

one or more partitions will need to be larger than the suggested minimum size listed. Sometimes, additional partitions will be required to further divide the filesystem. System administrators at each site will have to make these judgments based on an understanding of the issues we've discussed, on previous experience, and often on trial and error.

Conclusion

Although we've given some examples of server and client profiles, and some guidelines for combining services on multi-function servers, it is vital for each organization to define its own. It may be difficult to enforce a policy that *all* systems conform to defined profiles. However, when the majority of systems match, it makes the system administrator's job much easier. That increases the system administrator's capacity and results in fewer errors.

Using profiles is a bit like following the principles of object-oriented programming: each system is an "instantiation" of the profile (class). There are even analogues to "inheritance" and "multiple inheritance" (a generalized server profile inherits from intranet web, DNS caching, Samba, and other servers). System administrators who use system profiles wisely and consistently will enjoy increased productivity, reduced stress, and perhaps even some fun setting them up.

Further Reading

- *Sun Performance and Tuning,* Adrian Cockcroft, 1995
- Config HOWTO, by Guido Gonzato
- Intranet Server HOWTO, by Pramod Karnad
- Multi-Disk HOWTO, by Stein Gjoen
- Partition mini-HOWTO, by Kristian Koehntopp
- Pre-installation Checklist mini-HOWTO, by S. Parthasarathy

15

Automated Installation and Upgrade

THIS CHAPTER IS NOT ABOUT how to install LINUX on a single computer—that is specific to each distribution and should be covered by the vendor documentation. This chapter is about how to install LINUX on thousands of computers.

The general strategy is to boot each system to start an installation session from an appropriately configured install server. Information specific to each machine (such as hostname and IP address) may be required. This information may either be placed in one or more files before the new machine is booted, or supplied interactively during the install.

The install server will generally have several profiles for different types of systems. At a minimum, the install server will have one profile for client workstations and one for servers. Most will have profiles for more than one type of server, and some may even have profiles for more than one type of client. For details, see Chapter 14, "System Profiles." Also note that for each system profile, a distinct install profile may be required for different hardware configurations.

Alternatives

This centralized installation approach should be compared to manual installs and disk "cloning" techniques. The advantage of the centralized install server is that the configuration is tightly controlled by those who administer the install server. Manual interactive installs are subject to system administrator error and variation because men tend to follow written procedures unreliably, even processes that are described flawlessly.

Disk cloning is also subject to errors. The common problems associated with disk cloning involve using the wrong disk as a template. These problems are endemic because finding and updating all the disks used for cloning every time a system profile is changed is unlikely to be either simple or easy. Often, the disk used will be an outdated clone disk, reintroducing a problem that was previously corrected. In other cases, the disk will be up-to-date, but for the wrong system profile. Sometimes, disks are cloned from production disks and may include configuration information that is inappropriate for the new system. The centralized install server solves these problems.

Hardware Issues

Prior to the development of LINUX and other free UNIX operating systems, large-scale automated installs were restricted to RISC workstations running UNIX. These workstations were (and are) much more standardized in configuration and limited in peripheral options than today's PC. This simplified the job of automated installation, because it was quite straightforward to build a single system profile with the appropriate kernel and device support for the entire workstation community. This is still the case for LINUX on workstation hardware, but sites that run LINUX on PCs will suffer from the complexity that follows from much more diverse hardware.

Another complication presented by PC hardware is imposed by the PC BIOS. While the ability to boot from SCSI and ATAPI CD-ROMs is now common, support for network booting is still lacking. This requires that the install be supported by a local floppy disk or CD-ROM—which means a mandatory visit to the desktop. While desktop visits are common in Microsoft WINDOWS support, they are far less common in large LINUX environments. This is due to the greater ability to remotely administer LINUX systems via the network and to the higher ratio of desktop computers per system administrator in LINUX environments.

The hardware configuration issues that vary most are hard disk size, video cards, monitors, network adapters, and audio hardware. Physical memory also varies; however, this is a performance issue rather than a configuration issue.

The challenge, then, is to exploit the commonality that does exist and to dynamically adapt to the inevitable variations in hardware. Organizations having a purchasing policy that restricts desktop systems to comply with a standard will do best; those that have changed vendors several times or defer purchasing decisions to the users will encounter the most problems. It should be noted that even the largest PC vendors tend to change the internal components of computers shipping under the same model name and number. Usually, these changes are benign, but occasionally the new component will require a driver not supported under LINUX. The best defense is to specify to the vendor that LINUX be preinstalled on the system. While the configuration shipped by the vendor probably will not comply with your system profiles, one can at least be assured that LINUX will run on the hardware.

If the systems to be installed are already deployed, the next logical step is to inventory the systems using a spreadsheet or database. This is a time-consuming task, but well worth the effort. If the systems are running LINUX or some other form of UNIX, then the task can be automated. The dmesg command is useful here. There are also several products in the Microsoft WINDOWS and Novell spaces to inventory hardware, such as the Microsoft Systems Management Server (SMS). Comparing the hardware to the list of supported devices for the desired LINUX distribution will identify problems before the rollout begins. It may be difficult to justify why hardware needs to be purchased to support a software rollout, but being proactive make more sense than letting the project founder due to unanticipated compatibility problems.

Security

Crackers who gain root access to one system in a network usually gain access to many. They plant backdoors so that they can easily get back in even if the original hole is closed and the root passphrase is changed. The top target for a cracker is the build server. A backdoor installed in a build template is the ultimate penetration.

To protect against such an exploit, the disks on which the templates and packages are stored must be physically write-protected by means of a hardware jumper on each disk. The build server must be disconnected from the network before the jumper is changed to enable writes during the installation of new or updated profiles. It should be reconnected only after the disks are write-protected.

Kickstart

Red Hat's kickstart install mechanism is currently the most automated installation tool available for LINUX.[1] Kickstart can be used for new installs or upgrades to existing systems. It is implemented as part of the Red Hat installation program. Only local CD-ROM and NFS installs are supported. This should not present a problem, since the NFS mechanism is the most sensible choice anyway.

A network-based kickstart install requires DHCP or BOOTP, so this service must be available on every network segment on which installs are to take place. One machine

---

1. SuSe also has an automated installation tool, which is easier to use than Red Hat's, but less powerful. Both tools are likely to become more powerful and easier to use. Other automated installation utilities may also arise, so it should not be taken for granted that Kickstart is the best tool.

per net may be selected to perform this function in addition to its regular tasks, or a few systems with multiple Ethernet adapters can be dedicated to the task. For large environments, a few servers with (multiple) quad Ethernet adapters may be appropriate. These could also function as dedicated install servers. If the NFS install server is not on the same segment as the install client, then BOOTP or DHCP must provide a default gateway.

A kickstart install is driven by a configuration file, which can exist locally on the boot media or on a server. The authors strongly urge the placement of kickstart install files on the installation server. The contents of the kickstart file are documented in Appendix H of the *RedHat Linux 6.0 Installation Guide*.

The kickstart configuration file is order-dependent. The order generally parallels the normal installation sequence. If the installation determines that it needs information that is not present in the kickstart configuration file, it will prompt for those data interactively. Once the data are entered, the installation will proceed again in an automated fashion.

Here, we describe the keywords and the options to keywords that are used to constitute the kickstart configuration file. Note that kickstart expects these keywords in a particular order. We list them here in the expected order.

language

The language keyword specifies the language to be used for both the install itself and the language configuration of the operating system. Unfortunately, these cannot be different. So, for example, a system that will run LINUX in French must be installed using French.

network

The network keyword configures how the TCP/IP network parameters for the system should be found. The options are dhcp, bootp, and static. The static option may be used to enumerate the TCP/IP parameters.

Installation Method

The installation method is specified next. The two keywords available are cdrom and nfs. Other installation methods are not supported. The nfs keyword requires --server and --dir arguments to specify the server to use and the path to the ISO9660 or NFS image on the server.

device

The installation procedure will probe and detect IDE controllers and PCI bus cards automatically. If there are other devices (primarily ISA cards) that will not be discovered otherwise, then the device keyword is used. The options are ethernet, scsi, and cdrom. The --opts parameter is used to pass along any needed module parameters, as specified in Appendix E of the *RedHat Linux 6.0 Installation Guide*. Multiple devices of the same type can be declared. The following example configures hosts that have one of three Ethernet cards and one of two SCSI drivers:

```
device ethernet 3c507 --opts "io=0x300, irq=9"
device ethernet eexpress --opts "io=0x270, irq=5"
device ethernet smc-ultra --opts "io=0x270, irq=5"
device scsi aha154x
device scsi 53c7xx
```

Normally, only one device of each class is discovered. If the configuration requires multiple adapters of differing types, the --continue clause is used to force further probing. The previous example can be modified to attempt to discover two SCSI controllers:

```
device scsi aha154x --continue
device scsi 53c7xx
```

It is not necessary to use the --continue option to detect multiple instances of the same adapter.

keyboard

The keyboard keyword is used to specify a keyboard map. The kbdconfig command can be used to determine the keyboard map currently in use. The most common value is us.

noprobe

The noprobe keyword disables auto-probing of devices. Use this only if the system cannot be successfully probed by LINUX. It will be necessary to specify device statements to configure the system.

zerombr

The zerombr keyword takes a single parameter, either yes or no, that controls whether the installation will clear the Master Boot Record (MBR). yes is recommended if it is uncertain whether the current MBR is valid. The most common reason not to zero the MBR would be a dual-boot configuration, where a partition is known to contain a valid operating system.

clearpart

The clearpart keyword determines whether the partition table information should be cleared. It is an optional keyword. The options for this keyword are --all, which clears all partitions, and --linux, which clears just the LINUX-related partitions.

Partitioning with part

The part keyword is used to specify the number and size of LINUX partitions on the boot device. One part statement is issued per partition. The arguments are the mountpoint (or swap for swap partitions), the size of the partition, the --grow option, and the --maxsize option. The --grow option indicates that a partition can be resized to accommodate larger devices, while the --maxsize option limits the growth to an absolute value. If multiple partitions are given the --grow option, then the additional space will be split evenly among them.

Installation or Upgrade

The next statement in the config file must indicate whether a system is being installed or upgraded. Systems that are being upgraded only need to have the following keywords defined: installation mechanism (cdrom or nfs), any needed device specifications, keyboard type, the upgrade keyword itself, and the lilo statement.

Mouse Configuration

The mouse keyword configures the system mouse. The arguments for the mouse keyword are identical to the mousesetup command. The --kickstart option is mandatory. If no mouse is detected, a serial mouse on com1 (/dev/cua0, /dev/ttyS0) is assumed. The various mouse types can be found by running mousesetup --help on a running LINUX system.

Setting the Time Zone

The system-wide time zone is set with the timezone keyword. The database of time zone information is stored in the /usr/share/zoneinfo directory. For example, the timezone statement for the Eastern United States is as follows:

```
timezone US/Eastern
```

There is an option that bears some explanation: the --utc option specifies that the time in the computer's clock reflect Coordinated Universal Time (UTC, formerly known as Greenwich Mean Time). UNIX systems have traditionally represented time internally as the number of seconds from January 1, 1970, in UTC. The internal time is then offset by the local time zone data to display the correct local time. As a practical matter, this value should be set on laptops and palmtops so that it is possible to set the time zone correctly during travel without actually adjusting the time. The --utc option should not be set on computers that are configured to dual boot Microsoft WINDOWS operating systems. These operating systems lack proper time zone support and expect the hardware clock to reflect the local time zone.

X Window System Configuration

The xconfig keyword configures the X WINDOW system. Normally, video hardware is probed to automatically determine its configuration possibilities, and the purpose of this keyword is to specify a monitor type. The --monitor parameter introduces a monitor type. However, certain video hardware may not probe properly, so it may occasionally be necessary to specify a particular card with the --server option. Running Xconfigurator --help will display the possible choices of monitors and graphics adapters. This is a typical example for an adapter that probes properly:

```
xconfig --monitor "nokia 445xi"
```

Finally, it is possible to support monitors not listed in the monitor database by specifying the monitor's frequencies with the --hsync and --vsync options. Multiple frequencies can be specified by listing them delimited with commas, and ranges may be indicated with dashes. Here is an example of a system where the adapter is specified explicitly and whose monitor is not listed in the database:

```
xconfig --server "8514" --hsync "30.0-102.0"  --vsync "50.0-120.0"
```

Setting a Root Password

The root password may be set with the rootpw statement. It may be specified as being in an encrypted or unencrypted form. The --iscrypted option specifies that the password is encrypted. The authors suggest using the encrypted form as a practical security measure.

Configuring NIS

The auth keyword configures password security and NIS. The options are as follows:

- --useshadow This option enables the shadow password mechanism. It is recommended for security reasons.
- --enablemd5 This option enables a cryptographically stronger password mechanism. It is recommended for security reasons.
- --enablenis This configures the system to use NIS. If this option is given, the --nisdomain option will be required.
- --nisdomain This option takes one argument that specifies the NIS domain name.
- --nisserver The option provides the name of the NIS server to which the system is to bind. If this option is not used, the system will broadcast to find a NIS server.

LILO

LILO is the standard mechanism for booting LINUX on Intel-based machines. The lilo keyword is declared at this point in the config file to install and configure LILO. The three configuration choices are mbr, partition, and none. These are introduced by the --location option. The mbr option is the conventional selection. This installs the LILO bootloader in the master boot record (MBR) for the disk, allowing LILO to act as the boot manager for all operating systems on the disk. The partition option indicates that LILO should be installed into the root partition. In this case, whatever boot manager is installed in the MBR will be used to launch LILO. If none is specified, it will be necessary to arrange for an alternative bootloader, such as `loadlin`. Finally, kernel boot options may be specified with the `--append` option.

Specifying Package Selections

The `%package` keyword enables the system administrator to specify the packages to be included during an install. Package names are listed one per line, until the end of the file or the optional `%post` statement is reached. In addition to package names, groups of packages (known as components) may be specified. The available components are defined on any Red Hat LINUX CD-ROM, located in the `RedHat/base/comps` file. The kickstart installation process will always load the "base" component. It is possible to create site-specific components by modifying the `RedHat/base/comps` file.

It is also possible to create site-specific releases by including updated or additional packages in the `RedHat/RPMS` directory and then referencing them in the `packages` section of the kickstart configuration file.

Post–Install Scripts

All larger sites maintain a set of localized customizations and conventions. The `%post` keyword introduces shell commands to be executed at the end of the installation process, so that these changes do not have to be made by hand. Some examples of typical post-install activities are configuring `ntp.conf` and adding automounter maps. If a set of customizations is extensive, then it is best to encapsulate them as a package and include the package in a customized distribution, as mentioned previously.

Automatic Kickstart Config Generation with mkkickstart

The `mkkickstart` utility can be a tremendous help. It generates a valid kickstart configuration file for the system on which it is run. For installations that are already running LINUX and are using kickstart to reinstall or upgrade systems, `mkkickstart` can be run on each system and the configuration files stored on the install server(s). The `mkkickstart` utility can also be used for rollouts of new hardware. For each type of hardware to be installed, install one system by hand and run `mkkickstart` to generate a template for that hardware. These will be used as part of an automated configuration file-generating mechanism described in the next section.

Implementing System Profiles

System profiles are abstract prototypes that describe system configurations. The kickstart configuration file contains concrete rules for building systems, containing many details that do not apply to a system profile. In fact, the only data needed to express system profiles is contained within the `part`, `%package`, and `%post` sections. Consider this profile for a mail server:

```
/   100MB
swap  256MB
/tmp  100MB
/usr  500MB
/usr/local 500MB
/var  100MB
/var/spool 500MB
```

We can express this using the part keyword in the following fashion:

```
part / --size 100
part swap --size 256
part /tmp --size 100
part /usr --size 500
part /usr/local/ --size 500
part /var --size 100
part /var/spool --size 500
```

This will work well for a system with a hard disk that is *exactly* 2056 megabtyes, which is not useful in the real world. However, by using the --grow and --maxsize options, it is possible to create a generalized partitioning scheme appropriate for a variety of disk sizes:

```
part / --size 100
part swap --size 256
part /tmp --size 100 --grow --maxsize 200
part /usr --size 500 --grow --maxsize 1024
part /usr/local --size 500 --grow --maxsize 1024
part /var --size 100 --grow --maxsize 200
part /var/spool --size 500 --grow
```

When applied to a system with a 4 gigabyte disk, this configuration will yield the following partition sizes:

```
/   100MB
swap  256MB
/tmp  200MB
/usr  1024MB
/usr/local 1024MB
/var  200MB
/var/spool 1292MB
```

This partitioning scheme may not be perfect, but it does reflect the profile. When the same partitioning statements are applied to a system with a 9 gigabyte disk, the following partition sizes are generated:

```
/   100MB
swap  256MB
/tmp  200MB
/usr  1024MB
/usr/local 1024MB
/var  200MB
/var/spool 6412MB
```

These partitions reflect the requirement of dedicating space to the mail spool directory, while allowing ample space for adding software and maintaining log files.

Also, the software required for the mail server profile needs to be installed. Specifying @server in the %packages section will be sufficient for a mail server. Finally, it may be necessary to modify some files after the install has completed. This is done by adding some lines in the %post section of the kickstart file.

It is probable that every mail server managed by a system administrator will have a different hardware configuration. This means that the kickstart configuration file could not be shared among systems. After all the work done to generate a decent profile, this would be a waste, and another possible source of errors.

Generating Kickstart Files

This problem of different hardware configurations requiring different kickstart files can be solved by generating the kickstart files dynamically based on hardware and profile. We develop a script to automatically edit portions of the configuration file by looking for structured comments and inserting the profile-specific data in the appropriate places. For each profile, a directory will be created, as shown in Figure 15.1. Each directory has three files that contain the appropriate statements for the part, package, and %post sections of the kickstart configuration file. A typical requirement is a common set of commands that need to be run at the end of every install, regardless of the system profile. Finally, we take kickstart files with appropriate hardware configurations and store them with comments replacing the appropriate keywords. The script takes two arguments: the hardware type and the system profile. The script then edits the configuration file and inserts the profile-related data as well as the common %post commands. The output is a complete kickstart configuration file that has the correct definition based on both the hardware used and the system profile chosen.

```
#!/bin/sh
#
# This script looks for a kicstart file as arg 1 with the following
# conventions. Partitioning, %packages, and %post sections are
# removed and replaced with comments which match the patterns below.
# The second argument contains is a subdirectory of $BASE which contains
# three files, partitions, packages, and post.  They are required.
# A common directory under $BASE is expected to have a post file.
#
# This is a bare bones example script.  Most sites would want
# to add serious error checking and perhaps factor the common packages
# for all configurations into the common section as well.

BASE=/a/sdegler

if [ ! -f ${BASE}/${1}/kickstart.template ]; then
  echo "usage: $0 hardware profile"
```

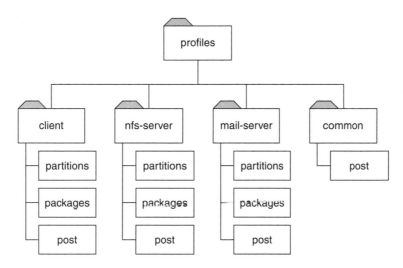

Figure 15.1 Kickstart profiles

```
  exit 1
elif [ ! -d ${BASE}/$2 ]; then
  echo "usage: $0 hardware profile"
  exit 1
fi

PROFILE=$BASF/$2

if [ -f $PROFILE/partitions -a \
        -f $PROFILE/packages -a \
        -f $PROFILE/post -a \
        -f ${BASE}/common/post ]; then
  cp $BASE/$1/kickstart.template /tmp/kickstart$$
  ed /tmp/kickstart$$ << EOF
/#Partitions Section/r $PROFILE/partitions
/#%Packages Section/s//%packages/
r $PROFILE/packages
/#%Post Section/s//%post/
r $BASE/common/post
r $PROFILE/post
w
q
EOF
  cat /tmp/kickstart$$
  rm /tmp/kickstart$$
fi
```

This process may seem like a lot of extra work. To some extent, it is. At a scale of dozens of systems, this technique for parameterizing configurations may seem like overkill. At a scale of hundreds or thousands, it is essential.

Versioning

Every organization large enough to automate the installation procedure will require its own version numbering scheme. This may be an extension of the numbering scheme of a LINUX distribution. For example, each time a new internal configuration is released to production, a number appended to the distribution's version number may be incremented. Thus, an organization might have an internal configuration numbered 6.1.3, which is the third internal release based on RedHat 6.1. An alternative is to base the version number directly on revision numbers from a version control system like rcs or cvs used to maintain the releases.

These internal releases may be based on updates from the distributor, but they will also often be based on software not released as part of the distribution. A good example is the cryptographic software that every organization needs for security but which cannot be included in many distributions because of export control laws.

Large organizations may also find and correct bugs and then need to roll them into production quickly. Sometimes, this will happen before the maintainer of the software has released a new version.

The organization may also need to make releases to meet its internal needs (that is, it is a requirement for the latest version of a package) or to address bugs that employees introduced via added software. Thus, there are several reasons why organizations may need versions of their configurations that may be revised independent of the LINUX distributions. For this reason, it is imperative to institute a version numbering scheme to provide for this when first setting up an install server. The release number should be embedded in obvious places, like /etc/motd, the kernel version number returned by uname -v, and so on.

Comparing Installs and Upgrades

Each LINUX distribution includes tools for installing the software. Most also include tools for upgrading a computer that is already running a previous version of the same LINUX distribution.

At the project management level, there is another way in which the words "installation" and "upgrade" are used. New systems are installed, and systems that have been running previous versions of LINUX are upgraded. However, at the project level, it does not matter whether a machine is upgraded using the vendor's upgrade mechanism or install mechanism. As long as the user is able to return to the system and begin his work unhindered, it does not matter whether the system was incrementally upgraded or reinstalled from scratch.

There is a compelling advantage to completely reinstalling a system. The system is put in a known state, and whatever idiosyncrasies the machine may have had are removed. Systems tend to vary over time, and periodically bringing the workstation population to an identical configuration is a good thing. Therefore, the authors recommend using an install mechanism for desktop upgrades. The exception to this is when one or a few packages need to be upgraded to correct an urgent problem. Then it is best to use `rpm -U` or `AutoRPM` rather than the build server. This may generally be done while the clients are running, except in the case of kernels and kernel modules.

There are two ways to upgrade servers. If hardware is available, a new server should be built from scratch, configured, and tested. Then, over time, users are migrated to the new server. Once the old service is no longer in use, the hardware can be reclaimed and used in future upgrades. The authors refer to this as the *swing machine* upgrade. This is the ideal upgrade path. Unfortunately, budgetary constraints or unique characteristics of the service offered by the server may demand that the system be *upgraded in place*. This is always a risky endeavor since servers tend to be customized more than clients, and the customizations are very often key to the services provided by the system. The upgrade mechanism is preferred for upgrades in place because they present less risk. The system as a whole is still intact, and key system configuration files will not be deleted. This is less important for client workstations, but for key servers the capability to upgrade rather than reinstall is a highly desirable feature.

Further Reading

For more information on the RedHat Kickstart system, and how to modify it to suit specific needs, see the Kickstart HOWTO.

Information on RPM packages can be found in *Maximum RPM* by Edward C. Bailey (Sams Publishing, 1997).

That government is best which governs least.

~Thomas Jefferson (1743–1826),
attributed by
Henry David Thoreau

16

User and Group Administration

THE MANAGEMENT OF USER ACCOUNTS is central to system administration. It not only absorbs much of the typical system administrator's time, but it is one of the more common sources of grief. Some users are never satisfied with their accounts, be it their shell, their disk space quota, their username, or the configuration of their virtual desktop.

LINUX provides powerful tools for the administration of users and groups, which at small to medium sites make the task a bit less onerous than it traditionally has been in UNIX environments. In this chapter, we examine what these tools do, how they are used in practice, and how they interoperate with other tools. We also consider how to fashion user administration policies to meet business requirements.

The administration of users and groups at large sites presents some challenges, such as maintaining a consistent mapping of uids to users, that the standard tools do not meet. At the end of the chapter, we consider tools, strategies, and procedures for managing large user databases.

Users and uids

uids identify the owners of files, directories, and processes. Each numeric uid corresponds to a username (or login) and optionally to a userfullname. The mapping from uid to username is normally found in the /etc/passwd file on isolated machines, and in NIS or another distributed database on networked machines.

Generally, a username may be used to log in to one or more systems, although a few, called pseudo-logins, cannot log in to any system. A username typically belongs to a single person, and most persons have only one username (in any particular organization). root is an obvious exception, because more than one person uses root on most systems, and everyone who uses root should also have a personal username.

Just as citizens live best when governments leave them free to make their own decisions, users work best when system administrators leave them free to choose their own usernames. Some system administrators have tried formal schemes for assigning usernames, such as the first two letters of the first name followed by the first five letters of the last name. Every such scheme eventually results in clashes, which are usually resolved by something like appending a numeral to the username of whomever joined the organization later. Even without such complications, these schemes do little to facilitate resolving real names to usernames and are detrimental to morale.[1]

Each uid has a corresponding password, the hash of which is also stored in /etc/passwd, /etc/shadow, or NIS. Each uid also has other attributes, such as a default shell.

Pseudo-Logins

Pseudo-logins exist so that processes can run with the uid of the pseudo-login without any user being able to log in to any machine using the corresponding username. Some of the pseudo-logins found on most Linux systems include bin, daemon, adm, lp, mail, news, uucp, and nobody.

Additional pseudo-logins may be created if necessary. Some system administrators create pseudo-logins each with a username that matches a command to be executed as its shell. Examples include hostname, ifconfig, netstat, and who. Security concerns should be kept in mind any time a pseudo-login is to be created, especially if attempts to log in using that username will result in the execution of a command. It is important to document the reason for creating each pseudo-login.

Groups and gids

Groups provide a mechanism for aggregating users so that permissions may be repeatedly granted to a group of users without the need to enumerate the members each time.

The passwd file or map contains a gid field. This is a vestige of when Unix limited each user to membership in only one group at any given time. Information about the groups to which a user belongs is now derived from the group file or map.

The group file or map contains a list of entries, one for each group. Each entry contains four fields: group name, passwd, gid, and a list of the members.

---

1. glibc2 raises the permissible number of characters in a uid from 8 to 31. However, some applications remain limited to 8 characters, so the transition may take some time.

Adding Users

The command normally used for adding a LINUX user is useradd. Because the useradd command does not create NIS entries, the logical host on which to run it is the NFS server that will host the user's home directory. This will create a home directory for the user, based on the template home directory that the system administrators have set up in the /etc/skel directory. It will also create /etc/passwd, /etc/shadow, and, possibly, /etc/group entries that may, on the NIS master, be added to NIS.

We recommend against reusing usernames for at least one year and against reusing uids unless they reach their numeric limit, at which time assignment should start again from the bottom of the range. Avoiding reuse precludes a host of problems that may arise in case a former user's files need to be restored, or if other vestiges remain. Thus, we suggest assigning the next uid that is higher than that of all other users, until the upper limit is reached. The number of possible uids is presently limited to 2^{16} by the kernel; however, glibc permits 2^{32}. Most sites will never need to reuse uids even if constrained to 2^{16}.

Whatever procedure is adopted to add new users, it must be documented and, to the extent possible, automated. The same is true of modifying user account information, disabling users, and deleting users. All system administrators within an organization should be able to easily find the correct procedure on an intranet site.

Updating Users

The standard command for updating users is usermod. It accepts a variety of options. Generally, each option corresponds to a particular attribute of the user's account. For example, the command

```
usermod -G techpubs,marcomm jjones
```

would make the user jjones a member of the techpubs and marcomm groups. jjones would no longer be a member of any groups of which he may previously have been a member. The groups must exist.

Deleting Users

Deleting a user is rather simple, and nearly as easy. All one needs to do is this:

- Remove or redirect all the user's mail aliases.
- Back up and then remove the user's home directory and all its contents.
- Remove all other files and directories owned by the user. The find command may be useful for this.
- Remove the user's entries from /etc/passwd, /etc/shadow, NIS, and so on. The userdel command will remove such entries from local flat files. NIS attributes must be removed on the NIS master. See Chapter 21, "Managing NIS," for more details.

- Kill all processes owned by the user.

- Search other databases that might have account information, such as NDS, NT domains, RADIUS (remote access), or any Kerberos ticket servers.

Unless the user is a skilled cracker actively trying to thwart his removal, the user will be deleted. If any of the removed files or entries or any processes owned by the deleted user appear again, change the root passwords, check `cron` and `at` jobs, and repeat the deletion process.

This procedure may be fine for schools and ISPs, but it is unlikely to meet the needs of any business left with the account of a departed employee or contractor. Many of the files are usually valuable to the business. The employee may someday return. An important business process may depend on a `cron` job run by this person—although `cron` jobs on which business processes depend should be owned by pseudo-logins.

Therefore, businesses will generally not want to delete the accounts left by departing workers. Rather, they will want to disable those accounts, preventing their active use while preserving the files until they are adopted by others.

Eventually, disabled accounts will need to be deleted. We recommend that the user's home directory have permissions set to mode 0 a few days or a week before the directory is actually deleted. This should catch any dependencies upon files that would break upon their deletion.

Disabling Users

Disabling a user's account without deleting it is a matter of ensuring that all authentication mechanisms will not permit anyone to execute processes owned by that user. This is not a simple process, because LINUX does not have a unified authentication model.

Any process that runs as root can do anything as any user. One of the consequences is that any process running as `root` can implement any authentication mechanism. Increasingly, software written for LINUX uses PAM (Pluggable Authentication Modules), but much software does not. Therefore, the procedure for ensuring that a disabled user will not be authenticated depends on the software installed at the site.

The first thing to do when disabling an account is to prepend a character such as * to the password field in the `shadow` file or map. Adding a character that cannot be generated by the hashing algorithm in use (`md5` is far more secure than `crypt`) should disable any authentication based on the `passwd` entry. Another method of disabling `passwd`-based authentication is to expire the password. Test any procedure to be sure that it works as expected. Here are some additional steps that we recommend for most sites:

- Remove or disable any authentication credentials, such as those of Kerberos, that may be in use.

- Change the default shell to `/bin/false`.

- Change the user's shell to a *binary*—not a script—which may be called `/usr/sbin/nologin`. This should contain only a few `write()`s and one `exit()`

and should not be linked against any standard libraries (which may have security vulnerabilities).

- Review all `cron` and `at` jobs owned by the user. Delete any personal jobs. Transfer to a pseudo-login each job that performs a valuable business function.

- Review all running processes owned by the user. If they perform a business function that is to be continued, restart them using a pseudo-login. Other processes should be killed. To kill all processes owned by a user, run the following on each machine:

```
ps -u | while read user pid rest; do
kill $pid; done
```

- Check files such as `.forward` that may be used to gain access. Remove or disable files that exist to grant access, such as `.rhosts`. If the account is likely to be reenabled in the future, setting such files to mode 0 is a good solution.

It should then be possible to reenable the account by removing the extra character from the password entry and changing the user's shell to one that permits logins.

System administrators should be prepared to back up a user's home directory on short notice. Sometimes management will ask that a copy be made before terminating an employee. It may be important to ensure that a recent copy is retained before a potentially disgruntled person has an opportunity to corrupt valuable data. This may also be true of databases.

Shadow Passwords

The information in `/etc/passwd` and the NIS `passwd` map must be world-readable so that processes can correlate usernames to uids. Traditionally, the hash of the password occupied the second field of the `passwd` file or map. Unfortunately, this provided anyone with access to the system an opportunity to run attacks against all the password entries.

To prevent such attacks, the hashed passwords have been moved out of the `passwd` files and maps into `/etc/shadow` and the `shadow` map, which are readable only by root. This makes systems considerably more secure against crackers who have either authorized or unauthorized non-root access to a system. Without the use of shadow passwords, once a cracker had access to one account, he could readily gain access to many others, except where the strictest rules are enforced to ensure strong passwords.

If, rather than using `useradd`, a new user is added by editing the `passwd` file directly, `pwconv` must be run to create a matching entry in the `shadow` file. Only then can a password or passphrase be set.

We strongly recommend the use of shadow passwords on all LINUX systems—even those not connected to the Internet. Failing to use them is tantamount to publishing all the passwords.

Password Aging

The aging of passwords is enabled by the shadow suite. The `shadow` file or map contains entries that specify when each password or passphrase will expire and how much notice to give each user. Failure to change a password will result in the automatic disabling of the account a specified number of days after expiration.

The command used to change user password expiration information is `chage`. Several command-line options are available. If none are specified, `chage` prompts the user interactively.

Quotas

It is often necessary to enforce disk space quotas to ensure that one or a few users do not fill a disk partition. Quotas are also useful to ensure that users consume only the disk capacity for which their departments are willing to pay.

It is possible (and recommended) to set two limits for each user. Upon hitting the lower limit, the user is warned. Upon reaching the higher limit, the user may no longer write to disk until space has been freed or the limit raised. It is also possible to allow the temporary use of space.

Quotas are set by editing the `/quota.user` file. Quotas may also be set for groups of users by means of `/quota.group`.

Mail

All the mail for each user should be delivered to one place. This location must be specified (explicitly or implicitly) each time a user is added.

Each user should have an entry in the `aliases` file or NIS map. It is essential to ensure that these entries are unique in the organization. In other words, there should never be conflicting entries in `aliases` files or maps used by different domains or departments.

In small organizations, we recommend setting each alias to

```
user: user@mailhost
```

Then mailhost should be set as an alias in `/etc/hosts` or the `hosts` map. There should not be a machine whose true hostname is mailhost.

In organizations large enough to require separate mailhosts serving each department, we recommend setting each alias to

```
user: user@mailhost.subdomain.domain
```

where `subdomain` corresponds to the NIS domain, to the DNS subdomain, and to the functional department; and where `domain` corresponds to the DNS domain for the organization. In this scheme, the mailhost alias must be set correctly in each NIS domain's `hosts` map and in each corresponding DNS subdomain.

NIS

All but the smallest installations will probably use NIS or a similar system to store user and group information. There are complications involved with using NIS and the shadow suite.

Of course, NIS servers can provide `shadow` maps to clients. The objective of the shadow suite is to allow only root to view the encrypted passwords. So `ypserv.conf` needs entries like these:

```
# Host              : Map             : Security   : Passwd_mangle
*                   : shadow.byname   : port       : yes
```

This should ensure that non-root users who request the `shadow` map via NIS see only an x in the password field. The mechanism for determining whether or not the user making the request is root on the client machine is the port number. Only root should be able to use port numbers 0 through 1024.

If unsecure machines (such as Windows NT)—with which any user can use any port— are present on the network, then the `/etc/ypserv.securenets` and `/etc/ypserv.conf` files must be configured to ensure that NIS maps will be passed only to trusted Unix machines and not to any other machine that may request them.

When loading the NIS `passwd` map from a flat file, check that the `minuid` variable in `/var/yp/Makefile` is set correctly. Any user in the flat file (such as root) with a uid less than the set limit will not be loaded. The same is true for the `mingid` variable and the `group` map.

Large Databases

Large installations are faced with complications that do not arise when the scale is smaller. Consider a site with 100,000 users and 100,000 workstations. DNS can easily handle name service—after all, DNS offers reliable name service for the whole Internet. But how to maintain uid consistency? Maintaining 100,000 copies of a `passwd` file with 100,000 entries is not feasible. Nor is maintaining a single NIS domain with 100,000 entries in the `passwd` map.

There must be a database of users, hosts, and so on from which NIS maps are pulled. The database must be configured to maintain data integrity. Additionally, permissions may be granted to each system administrator to change only the subsets of the data that are in his domain. Relational databases meet these requirements.

One tool for maintaining a relational database of network information is MESA,[2] a commercial product developed for SunOS/Solaris. It appears not to be marketed currently. Perhaps the creators can be encouraged to open the source code.

---

2. `http://www.esm.com/`

While it doesn't address the needs we've discussed for very large sites, the psntools package[3] is a set of utilities that partially automate the administration of user accounts at sites with between 200 and 4000 users. Written for the needs of educational institutions where users arrive and depart in large groups, it may be sufficiently flexible to be useful in other environments.

passwdd[4] is a tool for synchronizing passwd files that may be of use to small and medium-sized organizations.

ISPs running LINUX may find a package called ACUA[5] useful. It enforces access controls and session time limits, generates statistical reports, and provides notifications and warnings to users.

3. http://www.psn.ie/users/ad/psntools/

4. ftp://ftp.varna.net/pub/linux/passwdd/

5. http://acua.gist.net.au/

III

Services

17

Network Services

THE OPERATION OF A NETWORK COMPUTING ENVIRONMENT depends on many services provided by various software components. Network services are provided to applications both on the same host and on other hosts. This chapter explains the purpose, function, and configuration of these services, which fall into two classes, system-level services and user-level services.

Some of these services are necessary for computers to participate in the network computing environment, even before any user-level applications are running. These system-level services enable the computers in a network computing environment to function as a coherent whole. System-level services include DNS, RPC, NTP, and NIS.

Other services are needed only to support user-level applications. These application-level services include mail, news, printing, FTP, http, remote shells, and file services. Application-level services shape the users' view of the network computing environment.

System-Level Services

System-level services are not used directly by users. Rather, they form an integral portion of the network computing environment by providing service to both operating systems and applications. The delivery of these services to all systems within an organization lays the groundwork for the higher level services. Reliable delivery of these services makes the network computing environment stable and predictable.

DNS

The Domain Name Service (DNS) provides translations of hostnames to IP addresses. It also provides reverse translations of IP addresses to hostnames. The Domain Name Service came into being when users of the (then) Arpanet realized that they could no longer accurately maintain host information in a single file that had to be copied to every machine on the Arpanet every time a host was added, changed, or deleted. DNS delegates hostname management to the system administrators responsible for the systems. DNS has scaled with the rapid growth of the Internet.

The hierarchical structure of DNS comprises hosts at the leaves and domains at the branches. A hostname presented with its domain is known as a Fully Qualified Domain Name (FQDN). The hostname is written to the left and the branches of the domain are separated by periods. For example, the name `sunsite.unc.edu` refers to a host named `sunsite` in the `unc.edu` domain, which is part of the `edu` top-level domain. At the root of the DNS hierarchy, a DNS NS (Name Server) record points to the `edu` domain. Within the `edu` domain, another set of NS records points to the `unc` domain. The `unc` domain contains the host `sunsite`. A name server that carries out this recursive search will normally cache all of the data it learns along the way. Subsequent queries will not need to access any other server. All cached data has a lifetime associated with it and will expire after that period elapses.

The root name servers are preloaded onto every server. These systems are essential to processing queries and cannot be learned dynamically. The root servers are comparatively static, but current data is always available at

```
ftp://rs.internic.net/domain/root.zone.gz
```

DNS is one of the fundamental services that a system administrator must set up within any organization. DNS services are implemented by configuring and running `named`, the name server. The `named` dæmon is distributed as BIND (Berkeley Internet Name Dæmon). The BIND distribution contains the name server as well as the client side software, known as the resolver. BIND is available from the Internet Software Consortium (ISC).[1]

BIND uses ASCII data to implement the name database. These data are split into a number of zone files. BIND defines a zone as a domain and any subdomains that are administered by the same server. One of the quirks of DNS is that the reverse translations appear in different zone files than the forward translations. This means that a system administrator must edit two files to change any hostname. Many system administrators

1. `ftp://ftp.isc.org/`

find this cumbersome and prefer to manage a hosts(5) format file and use the h2n utility to generate zone files from it.

An instance of named has one of three possible relationships with any zone. It can be a primary, secondary, or caching server for a particular zone. Typically, a name server operates simultaneously in multiple modes, since many servers operate as caching servers for zones for which they are neither primary nor secondary.

The resolver is typically integrated into the C runtime library libc in a manner that is transparent to users. Some implementations of libc permit the system administrator to configure the order in which name services are consulted to resolve hostnames and other system data. The name service switch file /etc/nsswitch.conf is used to store this configuration information.

Details for configuring and managing BIND can be found in the references at the end of this chapter.

NTP

The Network Time Protocol (NTP) is used to synchronize time among computers on the network. This is especially useful with PC hardware, because their internal clocks tend to drift significantly. NTP should be configured to use an accurate source of Universal Coordinated Time (UTC). There are three basic choices for a good time source.

- WWV or WWVB radio receivers. NTP supports a wide variety of radio clocks. These devices listen to a signal transmitted in the United States by the National Institute of Standards. The disadvantage of radio clocks is that the signal is often poor in densely populated areas. Also, for the highest degree of accuracy, it may be necessary to correct the signal, requiring accurate knowledge of the site's latitude and longitude.

- A GPS receiver. Similarly to radio clocks, GPS receivers listen to an external signal for accurate time information. In this case, the source is the U.S. Global Positioning System, a constellation of satellites in orbit above the earth. These satellites broadcast such accurate time information that precise locations can be calculated by triangulating from several GPS satellites. The military uses a high-quality encrypted signal from these satellites for navigation and targeting. They also distribute a lower grade signal for non-military use, which commercial products use. The time signal is still highly accurate. GPS receivers work anywhere on the Earth's surface.

- Internet NTP Servers. A large number of high-quality time sources are available from the Internet. The NTP home[2] has links to these sources. This option has the advantage of being free. While it is theoretically possible for someone to spoof Internet time, the basic NTP filtering algorithm is designed to throw out packets

2. http://www.eecis.udel.edu/~ntp

that are way off (this is for accuracy, not security). In addition, a site can arrange to have a public server encrypt the data using a private key.

NTP defines 16 levels (called strata) to describe the distance a system is from a high-quality time source. NTP servers are configured to form a network or tree of time servers, with the top being the time servers with the lowest stratum (closest to the time source). Only the largest organizations will need more than three or four strata to reach all systems.

BOOTP, DHCP, TFTP, and RARP

This is a collection of services that perform operating system related tasks. BOOTP and DHCP support automated IP address configuration for LINUX and other systems. BOOTP supports static mapping of Ethernet addresses to IP addresses, while DHCP provides dynamic address allocation. Unfortunately, DHCP cannot yet update DNS, which will be needed for many site configurations. If DNS is not updated to follow IP address assignments, then hosts will change names when they are issued new IP addresses. This interferes with hostname based authentication. If a site grants all client workstations the same permissions to resources, then this may not be a problem, and using DHCP for client workstations is quite feasible.

In addition, both DHCP and BOOTP can be used to assist in network-based system installs, such as with RedHat's Kickstart installer. See Chapter 15, "Automated Installation and Upgrade."

Another tool used to assist installs is The Trivial File Transfer Protocol (TFTP). TFTP is typically used to download files from a server to a client during the install process. It is unsuitable for a secure environment, and care must be taken not to allow TFTP to be used to steal or alter files on the server.

Finally, the Reverse Address Resolution Protocol (RARP) is used by some systems to discover their IP addresses. LINUX does not require RARP services. This service is provided to support network devices that may need it. Sites that do not need RARP should disable it, as with any unneeded service.

RPC

A Remote Procedure Call (RPC) service provides applications with the ability to perform subroutine calls to other processes, which are typically running on other computers. The Open Network Computing Remote Procedure Call (ONC RPC) service has become a standard in the UNIX community. Many other RPC protocols exist, but ONC RPC benefits from the popularity of the applications that have been layered on top of it. NIS and NFS are both implemented using ONC RPC.

The RPC service uses the concept of program numbers to identify RPC-based services, The RPC port mapper dæmon maps program numbers to TCP or UDP ports, as needed. Each RPC service registers with the portmapper on its host and provides its program number and the port to which it is listening.

NIS

The Network Information Service (NIS) provides to all systems within a NIS domain unified system data regarding users, groups, mail aliases, and other system information. See Chapter 21, "Managing NIS," for details on NIS.

LDAP

The Lightweight Directory Access Protocol (LDAP) was designed to provide services similar to DNS and NIS. LDAP overcomes the limitations of both services, permitting richer data than is available from DNS, and having a hierarchical structure, unlike NIS. Years ago, developers of MIT's Athena project used DNS to create a service known as hesiod. hesiod used DNS txt records to manage user and group data. Unfortunately, hesiod was not widely adopted, and the practice of using both NIS and DNS in larger organizations persists. LDAP should be able to fulfill a similar role, but progress has been slow. Support for LDAP as a naming service has not been integrated into libc, so use of LDAP is restricted to programs which explicitly communicate with it. Not many programs do, so LDAP currently exists in a dormant state, waiting for the Internet community to decide which directory service to use and with which data to populate it.

Application-Level Services

A range of network services directly support user-level applications. These are distinct from the system-level services described previously in that the former rely on the latter. Application-level services include mail, news, printing, FTP, http, remote shells, and file services such as NFS and Samba. Because mail, printing, and NFS are covered in chapters of their own, this section focuses on the other application-level services.

Samba

Samba provides file and print services to Microsoft WINDOWS clients. Deploying Samba allows the system administrator to employ LINUX servers as an organization's primary file and print servers. This obviates the stability problems inherent in attempting to use WINDOWS NT servers. Samba is also able to provide NT domain services, further lessening the need for WINDOWS NT systems and thus improving the reliability of the computing environment.

Samba is configured via the smb.conf file. We defer to the Samba documentation, which accompanies the software.[3]

---

3. http://www.samba.org/

NetNews

Network News (NetNews) is the mainstay of discussion forums on the Internet. Although it is being supplemented by chat programs like IRC (Internet Relay Chat), and web-based mail archive browsers, NetNews still handles most of the discussion traffic on the Internet.

The Network News Transport Protocol (nntp) is the mechanism by which news servers pass the latest postings to each other. There are two software packages used to provide NetNews within an organization: INN[4] and nntp,[5] which should not be confused with the protocol of the same name. INN is more widely used and more vigorously maintained.

Remote Shells

Several programs are used to log on to remote computers and establish an interactive session. The oldest and most popular is telnet, which is available for virtually any computer that runs IP. The r-commands, or remote shell programs, were written for the Berkeley System Distribution, and are available on most UNIX systems. The r-commands consist of rsh, rlogin, and rcp. The r-commands support host-based authentication, which should not be used, and is in general a huge security hole. The big advantage of host-based authentication is that no password challenge takes place. This permits rsh and rcp to be invoked from shell scripts, thus allowing network tasks to be automated. The Secure Shell (ssh) utilizes public key cryptography to establish a session with an authenticated host. ssh extends the capabilities of the r-commands to include port forwarding and X WINDOW display forwarding. This allows users to execute a variety of commands, using ssh to provide an encrypted path to a remote machine. The rsync file distribution utility and the cvs version control system are examples of tools that can use the ssh command to provide themselves with a secure channel.

FTP

The File Transfer Protocol is one of the earliest services provided on the Internet. It quickly became one of the most popular as well. Most FTP servers provide *anonymous FTP*, which allows anyone to access the shared portion of a server's files. Care must be taken to limit the portion of the system that is accessible via anonymous FTP.

System administrators who support public FTP servers must aggressively monitor their systems for intrusion and tampering. The FTP dæmon ftpd should be run chroot'ed on public servers. This reduces the possibility that the ftpd dæmon itself can be exploited to alter or access sensitive files. Additionally, the ftpd dæmon must be updated whenever new security fixes become available.

---

4. http://www.isc.org/inn/

5. http://www.academ.com/academ/nntp/

http

The World Wide Web is based on the HyperText Transfer Protocol (http). This protocol defines mechanisms for the transfer of web pages, images, and other files. It depends on several lower-level protocols, including TCP, DNS, and RPC.

The software most commonly used to provide http services is Apache. A properly configured LINUX system running Apache and the needed underlying services is an excellent WWW server. Most of the configuration requirements are imposed by Apache. Here, we discuss system configuration issues that are independent of Apache.

WWW servers come under attack more often than other hosts. Therefore, the prudent system administrator will disable all services not essential to the proper functioning of the server. Unless there is a compelling reason otherwise, ensure that Apache runs as user nobody. Never run any WWW server as user root. As with FTP, the files served should be in a directory structure protected by chroot.

Provide a /var or /var/log partition with enough capacity to store the copious logs that a WWW server can generate. Servers with light loads may be fine with a 100MB /var partition. Heavily loaded servers may require a /var/log partition of 500MB or more.

Further Reading

- *DNS and BIND,* 3rd ed., Paul Albitz and Cricket Liu, 1998
- *sendmail,* 2nd ed., Bryan Costales with Eric Allman and Neil Rickett, 1997
- *sendmail: Theory and Practice,* Frederick Avolio and Paul Vixie, 1995
- *Understanding and Deploying LDAP Directory Services,* by Tim Howes, Mark Smith, and Gordon Good, 1999
- *Samba: Integrating UNIX and Windows,* by John D. Blair, 1998
- *Teach Yourself Samba in 24 Hours,* Jeremy Carter et al., 1999
- RFC 821, "Simple Mail Transfer Protocol"
  http://www.cis.ohio-state.edu/htbin/rfc/rfc821.html
- RFC 822, "Standard for the format of ARPA Internet text messages"
  http://www.cis.ohio-state.edu/htbin/rfc/rfc822.html
- RFC 1035, "Domain Names - Implementation and Specification"
  http://www.cis.ohio-state.edu/htbin/rfc/rfc1035.html
- RFC 2132, "DHCP Options and BOOTP Vendor Extensions"
  http://www.cis.ohio-state.edu/htbin/rfc/rfc2132.html
- RFC 2251, "Lightweight Directory Access Protocol (v3)"
  http://www.cis.ohio-state.edu/htbin/rfc/rfc2251.html
- The Network Administrators' Guide, Olaf Kirch,
  http://www.kernelnotes.org/guides/NAG/

- Clock mini-HOWTO, by Ron Bean
  `http://metalab.unc.edu/LDP/HOWTO/mini/Clock.html`
- The NTP Usenet Newsgroup comp.protocols.time.ntp
- NTP FAQ #3, notes from the newsgroup collected by Ulrich Windl
  `http://www.eecis.udel.edu/~ntp/database/FAQ/faq3C.htm`
- Diskless HOWTO, by Robert Nemkin
  `http://metalab.unc.edu/LDP/HOWTO/Diskless-HOWTO.html`
- DHCP mini-HOWTO, by Vladimir Vuksan
  `http://metalab.unc.edu/LDP/HOWTO/mini/DHCP.html`
- NFS HOWTO, by Nicolai Langfeldt
  `http://metalab.unc.edu/LDP/HOWTO/NFS-HOWTO.html`
- NIS HOWTO, by Thorsten Kukuk
  `http://metalab.unc.edu/LDP/HOWTO/NIS-HOWTO.html`
- An LDAP Roadmap & FAQ
  `http://www.kingsmountain.com/ldapRoadmap.shtml`
- Diagnosing Samba (DIAGNOSIS.TXT)
  `http://us1.samba.org/samba/docs/DIAGNOSIS.html` or within the Samba package.
- News Leafsite mini-HOWTO, by Florian Kuehnert
  `http://metalab.unc.edu/LDP/HOWTO/mini/News-Leafsite.html`
- For Providers (Rapid Knowledge Transfer for usenet news providers)
  `http://www.mibsoftware.com/userkt/forprov.htm`
- Ssh (Secure Shell) FAQ - Frequently asked questions
  `http://www.employees.org/~satch/ssh/faq/`

Do not get involved with sendmail. She is an exotic lover, whispering delicious promises in your ear, flashing her bright eyes at you. But she is insane, and will draw you down into her madness.

~Andrew Molitor

18

Mail

EMAIL HAS ECLIPSED TELEPHONY, facsimile, and direct personal interaction as an essential vehicle for business communication. The operation of many businesses has come to depend on the reliable delivery of email. With this in mind, we examine the software agents used by computers running LINUX to deliver email, in order to ensure its secure, reliable delivery.

First, we must distinguish between mail transfer agents (MTAs), mail delivery agents (MDAs), and mail user agents (MUAs). MTAs transfer email from one computer to another and are the agents by which email is delivered across organizations and over the Internet. qmail and sendmail are the MTAs commonly found on LINUX machines.

Once a message has reached the destination host, the mail delivery agent delivers it to the recipient's mailbox. /bin/mail and procmail are examples of MDAs.

MUAs are the programs with which users read, compose, edit, and forward email. When a user clicks the Send button, the MUA attaches some headers to the body of the message and passes it to the MTA running on the machine. The MTA then attaches additional headers and attempts to deliver the message to the destination host.

sendmail

sendmail was first written in 1981, in order to deliver mail among BerkNet,[1] UUCP, and the ARPANET,[2] which then still ran NCP (Network Control Protocol) as well as TCP (Transport Control Protocol), which superseded NCP. sendmail did an excellent job of delivering mail among these various networks and earned its place as a widely-used piece of software upon which the Internet depended.

Over the intervening decades, sendmail has grown ever larger and more complex, even as the requirements have become simpler with the standardization of protocols. This large, complex piece of software runs as root and must interact promiscuously, accepting connections from unknown machines across the Internet. Thus, it should be no surprise that sendmail has been the cause of more computer security problems than any other piece of Open Source software.

Although sendmail still runs on most of the mail servers on the Internet, and is still the most widely used free software in the enterprise, sendmail should be avoided if possible. Its use requires extreme vigilance in seeking news of new security holes. With each new hole discovered, a new version of sendmail must be compiled and installed. At large sites this may require considerable effort, because testing must be done to ensure that the new version doesn't break anything. Then it must be packaged for mass installation and the package tested as well. Note that not only the external mail gateways must be kept up-to-date. As we discuss in Chapter 7, "Security Policy," it is no less important to defend against attacks from within.

If bureaucratic or technical considerations require that sendmail be run, ensure that the version[3] installed has no known security holes by checking the website of your LINUX distribution and checking http://www.sendmail.org/. There are also mailing lists (we list some in Chapter 8, "Enforcing Security") by which to keep apprised of security problems. Then be ever-vigilant.

sendmail Configuration

sendmail gathers its configuration information from a single file, sendmail.cf. Current versions include an m4 macro facility for generating sendmail.cf files. The m4 package should be used, because it facilitates maintenance of any sendmail.cf file generated by it.

It is essential to maintain each .mc file from which a production .cf file is generated. When a .cf file needs to be updated, it is all too common that the original .mc file has been lost. We recommend distributing the .mc file as part of any binary sendmail package.

---

1. A network then used within the University of California, Berkeley

2. The predecessor of the Internet

3. To check which version of sendmail is installed on a particular host, telnet to port 25 of that host. Of course, the banner that announces the version can be overridden, as can any method of checking the version.

In other words, everywhere a `.cf` file is found, its corresponding `.mc` file should also be present.

To prevent mail bombs and secure against other exploits involving mail, mail should never be delivered to a mailbox or spool file owned by `root`. Ideally, mail for `root` should be delivered to an account that is not a member of the `wheel` group. Because this is not convenient, mail for `root` is usually forwarded to the accounts of the system administrators who manage mail.

qmail

qmail is a simple MTA first written in 1996 to provide a secure alternative to `sendmail`. qmail comprises several smaller binaries, each of which performs just one task. Only tasks that must be run as root are run as root. This presents several advantages over `sendmail`'s one large monolithic binary. The likelihood of bugs is reduced because each binary is smaller—in fact, all the qmail sources together contain less than one fourth the number of lines of code as those of `sendmail`. It also is inherently more secure, both because the compromise of one executable does not necessarily imply the compromise of all of them and because most of the functionality does not run as root.

qmail Configuration

The configuration of qmail is completely different from that of `sendmail`. Where the latter bundles all of its configuration options into a single file of notorious complexity, qmail is configured by means of many simple files, each of which determines a single aspect of qmail's behavior.

This makes qmail considerably easier for the novice system administrator (as well as some senior system administrators) to manage. The disadvantage is that the large number of files adds to the complexity of packaging qmail for installation throughout the enterprise.

qmail Installation

Large organizations should produce their own packages for qmail installation, in order to include as much of the required local configuration information as possible.

Departmental mail servers will have a common configuration that is quite different from the common configuration that clients and other servers will have. This difference may be provided for either by having a different package for mail servers or by breaking the distribution into two packages: binaries and config files. In the latter case, there will be alternative packages for server and client config files. We recommend this because it allows the base package to be revised without having to change the configuration package. In addition, a system's role can be determined by inspecting the packages.

Mail Service Structure

Reliable and timely delivery of email within an organization requires that mail service be structured without any single point of failure that might interrupt mail service for the whole organization. In other words, the failure of any one mail server, DNS server, NIS server, or network should not delay delivery of all email.

Departmental Mail Servers

Each operational department should have its own mail server. This may run on hardware dedicated to mail alone, or it may run on hardware that also provides services such as DNS and NIS. This choice will depend on the requirements and budget of the organization.

Departmental mail servers should direct mail for any given internal recipient to that user's departmental mail server. For this to work, each mail server must be able to resolve user names to fully qualified email addresses. The alias information by which this is accomplished is usually taken from the `aliases` NIS map, though it may also be taken from the `aliases` file.

Mail should never be transferred to a client workstation for storage. Doing so would violate the principle of never storing any user data on client machines. Rather, mail should be stored on the mail server until it is no longer needed, and copies should only be sent to client machines to be read. In order to accomplish this, POP or IMAP or both should be supported on each departmental mail server. IMAP is preferred, but some MUAs don't yet support it. Ensure that users do not have the option of saving mail locally. Some system administrators export the mail spool via NFS for each client to mount. Doing so is unreliable and usually leads to grief.

It is usually acceptable for departmental mail servers to be single points of failure for their department's mail. Incoming mail will queue until service is restored.

External Mail Gateways

Mail destined for users outside the organization should be directed by each departmental mail server to external mail gateways. Large organizations will typically have two such servers for handling outgoing mail, with DNS pointing at both of them in round-robin fashion. Incoming mail will typically be received by either of two servers, also served by round-robin DNS. These will then consult the `aliases` map and direct mail to the appropriate departmental mail server.

Large organizations will run incoming and outgoing mail servers on separate hardware both to prevent faults in one from affecting the other and to facilitate the diagnosis of any problems that may occur. For these reasons, smaller organizations that can afford only two external mail servers are better served by having one for incoming mail and the other for outgoing mail than by having each machine provide both services. Simplicity is usually more important than hardware redundancy.

procmail

procmail is a mail delivery agent that processes mail according to rules specified in a .procmailrc file. It is most often used to sort mail into different folders based on the sender, the subject, or the content. It is also used to selectively forward mail, and to start programs upon the receipt of some or any type of mail message. For example, procmail can forward to a pager the first 80 characters of every message that meets specified criteria. procmail is also capable of managing mailing lists.

System administrators can set procmail to be the default MDA. This will enable users to create .procmailrc files containing rules for how they would like their mail to be processed. Note that procmail, by default, will deliver to the usual spool directory any mail for users who don't have a .procmailrc file. The software and additional information may be found at http://www.procmail.org/

Spam

Spam is unsolicited email, usually sent to large numbers of recipients. The term also refers to messages posted to Usenet, often to large numbers of newsgroups, which are off-topic. Here we discuss unsolicited mail and what may be done to stop it.

The first thing that every system administrator responsible for external mail gateways should do is ensure that they cannot be used as relay hosts. Spammers often use someone else's external mailhost to send hundreds of thousands of messages. Sites that unwittingly are used by spammers to relay mail are often cut off from large portions of the Internet. Explaining to management that half the Internet couldn't buy anything from the company's website because a spammer used the misconfigured mail gateway to relay 400,000 advertisements is not likely to be a pleasant experience.

Sites running qmail are not vulnerable to spam relayers. Sites running sendmail should ensure that they are running version 8.9.0 or higher, because these disable relaying by default. See http://maps.vix.com/ for more information on spam relaying and how to fight it by automatically denying service to purveyors of spam and those who abet them.

To protect users whose email addresses have fallen into the wrong hands, we recommend installing software on departmental mail servers that uses pattern files to determine whether an incoming message is from a known valid sender, a known spammer, a probable spammer, or an unknown sender. This software then either accepts the mail, drops the mail, or bounces the mail with a polite explanation that, in an effort to combat spam, the mail is being returned because the sender is unknown. The bounce message should include instructions for resending the mail so that it will be accepted. Maintaining the pattern file of known good senders may be tedious, because entries for senders from most companies will generally match any user in the domain, while entries for senders at ISPs should match only that user. This is an excellent task for a junior system administrator.

There are several such software packages, most of which are built on top of `procmail`. Here are some:

spamgard. `ftp://ftp.netcom.com/pub/wj/wje/release/sg-latest.tar.gz`

Spam Bouncer. `http://www.hrweb.org/spambouncer/`

SpamDunk. `http://www.interlog.com/~waltdnes/spamdunk/spamdunk.htm`

JunkFilter. `http://www.pobox.com/~gsutter/junkfilter/`

Use Policies

Every organization should publish its email use policy on its intranet, making clear what is and what is not permitted. It should also specify the penalties for specific violations. For example, sending erotic email to one's spouse might or might not be allowed but, even if prohibited, would generally not invoke the same response as launching a denial-of-service attack against a personal enemy or sending spam soliciting a scam.

The authors are familiar with one organization that explicitly disallowed almost every use of external email. Specifically, external email was prohibited for any contractual business and all non-business use. Such a policy is unduly general and can lead to abuse. It is the responsibility of management to provide a use policy that is realistic and enforceable. Both human resource and corporate security professionals have access to industry guidelines and recent court rulings that can be used as a basis for developing an effective and enforceable use policy.

Email policies must cover more than just what sorts of email may be sent. Various difficulties may arise. One issue that arises frequently is what do with email that arrives for an employee who has become incapacitated. Just as with paper mail, many employees receive personal mail at work. The organization has a legitimate reason to open and read mail that may be business-related, whether that mail arrives in a paper envelope or an electronic one. In each case, it is often possible to distinguish business mail from personal mail from the envelope—but not always. Thus, a clear policy must be in place. At a minimum, it should establish that the company owns all mail received and has the right to read all mail received. It should also specify the circumstances under which that right will be exercised.

The objective is to ensure that neither the system administrators nor the organization may be prosecuted for taking reasonable actions, as well as to fairly let everyone know what is expected of them and what they may expect. Laws vary among jurisdictions and over time, so it is appropriate to have the draft policies reviewed by legal counsel.

The objective should not be to prohibit private use of email, but rather to make clear that privacy is not offered by corporate policy. Some organizations have made it a dismissable offense to receive "offensive" email. This is just another example of hiding a "terminate for any cause" clause in an email policy. You may receive email from unknown persons who found your address in mail that was forwarded. Determining how the address came to be known to the sender is usually impossible. Therefore, persons should never be held responsible for email they receive, even if the email received would have been illegal to send.

Also, the current email infrastructure of the Internet makes it easy to send mail pseudonymously. Therefore, care must be taken before holding someone responsible for email he appears to have sent, because heinous email is likely to have been sent by someone whose name does not appear in the headers.

Many organizations will want to archive all incoming and outgoing mail. The presumption should be that once deleted messages are more than a week old, the probability of ever having to refer back to them will be low. Therefore, email should be archived on read-only media that is kept offline, such as DVD-R. Each departmental mail server should separately archive incoming, outgoing, and local mail. This should obviate any need for the external mail servers to archive mail they receive.

Accordingly, we recommend that employees maintain personal email accounts outside the control of their employer. Many such accounts now offer http access, making them easy to use from any browser.

Privacy Ethics

While organizations must maintain the right to read email, system administrators should strive to respect the privacy of users. We suggest that system administrators who are requested to read the files or email of others insist that a reasonable attempt be made to inform the user. Each request should be made in writing and should include what specifically is to be sought and the purpose of the search. The authors also refuse to provide access to email unless corporate security officers and/or law enforcement officials are notified and present. Members of SAGE are also expected to abide by the set of professional ethics published by the organization.

If a system administrator wonders whether or not reading someone else's mail is justified, it probably is not. When it is justified, it will be obviously justified, and managers should not hesitate in signing their names to the directive. Each of the authors has risked a job over this issue, and none of us have any regrets about having done so.

Troubleshooting Electronic Mail

Debugging email problems can test the depth of a system administrator's skill and the breadth of his experience. A vast array of problems can occur at the source, destination, and any intermediate point in the path of a mail message. Additionally, problems related to routing or capacity have a tendency to snowball, creating problems larger in scope than the original failure. The system administrator must quickly identify which component is failing on which host to minimize the effect of these types of problems.

When confronted with a mail problem, the first task is to gather information on the scope. If one user complains about not receiving mail, immediately check to see if other users have the same problem. If multiple users complain about the same problem, the system administrator must attempt to find a correlation. Do they all use the same mail server? Are they all on the same IP subnet? Hopefully, the system administrator will gain a good feel for the scope of the problem and use this information to focus the initial troubleshooting effort.

Begin the actual troubleshooting by identifying which subsystem is failing. Is it the user agent, the transport agent, or the delivery agent?

If mail is bouncing, read the error message in the bounce. This sounds inane, but most junior and intermediate system administrators fail to read the error messages. If the error message doesn't make sense the first time, read it again. Almost all bounced messages really do indicate the source of the problem. Also, be sure to inspect the full message headers. Most mail user agents suppress the display of most header information, so you may need to turn this behavior off or look at the mail message directly with a text editor.

If mail is slowing down, look for mail routing loops. All mail transport agents provide logging facilities, and the logs should be inspected for useful hints.

Because failures and misconfiguration of either NIS or DNS can lead to mail failures, don't limit the search to only the mail system. Check for full disk partitions as well.

Be flexible in your approach—if a theory is not working out, backtrack and re-examine the symptoms. Also, if the source of the problem leads out of your administrative domain, try to alert the postmaster for the machine(s) in question. Remember, your users don't really care about the arbitrary boundaries created by corporations and their support organizations. They just need their mail to work.

We present a few of the common problems organized by component.

User Agent Problems

- Bad recipient addresses. This kind of failure generates a user unknown bounced mail message, sometimes several days after the message was sent. A good directory service can virtually eliminate this problem within an organization, but there will always be undeliverable addresses on the Internet. Sometimes a mail administrator's job is to inform users, "Yes, that email address really doesn't work."

- Bad sender addresses. This results in mail that cannot be replied to. User agents often let the user configure the return address to use when sending mail. Users may get this wrong, especially if the upper-level mail servers do a lot of header rewriting. Check message headers to see if the sender addresses match in the envelope and the message.

- Corruption of mail folders. This can occur due to bugs in the user agent, full disk conditions, or bad interactions with mail delivery agents.

Transport Agent Problems

- Bad mail aliases. These can result in bounces and loops. Definitely try to avoid bounces on the names mailer-daemon, root, and postmaster, because these can lead to serious loops.

- Bad header rewriting rules. This can lead to the corruption of email addresses, and looping. Test configuration files thoroughly before deploying them.

- Failure to accept mail or queue mail. Frequently caused by full disk or high system load conditions, and a common secondary effect of the other aforementioned problems.

- Hangs during operation. Most commonly caused by NIS or DNS failures, and occasionally by corrupted `passwd` or `group` files.

Delivery Agent Problems

- Corruption of mail folders. This can occur occasionally as a result of a buggy delivery agent, but it often occurs in conjunction with other delivery agents or a user agent. The most common cause is two programs accessing a mail folder simultaneously but using incompatible file locking mechanisms.

- Agent hangs during delivery. Most likely caused by file locking problems, especially if the mail folder is mounted via NFS. The authors strongly recommend against NFS exporting and mounting of mail spool directories.

19

Printing and Faxing

Many junior system administrators find Unix printing difficult to configure. It need not be so. Linux uses the BSD printing system, which is not as difficult to administer as some believe. While the BSD printing system may be antiquated, System V printing has proven to be less reliable, even when supported by the largest commercial Unix vendors. This chapter explains the components of the Linux printing system, and how each relates to the others.

The user-level print command is lpr, which may be invoked by an application or directly on the command line. lpr consults the printcap file to learn which spool directory to use for the specified printer, and then hands the job to the local lpd dæmon by writing it as two files to the appropriate spool directory. If the printer is locally attached (such as by a serial or parallel port), then lpd writes the job to the device specified in the printcap file, deleting the spool files only when the printer has acknowledged receiving them. If the printcap file specifies that the printer is attached to another host on the network or is itself a host, then lpd passes the print job across the network to the lpd dæmon on the remote host or printer before deleting the job from the spool directory.

lpr

Every print job is handled by lpr.[1] Typically, lpr is invoked by an application, a script, or directly on the command line. lpr never actually prints anything; rather it queues the print job, placing it in a spool directory to be processed by lpd.

The most common argument to lpr is the -P option used to specify the printer. If -P is not used, the default printer environment variable, PRINTER, is used. If PRINTER is not defined, then lpr defaults to using lp, which should be defined as an alias for the default printer.[2] The -m option instructs that a notification be sent to the user via email upon completion of the print job. The -s option is useful when printing very large files. It creates a symlink in the spool directory rather than a copy of the file.

Other arguments can be used to specify the type of data to be printed. These are rarely used now because general-purpose filters have become sophisticated enough to automatically discover print data types and handle each correctly. If a data type is specified, lpr indicates it in the control file. Eventually, the lpd dæmon on the print host pipes the data through the filter specified by the corresponding entry in the printcap file.

lpr parses the printcap file, searching for the desired printer name to learn the correct spool directory for the specified printer. lpr then writes one data file and one control file to the spool directory. The data file begins df*nnn*, and the control file begins cf*nnn*, where *nnn* is the job number.

The last thing lpr does is open a socket to notify the local lpd dæmon that the job awaits.

Spool Directories

The print spool directories are normally found under /var/spool/lpd/ but may vary with the particular LINUX distribution. Ownership of the contents varies even more. It is safest to use the ownership and permissions expected by the applications included with the distribution. A directory owned by root may or may not still be functional if the applications expect it to be owned by lp.

It is rare that a spool directory will need to be created manually. Normally, this is done using the printtool application.

lpd

The line printer dæmon, lpd, arbitrates access to printers by providing the spooling and scheduling functionality needed to support printing in a multiuser environment. It is the core of the LINUX printing system. The lpd dæmon speaks the Berkeley lpd protocol over the socket, which is well understood and documented as RFC 1179. Most modern network printers support the lpd protocol.

---

1. It is possible, as root, to cat a file directly to a raw print device for debugging purposes.
2. In SysV environments, lp is a command comparable to lpr.

lpd is normally started at boot time by an rc script. The rc script should verify that lpd is loadable, kill any stale lock files, and start the dæmon.

The first thing lpd does is read the printcap file. Then lpd checks the queues by examining the spool directories for waiting print jobs. Once started, lpd listens for TCP connections from instances of lpd running on other hosts. Before accepting a print job from a remote host, lpd weakly authenticates that host by checking for an entry in the /etc/hosts.equiv or the /etc/hosts.lpd file.

The printcap file

The printcap file, which is normally found in the /etc directory, provides a layer of abstraction for printers. Each entry in printcap defines a virtual printer that may be connected locally or across the network. Multiple virtual printers with different characteristics can be created by defining multiple entries with different options in the printcap file for the same physical printer.

The local lpd dæmon accepts print jobs locally for any printer with a correct printcap entry.

The printcap file deliberately follows a format similar to that of termcap. Designed for fast handling by primitive software, each entry is one line, and the fields are separated by colons (:). The first field is a list of one or more names by which the printer may be selected. In order to accommodate long entries, lines may be continued by placing a backslash (\) at the end of any line to be continued. This form of line continuation is common in Unix shells and in many other Unix contexts, such as configuration files. (Caveat: Trailing whitespaces after the backslash usually do not work.) The following lines must begin with a tab and typically begin with another colon as well, which is not common in Unix shells.

Unneeded fields may be omitted. Thus, a minimally useful printcap entry for a locally connected printer is

```
lp|generic:lp=/dev/lp0:sd=/var/spool/lp0:sh:
```

Using the line continuation feature for clarity, the same entry is:

```
lp|generic:\
        :lp=/dev/lp0:\
        :sd=/var/spool/lp0:\
        :sh:
```

These functionally equivalent entries define a print queue that can be addressed as either lp or generic. Print jobs sent to this queue will be temporarily held as a file in the directory /var/spool/lp0, until lpd has verified that the device at /dev/lp0 (the first parallel port on an typical PC) has accepted all of it.

As noted above, the first field is a list of one or more names by which the virtual printer can be addressed. All other fields take one of three forms: string, numeric, or Boolean. String fields take an option after the equal sign (=). Numeric fields take an option after the hash sign (#). Boolean fields can take either `true` or `false` after the equal sign. A Boolean option may be specified without an assignment, in which case it is taken to indicate `true`. For example, `:sh:` and `:sh=true:` are interpreted identically.

Note that if a printer has enough memory to accept a complete job and its power fails after it has accepted the print job, then the print job is lost. The `lpd` dæmon is only responsible for seeing that the printer gets the job, not that the printer is successful in printing it. Since printers are power-hungry devices, providing them with uninterruptible power supplies is rarely worthwhile.

`lp` as a printer name has a special meaning to `lpd` as the default printer to use if a default printer is not otherwise specified.

`sh` suppresses headers—the pages that announce the owners of print jobs—so suppression saves one sheet of paper per print job. If headers are needed to identify jobs, consider using `sb` (short banners) to see one line descriptions, similar to those found at the top of modern faxes. `sh` and `sb` take Boolean values.

`printcap` entries for printers that are connected to another machine on the network or that attach directly to the network are similar. Replace the entry for the device (`lp=device`) with two entries, describing the address of the machine serving the printer and the name of the print queue on the remote host. Consider this example:

```
lp|generic:\
        :sd=/var/spool/lp0:rm=192.168.64.22:rp=lp:sh:
```

`rm` could alternatively be a host name or FQDN, as long as the name can be resolved properly. Using names is preferred, because a change of IP address for a network printer or the host to which a printer is attached should not necessitate a change in the `printcap` files.

Several `printcap` fields may be used to send control signals to the printer. The most common of these set the form feed character `ff`, issue a form feed before each print job `fo`, and allow special output after the print run (`tr` sets trailing info, and `hl` prints the header page last instead of first). There are many other minor options, possibly varying between distributions. If composing a new `printcap` file, consider the printcap(5) man page a reference.

Filters

The previous `printcap` examples have not attempted to correct data sent to the printer—to present the data to the printer in the format that it expects. For instance, text printouts may stair-step, and PostScript must be handled differently than PCL.

Parsing the data and transforming it into something that the specific printer understands is the job of a filter. `printcap` entries allow several types of filters—some specific to certain kinds of input data—`of` (output filtering) and `if` (individual filtering). Although these accept options, `lpd` gathers the options from other entries in the `printcap` file, so only the name of the filtering program or script must be specified.

For example, a standard HP LaserJet expects text files to include a carriage return at the end of each line. Raw text from a UNIX file will stair-step to the right, printing off the right side of the page. This is the natural result of line feeds being applied without a balancing carriage return to bring the print-head back to the beginning of the line. The following example includes a filter to correct the problem:

```
lp|generic:\
        :sd=/var/spool/lp0:rm=192.168.64.22:rp=lp:sh:\
        :pw=80:pl=60:of=/usr/local/bin/fixcrlf
```

The Perl script /usr/local/bin/fixcrlf adds a carriage return:

```
#!/usr/bin/perl -wp
s/([^\r])$/$\r/;
```

The same script written in Tcl looks like this:

```
#!/usr/bin/tclsh
## James T. Dennis, <jimd@starshine.org>
## filter to convert line terminations into MS-DOS compatible CRLF
## sequences. (Also useful as a printcap filter).

fconfigure stdout -translation  "crlf"
while { ![ eof stdin] } {
        gets stdin line
        puts stdout $line
            }
```

The example printcap entry sets /usr/local/bin/fixcrlf as the of filter. Thus, all non-blank lines in the data file are converted into lines ending with an ASCII 13 (carriage return) followed by the standard UNIX ASCII 10 (line feed). Binary content should not be sent through this filter because it would be ruined by having bytes added to the data stream.

A more intelligent filter program only makes changes that are appropriate to the current content type. Examples include apsfilter and enscript, which only make changes that are appropriate to the type of content flowing through them to the printer. There are also filters specific to particular printer models.[3]

It can be useful to have your printer track how much it is used, by whom, how much its pages cost, and so on. With the af (accounting file) set, the filters above (except those for of) can log traffic as necessary.

Several other common file formats are used for more elaborate documents. The most common is PostScript which is used as the native page description language for many printers. PostScript is particularly dominant among the high-end printers that are preferred by most businesses.

---

3. Many useful filters can be found at http://metalab.unc.edu/pub/Linux/system/printing/ including descriptive .lsm files to help make an informed selection.

PostScript is a sophisticated programming language for describing text and graphics. It can generate very high-quality output. Most word processing and other office applications for LINUX and UNIX can generate PostScript output.

However, when using PostScript printers, we often face a problem just printing plain text. Some printers will reliably detect whether a given print job is in plain ASCII or PostScript format. However, it's often wiser to rely once again on the filtering provided by our LINUX printing subsystem.

Several popular filtering packages for LINUX convert plain ASCII into the equivalent PostScript. They prepend and append bits of PostScript code around each page of the text. (Most of their internal complexity stems from tracking those page boundaries.)

The most common such packages for LINUX are apsfilter by Andreas Klemm,[4] the public domain nenscript,[5] its GNU enscript[6] clone, and H.P. Anvin's magicfilter. These are sophisticated packages that can do quite a bit of additional filtering. Generally, a given server would use only one of these. Most of them can automatically detect the type of file being printed. This allows one to specify almost any sort of file to an lpr command, even listing compressed text, DVI and PostScript files, and various sorts of graphics.

Prior to the introduction of "magic filtering" (where the magic numbers, such as those recognized by the file command are used to automatically detect the format of data as it passes into the print queues), every user invoking the lpr command had to supply options to their command to manually specify this information. Each application that invoked lpr also had to be written and/or configured to pass these arguments to the command.

The various "magic filtering" packages we've described may seem overly complex. However, they greatly simplify the *use* of printers for non-trivial document formats. In the long run, the benefits of easier use probably translate to fewer Help Desk calls to the system administrator (despite the incumbent hassles of initially installing and configuring these systems).

Because of the flexibility of these auto-detection features, these packages are also frequently used with non-PostScript printers. They still generate PostScript output, which they then feed into Ghostscript.

Ghostscript[7] is a package that implements the PostScript programming language in its own software. Normally, a PostScript printer has a relatively powerful CPU and quite a bit of its own memory. For many years, the PostScript printers in many offices were more powerful than any of the desktop computing systems and most of the early NetWare servers. With Ghostscript, the PostScript processing is done by the host system and translated into the native page description language (control and escape sequences) of any Ghostscript-supported printer. In these cases, PostScript is used as an intermediary

4. http://www.freebsd.org/~andreas/#APSFILTER

5. http://www.im.lcs.mit.edu/~magnus/nenscript/

6. http://www.gnu.org/software/enscript/enscript.html

7. http://www.gnu.org/software/ghostscript/

format between lpr and the native printer languages. Luckily, most common printers are supported by Ghostscript.

The other two major file formats used in UNIX and LINUX are troff and DVI.

The troff and nroff formats are most commonly used for man pages. The GNU groff package provides support for printing and displaying these files. The easiest way to print *roff files with groff is to let your "magic" filter package pass them through the grops (groff to PostScript conversion) filter. There is also a grodvi filter to generate DVI formatted output from *roff sources.

DVI (device independent) files are generated by TEX, LaTEX, and other programs. There are direct DVI drivers for many printers. This dviware (as TEXnicians call it) directly supports almost as many printers as Ghostview (and the dvips command/filter allows DVI files to be easily filtered to any PostScript printer or into any Ghostview print queue).

To reduce wasted paper, one can use mpage to force plain text files to be printed with two, four, or eight pages per sheet—actually that's per side of each sheet of paper. mpage has many options and produces its output in PostScript.

There is a set of psutils that can force multi-page printing of PostScript pages. (This is actually not a difficult trick because the PostScript programming language supports scaling, rotation, and translation primitives.) It's also possible to force duplex printing (putting print on both sides of each page) even on common simplex (one-sided) printers by feeding the same paper through twice, alternately filtering odd and even numbered pages.

For previewing files (another way to reduce wasted paper and toner—or ink for your non-laser printer), there are the xdvi, ghostview, and gv programs for the X WINDOW system. gv is particularly nice for previewing a PostScript document and for selecting subsets of the pages to be printed.[8]

Remote Printing

When lpd receives a print job destined for a remote printer, it opens a connection using TCP sockets to the lpd dæmon on the host specified by the rm= field of the printcap entry.

After the remote lpd dæmon has acknowledged receipt of the complete job, the local lpd dæmon deletes the files from the spool directory. Whether the remote lpd dæmon is running on a UNIX host or a networked printer is irrelevant to the local lpd dæmon.

Administrative Commands

LINUX includes the three administrative BSD print commands. lpq lists queued print jobs that have been spooled by lpr and are still awaiting action by lpd. lprm removes print jobs from the queue. lpc performs all other administrative print duties.

---

8. The authors used these programs extensively during the production of this volume.

lpq

The lpq command checks the spool area and reports on the print jobs that it finds. The job numbers reported by lpq are required to kill a print job using lprm.

The printer to check may be specified using the -P option, as with lpr. If it is not specified, the queue for the default printer is checked—the printer defined by the PRINTER environment variable, or lp if undefined. The -l option prints the information in long form.

lprm

The lprm command removes print jobs from a queue. As with other print commands, the printer is specified using the -P option; otherwise the default printer is assumed. One or more numeric arguments specified on the command line are interpreted as job numbers. The number of a job in the print queue can be learned using the lpq command. Arguments beginning with non-numeric characters are interpreted as user ids whose jobs are to be removed from the queue.

lpc

All other administrative tasks relating to existing printers are performed by the lpc command, which takes a variety of command options. Alternatively, lpc can be invoked without options, in which case it runs interactively, accepting commands at a prompt of its own.

A system administrator can use lpc to stop and start printers and to enable and disable queues. Unfortunately, lpc suffers from a number of commands with similar names that perform similar actions. Also, it can only control the queues on the local host—no provision is made to control remote print queues.

lpc accepts a help command that is not particularly helpful. Most of the other commands take a single argument, either the name of a printer or the all keyword. (Printers should never be named all.)

The other commands are described in Table 19.1.

Because lpc is notoriously unreliable, its use is less likely to resolve a problem than is a complete restart of the printing system. The commands

```
/etc/rc.d/init.d/lpd stop
/etc/rc.d/init.d/lpd start
```

can be used. As with most other dæmons, running the command

```
tail -f /var/log/messages
```

in another window or on another virtual console before issuing these commands is a good way to see error messages from the process.

Table 19.1 **lpc commands**

abort	Kills the active spooling dæmon and disables printing on the specified printer(s).
stop	Kills the spooling dæmon after the current job completes; then disable printing on the specified printer(s).
clean	Removes any files that are not part of a complete print job from a given queue (or all of them).
disable	Prevents new printer jobs from being entered into a given queue.
down	*stops* then *disables*. Any additional arguments to this command are taken as a "message" that will be printed by lpr to explain why jobs are being rejected from this queue.
up	*starts* and *enables* a queue.
enable	Accepts new jobs into this queue. (opposite of *disable*)
start	Spools jobs from this queue out to its printer. (opposite of *stop*)
status	Provides status information for the specified printer(s).
restart	Tries to kill and start a new lpd dæmon.
topq	Moves a specific list of jobs or users to the top of the queue.

Adding a Printer

There are several steps to be taken when adding a printer:

- Physically connect the printer to the host or network.
- If the printer is connected to a host, ensure that lpd starts during the boot process.
- If the printer is connected directly to the network, configure its hostname, IP address, and so on, as indicated in the printer's documentation.
- Add an appropriate entry to the printcap file, and distribute it to the hosts that may access the printer.
- Create the spool directories, ensuring that they have appropriate ownership and permissions.

Most system administrators use printtool to create both spool directories and printcap entries. This usually works well for the spool directories, but printcap entries occasionally need to be edited manually.

Print Server Configuration

Some printers may have several different entries in the printcap. Each of those entries can describe different filters and other aspects of the printer's operation.

Samba

As noted in Chapter 17, "Network Services," Samba allows a LINUX or other UNIX system to function as a print server for Microsoft WINDOWS and WINDOWS NT clients.

Using Samba, it is also possible to configure a LINUX system to spool its print jobs off to a WINDOWS NT or Microsoft WINDOWS print server.

Full details on configuring Samba print servers are included in the `Printing.txt` file that is included with the Samba source package.

Security

Most default installations of the printing suite depend on the port number for authentication using the protocol defined in RFC1179. There are many known techniques for defeating this security mechanism—it is inherently insecure. The traditional `lpd` dæmon is typically installed `suid` `root` despite reliance on insecure authentication.

A new implementation of RFC1179 is available for LINUX. It is called LPRng[9] (next generation) and it overcomes some of the security problems of older implementations. In particular, it is not necessary for LPRng's `lpd` to be installed `suid` `root`. However, doing so allows the system to work over a wider range of less exacting configurations.

Diagnostics

In its simplest form, printing is a matter of copying data (such as plain text) to some interface (usually a parallel port). In some cases we can test the lowest layer components of a system's printer subsystem by issuing a command like

```
cat /tmp/foo > /dev/lp0
```

where `/tmp/foo` is any short text file, and `/dev/lp0` refers to the first available parallel port.

There are several possible reasons for a lack of output.

The printer might not be attached to `lp0`. It might be an old serial printer (uncommon in recent years) or a new USB device. It might simply be on `/dev/lp1` or some other parallel port. Sometimes LINUX detects its ports in a different order than do other operating systems on the same system. Thus the MS-DOS `PRN` or `LPT1` does not necessarily correspond to `lp0` under LINUX.

It is also possible that the parallel port device drivers are not compiled into the kernel, and that the modular form of them is not loaded. As discussed in Chapter 10, "Configuring and Building Kernels," LINUX device drivers can be built into the kernel (statically), or they can be compiled as separate modules. These kernel modules can be loaded "manually" (using `insmod`), semi-automatically (using `modprobe`), or "dynamically" (using the `kerneld` dæmon or the `kmod` kernel module).

Note that the parallel port interface driver was completely rewritten between the 2.0 and 2.2 kernels. This resulted in a name change in the kernel configuration files (and their `menuconfig` and `xconfig` dialogs). The LINUX kernel 2.0 configuration files referred

9. `http://www.astart.com/lprng/LPRng.html`

to these as the lp devices, whereas the 2.2 and later kernels use parport drivers. Part of this was necessary to standardize the handling of parallel ports on systems other than PCs (x86-based computers).

Of course it could be that the printer is offline (a mode in which it won't accept any print jobs). Many printers have a control panel or set of buttons that can be used to switch them among various modes, usually including at least "ready" and "offline." Some of them also have LEDs or other mode and status indicators. Many printers switch to "offline" mode automatically when they run out of paper, reach the end of their ribbons, run out of ink in their inkjet cartridges, are low on toner, experience a jam in their paper feed mechanisms, or encounter other problems.

It's also possible for the interface inside the computer to be set incorrectly or damaged. There is often a cable from the interface card to the connector on the case of the computer. Parallel ports on PCs are also subject to the same sorts of IRQ and I/O port collisions as other devices in these systems. Ethernet adapters and sound cards are notorious for introducing these sorts of conflicts. Another occasional problem relates to the cable between the system and the printer. It may be defective, or it may have the wrong "pinout" (set of wire connections between one end and the other).

When trying to set up a new printer or troubleshoot problems with LINUX printers, this is the place to start. Talk directly to the devices (/dev/lp0) with the simplest commands available (cat). Until that works, nothing else will.

If cat redirected to the appropriate /dev/lp* device node doesn't work, then try building a kernel with the appropriate lp or parport device drivers statically linked into it. This is a common technique for eliminating any possibility of problems in the dynamic kernel module loading subsystems (kerneld for 2.0 kernels or kmod for 2.2 and later kernels).

The printing subsystems for LINUX (both lpd and LPRng) are extremely sensitive to the permissions and ownership of the various directories and files that are involved with them. As we've described, these subsystems have many "moving parts," and all of them must be coordinated correctly for anything to work.

The key to diagnosing printing problems is usually to *start with the basics.* Make sure that simple files print using simple cat commands. In cases where the printer must have its input in a specific format (non-text), it is possible to bypass lpr and any magic filters that are specified in the printcap file by manually piping data through the appropriate filter and redirecting that to a temporary file. Then transfer that temporary file to the appropriate host (using FTP or whatever) and cat it directly to the appropriate device/port.

This is why we've described the conceptual underpinnings of the printing subsystem to such laborious extents. It's important to understand how the data flows from the application, through lpr to lpd, through any filters specified in the /etc/printcap, and finally to the device. One can then walk through that process manually to find out where any failure is occurring.

As with any LINUX client/server subsystem, syslog is useful for troubleshooting printing problems. Any errors reported by the lpd dæmon are likely to appear in

`/var/log/messages`. As soon as you start your troubleshooting foray, choose an otherwise ideal virtual console or open an extra `xterm` with a shell session on the print server (and any one of the affected client systems for networking problems) and issue a command like this:

```
tail -f /var/log/messages
```

Error messages and warnings can then be monitored as they occur. The `lpd` dæmon may need to be restarted with the `-l` (logging) option. Also, a copy of `strace` can be attached to the running `lpd` process using a command like

```
strace -p 132
```

where `132` is the hypothetical PID (process identification number) of the `lpd` dæmon.

Unfortunately, the error messages and warnings from `lpd` are often cryptic and usually not helpful.

The system administrator who spends the time and energy to become proficient at configuring and troubleshooting print systems will be indispensable in most organizations. When the system works, it works well and tends to be reliable. When it is broken, it is one of the most frustrating and difficult sorts of problems a system administrator will ever face.

Winprinters

By far the worst and most common cause of printer problems at this level are the infamous winprinters or Microsoft WINDOWS GDI "driven" printers.

Normal printers have their own CPUs and some memory that is used to store fonts, perform some processing, and to act as a buffer. In the mid-1990s several companies started producing printers that were driven by very low-level instructions from the host computer. This requires proprietary sets of drivers to be running on the host system, and those drivers typically have been available exclusively for Microsoft WINDOWS. These printers cannot be used by any other systems—even MS-DOS systems. Naturally, these printers are sold at a lower price than their "real" cousins, and so are very popular low-end peripherals.

Winprinters are not suitable for use on multi-user systems. Even if the drivers become available for LINUX the computing overhead on the CPU and the timing and latency requirements of these devices makes them a very poor choice for business use. The point is moot since there currently are no drivers available for them and there have been historically unfavorable relations between the Open Source programmers who have expressed an interest in developing such drivers and the manufacturers who would have to provide the requisite specifications and documentation.

In the Printing HOWTO there are notes on support for some GDI and PPA printers using special filters. There is also a section of that HOWTO with links to lists and databases of supported printers.[10]

10. `http://www.picante.com/~gtaylor/pht/printer_list.cgi`

Also refer to the Linux Hardware Compatibility HOWTO[11] for any question about hardware that's supported under Linux.

If there is any doubt regarding whether a device is a "winprinter," the best test is to boot the system under MS-DOS (or connect the device in question to a PC and boot that under MS-DOS) and try to use the old Print Scrn key, or a command like this:

```
COPY AUTOEXEC.BAT PRN
```

If this doesn't work and the printer is properly powered up and "ready," and the cable between it and the computer is good, then it's almost certainly a "winprinter." Return it for a refund and get a "real" printer.

Faxing

Most modern modems are capable of sending and receiving faxes. Using the popular mgetty package, Linux can receive faxes through such modems, and it can distinguish between incoming fax, data, and other calls. With a bit of configuration, a single modem can be configured for dial-in shell, networking, uucp, and incoming faxes—even voice and DTMF remote control (with some modems).

The mgetty package includes a sendfax program and a small suite of utilities for managing the incoming and outgoing fax queues. More sophisticated free fax management packages include Ed Casas's efax[12] and Sam Leffler's HylaFAX[13].

Many of the filtering and file format conversion issues that relate to printing recur in the management of fax systems. There is still the need to arbitrate access to the physical devices and interfaces (the printers in the one case and the modems in the other) and to detect and convert a variety of file formats into a suitable format for those devices. The "universal" format for faxes is TIFF (tagged image file format). It dominates the faxing world to a degree that is far greater than PostScript's prevalence on printers.

Unfortunately, the Linux Documentation Project doesn't offer much on the subject of faxing. There is a short Linux simple fax printer server mini-HOWTO[14] that describes a very simple configuration with efax.

For the most part, the system administrator should rely on the documentation that's included with the fax package he selects. efax is fairly small and lightweight. mgetty is a bit more complex, but most of that relates to its ability to manage other sorts of incoming data calls. HylaFAX is a large, complex professional system. However, its web site contains very extensive documentation. It is the free fax system of choice for most businesses.

There are also many utilities for viewing and printing incoming faxes. In particular, there are some very nice programs for KDE and GNOME, which offer attractive interfaces for the fax subsystem. These are changing so rapidly that the best way to find them is

---

11. http://metalab.unc.edu/LDP/HOWTO/Hardware-HOWTO.html

12. http://casas.ee.ubc.ca/efax/

13. http://www.hylafax.org/

14. http://metalab.unc.edu/LDP/HOWTO/mini/Fax-Server.html

to point your web browser at freshmeat[15] or any of the many other search engines and portal web sites that are devoted to LINUX software.

The same modem can be used for outgoing terminal emulation, PPP and/or SLIP networking, sending faxes, and supporting other protocols.

With its other networking facilities, it is relatively easy to configure a LINUX system as a gateway between various protocols—allowing us to configure magic "mailing addresses" and lpd spools to feed faxes to our modem.

We can even participate in an international Internet cooperative to spool our long distance faxes through volunteers within their dialing areas (http://www.tpc.int/). (Naturally if you make significant use of that service, you should consider configuring one of your systems to donate some of its "bandwidth" to the project).

Further Reading

The Linux Documentation Project has two HOWTO documents on printing. The Linux Printing HOWTO[16] covers the issues relating to the configuration of print servers and their client systems, and the The Linux Printing Usage HOWTO[17] describes how to use the printing system. Generally, only the system administrator would need to read the Printing HOWTO, but he might refer users to the latter.

In addition there is an excellent LPRng-HOWTO[18] that covers the installation, configuration, use, and troubleshooting of LPRng, as one would expect. However, this document also provides some of the best explanations of the BSD lpd and AT&T SYSV lpsched available.

---

15. http://www.freshmeat.net/

16. http://metalab.unc.edu/LDP/HOWTO/Printing-HOWTO.html

17. http://metalab.unc.edu/LDP/HOWTO/Printing-Usage-HOWTO.html

18. http://www.astart.com/lprng/LPRng.html

All art, and most knowledge, entails either seeing connections or making them. Until it is hooked up with what you already know, nothing can ever be learned or assimilated.

~Ralph Caplan

20

Working with NFS

THE NETWORK FILE SYSTEM is the set of building blocks for creating a filesystem hierarchy shared across the network. In LINUX, all files are visible as a single tree structure descending from the / directory, also called the root directory. The `mount` command is used to attach filesystems to this tree. NFS clients mount filesystems provided by one or more NFS servers using either the automounter or entries in `/etc/fstab` to specify the filesystems to be mounted. An NFS server provides NFS service for one or more filesystems that are locally mounted on the server. The `/etc/exports` file specifies the hierarchies to be exported and the access controls applied to them. Access to NFS mounted filesystems is transparent to users and user processes. From the user's perspective, NFS filesystems exhibit the same semantics and behavior as locally mounted filesystems.

NFS Basics

In the simplest case, there are only a few things one needs to do to use NFS. On the server, add the filesystems to be exported to the `/etc/exports` file and start NFS with the `/etc/rc.d/init.d/nfs start` command. On the client, specify in `/etc/fstab` the filesystems to be mounted and the directories where they are to be mounted. The structure of these files is documented in the exports(5) and fstab(5) man pages. There are a large number of NFS mount options, but the defaults are appropriate for most situations.

If a filesystem is needed only on a temporary basis, the mount command may be used directly, bypassing the fstab file. Filesystems mounted in this fashion will not be mounted during subsequent reboots of the client.

Managing NFS Mounts with the Automounter

At smaller sites, the system administrator typically will begin by mounting a few filesystems using the fstab method. As the number of filesystems and servers grows, this technique becomes cumbersome, and the automounter becomes the preferred mechanism for managing NFS mounts.

The automounter has several distinct advantages. It defers NFS mounts until they are actually needed, which can prevent mount storms if a large number of NFS clients reboot at the same time. It also unmounts filesystems that are not in use after a specified period of time. This often helps the administrator move data between servers while minimizing interference with processes running on client workstations. Finally, the automounter maps are reread every time a new mount request is processed, so one can make changes on-the-fly, and the new mapping will take place the next time the filesystem is mounted. However, if the automounter crashes or encounters a serious bug, the system may have to be rebooted to clear up the resulting problems. This occurs very infrequently, so it rarely presents a reason to not use the automounter.

There are two flavors of automounter available to Linux users: amd (also known as am-utils) and autofs. The amd automounter uses an older technique for managing mounts. The amd automounter cannot mount filesystems directly where the mount points indicate; instead, a symlink is placed at the mount point, which points to an alternate location where all automount mounts are made. This directory is normally specified as /a, but another location can be specified on the command line. amd has been ported to a large number of platforms and may be the best choice in heterogeneous environments that share a single set of maps. The autofs automounter is a more modern implementation and is preferred. It is implemented as a filesystem, so there are no annoying symlinks. Thus, automounted files appear exactly as indicated by the automount maps. Also, the format of the autofs maps are simpler and easier to maintain. If one chooses to support both the amd and autofs automounters, we recommend that one set of maps be generated programmatically from the other. The authors use a utility called automount2amd to generate amd style maps from autofs style maps. One automounter map is required per mount point. The format of an autofs map is as follows:

```
key options source
```

The options field can be empty. A typical home directory tree might look like this:

```
steve hard,intr server1:/vol1/&
lisa   server1:/vol1/&
bob    server2:/vol2/&
janet  server1:/vol3/&
batch hard,intr server1:/vol1/&
```

The ampersand at the end of each line is an example of map key substitution, where the key itself is substituted for the ampersand in the source string. A more complete description of the autofs map syntax can be found in the autofs(5) man page.

Managing Access Control

Another issue, particularly in larger NFS environments, is the management of access control. It is a security risk to export writable NFS filesystems such that they can be accessed by any host. However, enumerating every NFS client machine in an organization may not be tenable either. There are two mechanisms available in LINUX to specify groups of clients that may be granted NFS privileges in order to simplify access management in larger environments. The first mechanism is the use of wildcards. If all of a group's machines (and no others) reside in the same DNS domain, a wildcard may be used to specify them. For example, this /etc/exports entry would permit all systems in subdomain.domain to access /work/project2:

```
/work/project2 *.subdomain.domain
```

Where NIS is in use, netgroups may also be used to specify access lists. The following /etc/exports entry would allow all systems in the NIS netgroup myhosts access to the /work/project3 hierarchy:

```
/work/project3 @myhosts
```

User Id Mapping

A basic security mechanism (and perhaps the only effective one) built into NFS is the practice of mapping UID 0 (root) to a user-level id. Normally root is mapped to the user nobody with a value of -2 (65534). This is the default behavior unless the no_root_squash option is specified. Several additional options provide a great deal of flexibility. The anonuid and anongid options can be used to set the anonymous user id and group id, which may be helpful in maintaining compatibility with other UNIX systems. The squash_all option can be used to force all users and groups to the anonymous value. The squash_uids and squash_gids options allow a list of uids or gids to be specified for remapping, not just uid/gid 0. These options can be used to provide security by selectively removing write access to publicly shared areas. One could also use these facilities to manage access from PC/NFS, an NFS implementation for Microsoft WINDOWS operating systems. A better solution for providing file services to PCs running Microsoft WINDOWS is samba(8), which is discussed in Chapter 17, "Network Services."

NFS Server Processes

The server side of NFS is also based on ONC RPC, so the port mapper must also be running on each server. In addition, four user-level processes are required. `rpc.statd` supports the NFS lock manager, while `rpc.rquotad` deals with NFS disk quotas. The `rpc.mountd` dæmon handles NFS mount requests. Finally, `rpc.nfsd` notifies the kernel to start processing NFS file requests. These processes are started by the `/etc/rc.d/init.d/nfs` script during system boot. This script also facilitates on-the-fly administration with several useful options: `start`, `stop`, `status`, `restart`, and `reload`.

NFS and File Locking

NFS file locking is supported in the LINUX kernel[1] by means of `rpc.statd`. Note that support for locking files via NFS has always been fragile and may not stand up to the rigors of a production environment. The problems are design issues and are not likely to be resolved. If NFS file locking is needed, try it. It should work fine for simple cases and lower volumes. If problems arise, try to find another solution.

The NFS Stateless Model

A key concept behind the design of NFS is that it is (mostly) stateless. The primary benefit of this approach is that there are no complex protocols for restart and recovery. The disadvantage is that when a server crashes or becomes unavailable, processes get stuck in the disk wait state (see the ps(1) man page) and will not respond to signals. When NFS service is restored, the system calls complete normally (with the exceptions noted below) and processes resume where they left off. If the system administrators or users have been trying to kill these processes, then the signals will be received after the problem has been resolved! Once the administrator becomes familiar with this behavior model, many small tragedies can be avoided by simply taking no action until the NFS server or network problem is resolved.

Two NFS `mount` options modify this behavior. The first option is the keyword `soft`, which causes NFS file operations to return failure codes after a major timeout occurs. A major timeout occurs after `retrans` number of retries have failed. By default this number is 3, but it can be specified as a mount option. The `soft` mount option should be used with extreme caution, because it can lead to data loss. The second mount option is the keyword `intr`, which allows signals to be received during major timeouts. The `intr` option is far better because it allows the system administrator to decide whether intervention is needed, rather than automatically returning an error. These options and many others are documented in the nfs(5) man page.

If the NFS server has lost disk data or will be down for a long time, then a more aggressive approach is warranted. What is done at this point depends on the length

---

1. The 2.0 (and earlier) kernels do not support NFS file locking.

of outage that is tolerable by the user community and the contingency plans for the environment. Users whose files or filesystems are missing will experience errors due to stale NFS file handles. Stale filehandles occur when clients have files or directories open that are no longer available on the server. The server marks these file descriptors as invalid, and the processes on the client machine that refer to them fail with the ESTALE error code (see errno(3) and /usr/include/asm/errno.h for system error codes). Stale file handles may also occur if multiple clients are reading and deleting files in the same directory. Note that this aspect of NFS varies from the normal UNIX file semantics.

NFS does try to hide this side effect of its stateless design by special treatment of deleted files. File removals are translated into rename operations that create .nfsxxxxx files in the users' home directories. This allows a client program to open files, remove them (really unlink(2) them), and continue to read and write to them. When the process exits, the .nfsxxxxx files are removed. This mimics the semantics of local filesystems, where open files are reference counted by the operating system.

Debugging Techniques and Analysis Tools

A common message seen when problems occur with NFS is

```
NFS server xxx not responding, still trying
```

This occurs when the server has not responded to the client within the number of retries specified by the retrans parameter of mount. This value defaults to 3 on most systems. If this message repeats several times, the server or the network is down hard. However, if users see this message alternating with

```
NFS server xxx Ok
```

either the server is overloaded or the network is losing packets.

To diagnose an NFS server problem, start by collecting some basic information:

- Is the server still up?
- If so, does the server accept logins?
- Does rpcinfo servername indicate that the portmapper and rpc services are in order?
- Are all clients affected, or just a subset?

The first task is to determine whether the problem lies with the server or with the network. Diagnoses of NFS problems often lead directly to debugging the network. For instance, if a system administrator becomes aware that all affected NFS clients are on the same IP subnet and clients on all other subnets are fine, the focus of debugging immediately will shift to the network.

Problems encountered while mounting filesystems can generally be resolved in a straightforward fashion. If the mount hangs, use ping to verify that the server can be reached. If it is reachable, then try rpcinfo -p xxxx, where xxxx is the name of the server. The nfs and mountd ports should appear.

If the mount fails with the error message `permission denied`, then it is time to examine the `/etc/exports` file and determine if there is a problem with the mount entry in question. Log onto the server and issue the `exportfs` command. The output reflects what the server currently has exported, along with the export options. If there is an obvious problem with the exports, edit the `/etc/exports` file and reexport all the filesystems using the `exportfs -a` command. On the other hand, if the output looks good, then perhaps there is a problem with the underlying data. For example, consider the following wildcard export statement:

```
/vol1  *.subdomain.domain(rw)
```

In this example, the client mars.subdomain.domain is having a problem mounting /vol1 from this server. One possible reason is that DNS might not have the correct reverse name mapping. When the server gets the mount request it will call gethostbyaddr(3) on the IP address of the client. If the response does not match the wildcard pattern, the mount will be refused. For example, the following mappings have an error:

```
mars# nslookup mars
Server:  venus.subdomain.domain
Address:  192.24.12.164

Name:    mars.subdomain.domain
Address:  192.24.12.120

mars# nslookup 192.24.12.120

Name:    mars.domain
Address:  192.24.12.120
```

Here the reverse mapping returns a fully qualified domain name that does not match the entry in `/etc/exports`, which will cause the mount to fail. A similar error may crop up in NIS. Here is the `exports` line again, using a netgroup:

```
/vol1 @nfsclients(rw)
```

The netgroup(5) file format is subject to numerous typos. Again, verify that the IP address-to-hostname mapping is correct as in the wildcard case, and also verify that the netgroup nfsclients is correct. Look for missing line continuation characters and tab characters in inappropriate locations.

The automounter may also be a source of errors. The two common problems stem from typos in the automounter maps themselves and export permission problems, as discussed in the preceding sections. Infrequently, the automounter itself may hang or malfunction, in which case it may be killed with the `-USR2` signal and restarted. Otherwise, a reboot will be required.

Port Mapper

If the port mapper dies, all processes that register with it must also be restarted. A common tactic at this point is to reboot the system, since this often meets with more success than trying to find and restart everything.

Analysis Tools

Table 20.1 presents a set of tools frequently used to debug NFS-related problems.

Table 20.1   **NFS analysis tools**

Command	Use
ping	This utility is used to verify basic connectivity to the client or server host. If ping succeeds in reaching a host, there still may be problems with upper-layer programs.
traceroute	If ping fails, traceroute will help determine the location at which the failure occurs. traceroute is most useful in identifying network hardware and routing problems.
tcpdump	tcpdump is a network sniffing program. Its utility as a general-purpose sniffer may be negated by switched networks, but it is still a standby for packet-level debugging at each end point of a problem. Note that IP-level encryption, if present, must be disabled for tcpdump to be useful.
rpcinfo	rpcinfo can be used as a ping of the RPC network layer and can be used to view the programs registered on a system.
fuser	This shows the running processes that have a particular file descriptor open, which can be used to determine which processes are keeping a mount point busy.
lsof	Similar to fuser, but generally much more informative. A must-have for the system administrator's toolbox.
nfsstat	This utility dumps kernel statistics on NFS and can be used to collect historical data or for real-time analysis of the NFS subsystem.
nfsstone	A utility for measuring NFS performance. Available from various sites on the Internet.

Providing a Common File Hierarchy

Many NFS environments are the product of unplanned growth and layers of short-term solutions. Any business expected to grow beyond two or three servers needs a long-term plan for how the global file hierarchy will look and how it will scale. This initial plan for the NFS environment may be flawed, but it will still yield better results than actions taken in the absence of a plan.

Here are some guidelines for setting up a shared file hierarchy:

- Applications and their static data should be maintained together.
- Home directories and shared data directories should be maintained together.
- If a software development environment is present, it must be separated from the normal production environment.

Table 20.2 presents a possible hierarchy based on these guidelines.

Table 20.2   **NFS file hierarchy**

`/prod`	The directory for production applications and static data
`/prod/applix`	Third-party software installed on the server and visible to all
`/prod/data1`	Static data shared by users and applications
`/prod/scripts`	Startup scripts for all applications in production
`/dvlp`	The directory for development tools, present only on development systems
`/dvlp/nag`	Third-party libraries and include files
`/home`	The directory for home directories
`/home/fred`	Fred's home directory
`/home/salesdata`	Frequently modified data shared by the sales group
`/home/bob`	Bob's home directory. Won't get mounted on non-development machines because Bob is a developer.

More About Automounting

Often system administrators will be inclined to set up NFS servers with the filesystems mounted locally at the same point at which they are to be automounted. In the previous example, the /prod directory on a server may be exported to client systems, which will mount it at /prod. This is simple, elegant, and completely wrong. The server should have the same view of the global file hierarchy as the client.

If this server needed to mount an NFS partition at the same mount point from another NFS server, one would be forced to create a specialized automounter map for this particular server. The introduction of a specialized map for each server is complex, confusing, and unnecessary.

A better methodology is to arrange for local filesystems to be mounted at a different place. Let the automounter put everything in the correct place.

Consider the following exports file:

```
/vol1/prod hosta,hostb,hostc,this-server(no_root_squash)
```

along with this automounter map for /prod:

```
bin this-server:/vol1/&
lib this-server:/vol1/&
etc this-server:/vol1/&
```

This scenario invites the following questions: How difficult will it be to move the etc directory to the /vol2 filesystem? How difficult will it be to move the etc directory to another host?

This is certainly not the only viable model for automounting, but it is simple, effective, and well-tested. The motto for automount maps is "Stay out of your own way." And the principle of simplicity applies here as always.

Security

It is possible for anyone who gains root on any NFS client to impersonate a valid user (usually *other* than root) on any of the NFS servers that trust that system. Worse, on most LANs it is possible to impersonate any client on the LAN so that an NFS server is quite likely to trust any box that uses the "trusted" client's IP address. Consider this each time a decision is made about sharing a filesystem via NFS and about whether each filesystem needs to be shared read–write.

Further Reading

This chapter addressed most of the issues related to NFS and the automounter. For those wishing to further explore the topics discussed in this chapter, the following resources are recommended:

- *TCP Illustrated,* Volume 1 by W. Richard Stevens, published by Addison Wesley. All you need to know about IP, TCP, and UDP.
- *Managing NFS and NIS* by Hal Stern, published by O'Reilly & Associates. Although a little dated and SunOS 4.x-centric, this book is still the NFS and NIS bible.
- *Power Programming with RPC* by John Bloomer, published by O'Reilly & Associates. This book describes the nuts and bolts of programming with ONC RPC.
- The Internet RFCs. These are freely available from many sites on the Internet. The following RFCs provide a good starting point: 1014, 1050, 1094, and 1813.
- And of course, the sources for the kernel and the NFS utilities. Reading source code to understand the behavior of software requires a large investment of time, but it is the authoritative source.

Ignorance can go to the library.
Stupid needs to evolve.

21

Managing NIS

THE NETWORK INFORMATION SYSTEM (NIS) is a network service for sharing common system information. The data commonly managed by NIS include user password and group information, host-to-IP address mappings, mail aliases, and other system data that should be common among systems. By centralizing the administration of these data, NIS enables the system administrator to create a more homogeneous environment, while at the same time simplifying the task of updating and distributing these data.

NIS was created by Sun Microsystems for SunOS. It was orginally known as Yellow Pages (YP), but Sun had to change the name as a result of a lawsuit brought by British Telecom. They officially renamed YP to NIS, but they left vestiges of the YP naming conventions within the system. NIS is implemented using the ONC RPC (Open Network Computing Remote Procedure Call) networking protocol as the underlying mechanism.

Data sets in NIS are represented as one or more *maps*. NIS maps consist of key/value pairs arranged in accordance with the way various system library functions expect to access the data. For instance, two maps represent hostname information in NIS: `hosts.byname` and `hosts.byaddr`. These maps are a direct reflection of how hostnames are accessed by the system library functions `gethostbyname(3)` and `gethostbyaddr(3)`. Given a hostname, gethostbyname(3) yields an IP address, and given an IP address, gethostbyaddr(3) returns a host name.

All systems that share the same NIS database are members of the same NIS *domain*. Within a domain, a system can have one of three roles: client, slave server, or master server.

Master. The system is the source of NIS data for the domain. All updates to NIS data occur on this host.

Slave. The system maintains a copy of the master's database. It is updated when data is changed on the master.

Client. The system connects to a NIS slave or master server to obtain NIS data.

NIS domains differ significantly from DNS domains. Whereas DNS domains specify nodes on a graph, NIS domains are singular entities. There is no hierarchical relationship between two NIS domains, even if a naming convention might suggest that there is. In fact, there are no relationships between any two NIS domains at all. For example, it is possible to have two NIS domains with the names subdomain.domain.com and domain.com. These domains will not interact with each other in any way whatsoever. They could be named apple and orange and function identically.

This fact limits the scalability of NIS. Although there are those who would push NIS to its limit, it is best not to include more than approximately a thousand machines in a NIS domain.

NIS Client Processes

The NIS client process is ypbind. Since NIS is an RPC-based system, the portmap process must also be running on each client for NIS to function. The ypbind process initializes itself by parsing /etc/yp.conf for specific details on how to find a server for its given NIS domain. If the domain is not present in /etc/yp.conf or the file does not exist, the ypbind process broadcasts to find a server. The broadcast mechanism will only find NIS servers on the same IP subnet as the client. Once the client sucessfully binds to a server, it periodically checks the server and restarts the whole binding process if the NIS server becomes unavailable.

The ypbind process also expects the NIS domain name to be set. RedHat Linux systems store the NIS domain name in /etc/sysconfig/network as the variable NISDOMAIN. The domain name is set with the domainname command at system startup. This occurs in the /etc/rc.sysconfig script. Unlike many other Unix systems, merely setting the NIS domain name does not configure a Linux system to be a NIS client. The ypbind dæmon must be enabled via the chkconfig(8) command. For those who prefer a visual front end, the tksysv, ntsysv, and linuxconf programs offer graphical configuration of ypbind (and other dæmons).

NIS Server Processes

NIS provides the ypinit command to simplify the creation of slave and master servers. The ypinit -m command creates maps from the standard source files stored in the /etc directory. It is not advisable to initialize a NIS master with this command if the system administrator has placed files in an alternate directory. Instead, create the /var/yp/domainname file, where domainname refers to the NIS domain name, and create a /var/yp/ypservers file. Edit the makefile, supplying the correct values for YPSRCDIR and YPPWDDIR, and then (as root) run make in /var/yp.

Each NIS slave server runs the ypserv process, which stores the NIS maps in /var/yp/domainname. NIS slaves must be initialized with the ypinit -s *master* command, where *master* is the name or IP address of the NIS master. When new NIS slaves are created, it is vital that the host be added to the /var/yp/ypservers file. If it is not added, the new slave server will not receive updates from the master. Each NIS slave server will also normally be configured as a NIS client as well.

Many sites also configure slaves with cron jobs to poll maps from the master at periodic intervals. Sample cron jobs are distributed with LINUX in the /usr/lib/yp directory. The intent is to update the slave server in case there is a transient failure. These may not be necessary for all sites, particularly not for sites where the /var/yp/ypservers file is kept up-to-date.

A NIS master is similar to a NIS slave but has two additional roles. The first is to provide for the maintenance of NIS data, and the second is to distribute updated maps to the NIS slave servers. The master also functions identically to a slave server in that NIS clients may bind to it, because it runs the ypserv dæmon as well.

NIS Database Maintenance

The central file in the maintenance of the NIS maps is /var/yp/Makefile. The system administrator simply types make in the /var/yp directory, and the makefile is processed to update NIS. This makefile translates the text file representations of the NIS database into the NIS maps with the makedbm command. Then the maps are distributed to the slave servers with the yppush command. The yppush command itself uses the ypservers map to determine the list of slave servers, so the system administrator is strongly encouraged to keep this database current.

Another set of processes allows NIS to be updated from any host within the NIS domain. The yppasswd, ypchfn, and ypchsh commands enable users to update their password, full name, or shell respectively without the intervention of a system administrator. These commands communicate with the yppasswdd dæmon on the master and arrange for an automated edit of the password (and possibly shadow) maps, and then a push of the updated maps.

By default, the NIS master generates the NIS maps from the respective source files in the /etc directory. The NIS maps can be created from data in another location. Popular alternate locations are /var/yp/maps and /var/yp/ypfiles, but these are only conventions. If the map files are stored in an alternate location, the directory must be specified with the -D flag. As an example, /etc/init.d/yppasswdd would be modified to read /etc/init.d/yppasswdd -D /var/yp/maps.

These tools are often sufficient to manage NIS in a small environment. However, there is no mechanism to prevent two system administrators from simultaneously editing files, resulting in data loss. In larger environments where multiple system administrators manage the same NIS domain, a mechanism is needed to manage access and updates to these files. Typically, a front end is written to manage concurrent access by interacting with the Revision Control System (rcs). This technique has several advantages. First, rcs manages write access to the files simply by checking the file into and out of the rcs system. Second, previous versions of a NIS map can be recovered. Finally, rcs can provide an audit trail. This is useful when the origin or time of introduction of a map problem needs to be researched. The NIS front end program also must interact with yppasswdd to manage access to the passwd (and possibly shadow password) file.

NIS Database Distribution

As described, the NIS Makefile invokes yppush to distribute the maps to the slave servers. Optionally, the master may also run the ypxfrd dæmon. ypxfrd registers itself with the portmapper and waits for map transfer requests. When ypxfr is run on the slave servers, it checks for the presence of the ypxfrd program and will use it if present. Otherwise, the ypxfrd program makes a ypall(3) remote procedure call to transfer the map. The ypxfrd mechanism is far more efficient for a large NIS environment.

Custom NIS Data

The standard data distributed via NIS is briefly described in Table 21.1. Specific sites may choose to share some, none, or all of these maps. The best results—host independence for users and programs—are obtained by using the full suite of these maps.

In addition to the standard data, system administrators may choose to distribute additional maps via NIS. The most common of these maps are automounter maps for use by autofs(8).

However, the data distributed via NIS is not restricted to those formats understood by the existing applications. Nothing prevents a site from maintaining and distributing custom data via NIS. The applications that use these data have to be programmed to explicitly retrieve the data via NIS.

Implementation and Interoperability

The original SunOS NIS implementation used the dbm libraries, which imposed a 1000-byte limit on the size of data objects. Most UNIX vendors mimicked this implementation, including the size limitation.

Table 21.1 **Common NIS data**

Map	File Equivalent	Description
password	/etc/passwd	Correspondence of user name, uid, password, shell, and so on
group	/etc/group	Group names, gid, members, and so on
aliases	/etc/aliases	Shared mail aliases
hosts	/etc/hosts	Host data. Normally DNS obviates the need for this map.
networks	/etc/networks	Information on networks and netmasks
protocols	/etc/protocols	Data about IP protocols
services	/etc/services	Well-known ports for TCP and UDP
rpc	/etc/rpc	RPC program numbers
netgroup	/etc/netgroup	Access control lists
netids	none	Data derived from hosts, group, and passwd files. This set of data is specific to NIS.
auto.master	/etc/auto.master	The root automounter map
auto.home	/etc/auto.home	The automount map of home directories

The size limitation could be circumvented by creating nested definitions for large mail aliases and netgroups. Where such workarounds are in place, they should not be unraveled without due care.

The implementation of NIS available for LINUX (NYS)[1] is written with gdbm, which does not suffer from such data length limitations. However, when deploying NIS in a heterogeneous environment, any slave server running a dbm implementation will impose data object size limitiations. Also, do not use the ypxfrd dæmon if slave servers are not running LINUX or have a byte order different from that of the NIS master. See the ypxfrd man page for additional information.

Configuring NIS for High Availability

NIS contains critical system data, and systems configured to use NIS will hang or respond sluggishly if the NIS service becomes unavailable. Therefore, NIS should be deployed in a manner that ensures the highest possible availability. The key to providing highly available NIS is understanding how the ypbind process behaves when the server to which it has bound becomes unavailable.

The ypbind process attempts to *rebind* when a server becomes unavailable. Usually, this means that the client will broadcast to find another server on the local subnet. By

---

1. Up-to-date instructions on where to find NYS can be found in the NFS HOWTO.

deploying two NIS slave servers on every subnet, the clients will be able to rebind in the event that one server becomes unavailable.

It is common practice to modify the initialization scripts for each NIS slave to ensure that it will bind to itself. This can be done by specifying localhost as the server for the domain in /etc/yp.conf. Also, the start order of ypserv and ypbind must be altered such that the server starts first. This is done to avoid problems that can occur when both servers on a subnet are rebooted.

Debugging Techniques and Analysis Tools

By far, the most common problem with NIS occurs when slave servers become unavailable, and the clients that bind to them cannot find another server to which they can bind. Once that problem is remedied, as just described, NIS failures occur much less frequently. Nevertheless, problems can still arise.

If NIS map pushes do not seem to update all hosts, there may be a *rogue slave* server running in the domain. A rogue slave is a system that is running ypserv but is not listed in the ypservers map. To find the rogue slave, log onto a machine where the data are not current and issue the ypwhich command. This will output the name of the NIS slave to which the host is bound. Check the hostname against the ypservers map.

Another problem that can occur on NIS slaves is map corruption. This occurs most often as a result of disk-full conditions. Similar to the process just described, identify the offending slave by finding an afflicted client and issuing the ypwhich command. If the maps are corrupt due to lack of disk space, then the space must be freed and the maps transferred with ypxfr.

Finally, nothing prevents incorrect and incomplete data from being propagated via NIS. It is possible, for instance, to push out an empty map. This is especially exciting in the case of the hosts map. The system administrator can use ypcat -k to list entries with their keys. The practice of using rcs to maintain previous versions of the NIS source files is invaluable in this situation. It makes the difference between restoring service in a few minutes versus the hour or so that it may take to find the most recent backup tape from which to restore the file.

NIS Alternatives

NIS is the most common distributed database system for managing system information, and the only one currently available for LINUX. Here we note two possible alternatives: Netinfo and NIS+.

In March 1999, Apple Computer released Netinfo under an Open Source license. Apple acquired Netinfo when it purchased NeXT. Netinfo was developed by NeXT in 1988 as an improvement over Sun's NIS. At the time of this writing, the LINUX community had not yet adopted Netinfo, but it provides a viable alternative to NIS. The hierarchical domain structure of Netinfo overcomes most of the difficulties of maintaining consistent common data among NIS domains.

NIS+ was Sun's response to Netinfo. It includes some of the advancements made by Netinfo while maintaining some backward compatibility with NIS. However, both the design and the implementation were less than compelling. NIS+ is far less widely used than NIS. We mention it here because it does offer some advantages over NIS, and work on a LINUX implementation is in progress.

Further Reading

- *Managing NFS and NIS* by Hal Stern, published by O'Reilly & Associates. Although a little dated and SunOS 4.x-centric, this book is still the NFS and NIS bible.

- The Linux NIS(YP)/NYS/NIS+ HOWTO by Thorsten Kukuk. Distributed with LINUX and widely available on the Internet.

IV

Appendix

A

Emergencies

Tʜɪꜱ ᴀᴘᴘᴇɴᴅɪx ʟɪꜱᴛꜱ ꜱᴏᴍᴇ ᴏꜰ ᴛʜᴇ ᴍᴏʀᴇ ᴄᴏᴍᴍᴏɴ ᴇᴍᴇʀɢᴇɴᴄɪᴇꜱ that beset system administrators. Most of these are situations that should be considered in recovery planning. Practice recovering from these situations as part of normal training and recovery plan drills.

For each situation we describe the problem, and one or more solutions, a few brief pointers on prevention, and some references to other parts of this book that go into more detail.

Lost Root Password

This is one of the most common, and most easily remedied, problems under most forms of Uɴɪx. It's a FAQ for the comp.unix.admin newsgroup, and it appears there about once every week or two. Variations include the following:

- My /etc/passwd file is corrupt . . .
- I was editing /etc/passwd when the lights went out . . .
- We fired the last system administrator and he left without . . .

There are many ways to recover from this under Lɪɴᴜx.

Without Rebooting

If a rootshell prompt remains open on one of the virtual consoles, just use it to force a password change with the passwd command. For this purpose, a user privileged under sudo to run a shell or the passwd command as rootwould suffice. (See Chapter 8, "Enforcing Security," for more about sudo.)

Since ssh does not use /etc/passwd to authenticate when a public key is present, a host with the accompanying private key could allow access to the system. This assumes that the passphrase to the companion ssh key has not also been lost. (If the problem is a manifestation of firing the last system administrator, then change all the keys.)

Rebooting Without Root Account Access

Without these means of accessing the root account, it will be necessary to reboot the system into single-user mode, where the account can be repaired. Obviously, this will cause a service interruption, so follow your site's policy for notifying users.

Systems occasionally have a dedicated account to properly shut down a system, with a password of its own. If this password is known, or a user with sudo privileges is allowed to shut down the machine, then the system should be rebooted accordingly.

To reboot safely from the system console, just press CTRL+ALT+DELETE. If the X WINDOW system is active, it may be necessary to kill the X display server using CTRL+ALT+BACKSPACE first. Most LINUX systems are configured with a ctrlaltdel entry in their /etc/inittab. This is ordinarily set to trigger a safe shutdown. (This can usually be checked because the inittab file is normally "world readable".)

It is possible to compile a kernel with support for the Magic SysRq features to enable a forced sync, a umount, or a reboot. Although this configuration is not the default, the feature should be compiled into the 2.2 and later kernels in most servers and workstations. These features are documented in the /usr/src/linux/Documentation/sysrq.txt file (although, as with all things, this might change in future kernel sources).

The following is suitable for use with a typical PC and kernel:

1. ALT+SYSRQ+S   attempt to sync all mounted filesystems

2. ALT+SYSRQ+U   umount and remount in read-only mode

3. ALT+SYSRQ+B   reboot

If the system will not reboot using any of these "gentler" methods, then attempt to minimize the potential damage to the filesystems that can be caused by a hard reset. We recommend waiting until after hours before resorting to this. Because this last method will not dismount the filesystems cleanly, it will also entail an fsck session when the system comes back up. On a server with lots of disk space, this fsck may take hours.

Disable as many processes as possible to reduce the system's need to access the disk. Then, try to sync the filesystems. (Normal user accounts can usually do this. There might be a *sync* pseudo-user account in the passwd file with no password.) Then press the Reset button.

Booting into Single-User Mode

If the system has an *alternative root filesystem* and the root password to *that* is remembered, then boot from it.

Otherwise, interrupt the normal boot sequence to force it into single-user mode. The usual way to do this is to use the single option, which is a normal request to start the system in single user mode. (Details may differ for systems that aren't using LILO. See the documentation if another bootloader is in use.) For example, at the LILO: prompt, type

```
LILO: linux single
```

to load the linux stanza and pass its copy of init the single option.

However, some installations will have an sulogin command configured to require the root password for single-user access. This feature, if enabled, is enforced by init. (The directive to use sulogin is in the inittab file.) Stop LILO's boot sequence with SCROLL LOCK and add the parameter init=/bin/sh to the boot/command line. This bypasses the normal execution of init and just starts a shell. For example:

```
LILO: linux init=/bin/sh
```

In both of these examples the stanza name is linux. Pressing the Tab key at the LILO: prompt displays a list of available boot stanzas.

It's also possible that the system has passwords set in the /etc/lilo.conf file. These can be used to require a password to boot a particular configuration (to prevent casual users from getting into a particular MS-DOS or LINUX configuration on a personal workstation, and so on). Or the configuration can be marked as "restricted"—meaning that they can be booted without a password—but a password is required to override any of the boot parameters for that stanza. (See the lilo(8) man page for details on these options.)

Luckily, these password and restriction features of LILO are rarely used. They are not always needed for systems in a data center. However, if lack of a password prevents the system from being booted into single-user mode, move to "Plan B"—the boot diskette.

Boot into a shell using a boot/rescue diskette or a bootable CD-ROM, such as an installation CD-ROM. The toolkit of every LINUX system administrator should include a boot/root floppy (or possibly several). See Chapter 3, "Recovery Planning," for a full discussion on creating and maintaining rescue diskettes.[1]

Repairing the Root Password

Having successfully booted into a shell, mount the root filesystem (if you booted from a rescue floppy or CD-ROM) or remount it in read-write mode (if you used the single or init=/sbin/sh options).

---

1. The very popular "Tom's boot/root diskette" may be found at http://www.toms.net/rb/ along with pointers to other rescue floppy and "micro-LINUX" distributions.

To remount the root filesystem in read–write mode, use a command like this one (taking care not to include a space after the comma):

```
mount -o remount,rw /
```

If the layout of the system is unfamiliar, use the command fdisk -l to see a list of the available partition entries. Often, root will be the first *linux native* filesystem listed, although multiple root filesystems may be available. Keep mounting filesystems until a suitable /etc directory is found.

It should now be possible to edit the /etc/passwd *or* /etc/shadow file (whichever contains passwords on the system) to remove the root password.

Note that sometimes it is more difficult to remove the password than it is to simply change it to a known value.

If PAM or another authentication suite is configured to prevent null passwords, copy a hash corresponding to a known password. It does not matter whether the hash is copied from the same passwd file or from a different machine. The root account will now have the known password.

If the hard disk's root filesystem is mounted on /mnt (the system was booted from a rescue floppy), the chroot command can be used to allow commands like passwd to work on the intended copies of the passwd file. For example:

```
cd /mnt && usr/sbin/chroot . /bin/sh
```

The example uses a relative path to the chroot command in case the rescue floppy doesn't have a copy.

Once the root filesystem has been mounted in read-write mode, and chroot has made it the root for the shell process if necessary, the passwd command can be used to force a new password. This should also force any synchronized authentication methods and/or db hash files to be updated correctly.

If the /etc/passwd file is corrupted, copy a new one from a similarly configured machine or from the rescue disk. Failing that, there may be an undamaged /etc/passwd, vi recovery file, or other backup file available on the system. Note that these may be missing some recent entries. Examining the /etc/shadow (and on systems that are configured with one group per user, /etc/group) may indicate which users are missing. On NIS clients, there should be very few local user entries.

Remember that the vipw command makes a backup of the passwd file during editing sessions. If the vipw package is properly installed, then the /etc/rc.d/* scripts should check for the existence of a vipw backup and automatically restore it. These backup files should exist only while the vipw command is active, so the boot scripts are coded to presume that their existence indicates that a system was rebooted during a vipw edit session. Proper use of vipw can make it very unlikely that the /etc/passwd file will get corrupted in normal system operation.

I've Been Hacked!

This is a large and complex issue. Security incident response procedures are discussed in Chapter 8, "Enforcing Security."

If there is reason to believe that the root account has been compromised in any way (any SUID root program or root dæmon or other process has been subverted and forced to run any exploit code), then disconnect the system and do a fresh install of the operating system from write-protected sources such as a CD-ROM or the build server. (This is why the profiles on a build server should always be hardware-jumpered read-only, except when the server is disconnected from the network.) Then perform a restoration of the data and configuration files. Do not restore binaries from tape, because they may be compromised (contain trojan horses).

Configuration files that need to be changed from the image on the CD-ROM or build server should be carefully checked by hand. Many configuration files have scripting and programming statements or other features that can be used by an attacker to regain access. It is best to maintain copies of all configuration files after they were initially created and after all vetted changes. These copies should be kept on write-protected media (and printed copies should be kept on file as well).

Boot Troubles

Because there are several software components involved in the boot process, there are several distinct stages during which booting problems can occur. We discuss each separately.

Can't Boot Kernel: Stops in LILO

To prevent most LILO problems, always rerun /sbin/lilo when building new kernels or changing drives. Be sure to note any error messages or warnings that this command generates as it updates the MBR and its boot map files. Use the verbose option, -v, to see more detailed information as it runs.

Keep a boot floppy handy for situations where the LILO maps are damaged (including cases where a DOS boot sector virus has trashed the partition table and MBR). Backing up the MBR and partition table of a drive is described in the section "Damaged, Infected, or Corrupt MBR."

Keep a copy of /etc/lilo.conf, these MBR backups, and other small but crucial system files like this on the rescue diskettes. Be sure to keep them up-to-date as the system changes.

LILO Prints an Endless Stream of 010101010 . . .

The kernel/boot image is on a device that is not BIOS-accessible.

LILO Stops at L

LILO's first stage loader couldn't find the second stage loader. It also returns a disk error code, documented in `/usr/doc/packages/lilo`. Usually this means the BIOS and LILO did not agree on the disk geometry. If the BIOS supports LBA, enable it, set the `linear` directive to `/etc/lilo.conf`—or, if it's already in there, unset the directive—and run `/sbin/lilo` before rebooting.

Make sure that the boot partition is small enough to fit within BIOS-accessible cylinder boundaries.

LILO Stops at LI

LILO's second stage loader was found but is not loading correctly. This may also be disk geometry troubles or `/boot/boot.b` and your system map disagree—run `/sbin/lilo` and reboot.

LILO Stops at LIL?

The second stage loader was not at the address it found. Treat the same as LI.

LILO Stops at LIL

The second stage loader cannot read the system map file. Rerun `/sbin/lilo`.

LILO Stops at LIL-

The descriptor table found in the system map is bad—the `/boot/map` file is broken or was moved.

Problems Running `/sbin/lilo`

Various problems may arise while running the `lilo` command. Note that the `-v` option produces verbosity.

Invalid LILO Signature

An error message like

```
First boot sector doesn't have a valid LILO signature
```

typically indicates a corrupt `/boot/boot.b` file (or the `install=` directive in the `/etc/lilo.conf` file points to something that `lilo` thinks is not a bootloader).

An error message like

```
Chain loader doesn't have a valid LILO signature
```

typically indicates a corrupt `/boot/chain.b` file (or one of the `loader=` directives in the `/etc/lilo.conf` file points to something that `lilo` thinks is not a chain loader).

The boot.b secondary bootloader code is called by the MBR's primary bootloader code to boot a LINUX kernel image. All of the image= directives in a lilo.conf file implicitly use this loader.

The chain.b bootloader code is used to boot MS-DOS and other similar operating systems. It is used by other= stanzas in the lilo.conf file. Individual bootloaders can be set for specific stanzas using the LILO loader= directive. Read the *LILO Technical Guide* and the Multiboot Using LILO mini-HOWTO[2] and LILO mini-HOWTO[3] for details.

BIOS Drive May Not Be Accessible

Warnings like this:

```
Warning: BIOS drive 0x82 may not be accessible
```

suggest that some stanzas in lilo.conf refer to images and operating systems on a hard drive other than one of the first two on the primary controller. In other words, lilo.conf is configured to boot from a third drive, or a drive on a secondary controller.

Some PC BIOSs, and most SCSI extension firmware, can access some devices beyond the first two on the primary controllers. This is very system-specific.

This message from lilo is just a warning. No harm should come from trying it on a newly installed system. Indeed, so long as a rescue floppy is handy, it is a harmless experiment.

If the system cannot boot into that image try rearranging the partitions to fit the bootable partitions on either of the first two drives. Failing that, consider using an alternative bootloader such as LOADLIN.EXE or the GNU GRUB package.

Damaged, Infected, or Corrupt MBR

If the master boot record or partition table (which is actually part of the MBR) becomes damaged, it can be repaired. Usually this will not have affected any of the filesystems or data on the rest of the drive.

Foresight can make this job trivially easy. In other words, as with so many other emergencies, an ounce of preparation *before* the damage occurs is worth many pounds of heroic recovery effort.

The MBR and partition table can be backed up with a command like this:

```
dd if=/dev/hda of=$BACKUP_FILE bs=512 count=1
```

where /dev/hda is a reference to the first IDE hard disk (alternatively, use /dev/sda for the first SCSI hard disk) and $BACKUP_FILE is an arbitrary filename like /root /hda-mbr.bin. Here the block size is 512 bytes. We set the *count* to just one, because we want only one sector. If we failed to do that, then the dd command would default to dumping the contents of the entire disk.

---

2. http://metalab.unc.edu/LDP/HOWTO/mini/Multiboot-with-LILO.html

3. http://metalab.unc.edu/LDP/HOWTO/mini/LILO.html

Note that only the primary hard disk (/dev/hda or /dev/sda) has boot code in its MBR. All other drives will have partition tables, but the rest of the MBR will usually be empty. Nevertheless, it's a good idea to save information about all of the partition tables on a system. (They only take a half kilobyte each.)

To restore a drive's master boot record, simply reverse the if and of parameters in the dd command, so it looks like this:

```
dd of=/dev/hda if=$BACKUP_FILE bs=512 count=1
```

A partition table can also be rebuilt by hand using information previously saved or printed with the fdisk -l command. It's a good idea to store one copy of this inside the system case during initial setup (where it can't easily be misplaced as the system gets moved around).

Naturally, it is likely that the system will not be booting properly when it is time to use these spare boot record copies. So you'll want to copy these .bin files to your rescue diskettes (boot/root) and to any alternative root filesystem on each system.

These files are in binary. They are not human-readable and should not be edited with normal text editors. So, it's also handy to store a human-readable list of all of the partitions, with their sizes and locations. This is easily accomplished using these commands:

```
fdisk -l
mount
```

Just redirect the output into any convenient file. Also put the output from these commands in the /etc/README files. The mount command provides a mapping between the partitions and their mount points, indicating what should be on each partition.

Even without any of these rescue dump files, it's possible to restore a partition table by hand. Restoring the boot loader code to an MBR is very easy if using LILO—just run the /sbin/lilo command with a proper /etc/lilo.conf (the usual working one will suffice).

Restoring the partition table (the last 66 bytes of the MBR for every drive) can be a bit trickier if you don't know what partitions were there.

If you can find the beginning of any ext2 filesystem, then use fdisk to create a partition starting at that point and extending to the end of the drive. If the partition is larger than the filsystem, the LINUX filesystem drivers and e2fsprogs utilities will not complain and will not access the regions of that partition that lie beyond the end of the filesystem. You can then fsck and mount that filesystem and find out its size. From there you can go back into fdisk and adjust the size to the next cylinder boundary beyond the end of the real filesystem's size (use a calculator to figure out where it should end). From there, try to find the next filesystem (starting a new partition just beyond the one that you think you've recovered). Try stepping past the first recovered filesystem one cylinder at a time until fsck reports success finding a filesystem.

A few iterations of this, and perhaps some quality time with one of the Linux hex editors like beav or ext2ed, may save the risk and effort of rebuilding the system and restoring the data from backup tapes.

Newly Installed Kernel Doesn't Boot

Run /sbin/lilo to update the loader map. This contains information about the exact location on disk of files that the LILO boot manager will need to access before the system is completely launched, including the kernel (or, in the case of multiple /etc/lilo.conf stanzas, each of the kernels). This problem can happen when an automatic upgrade process does everything except run /sbin/lilo.

If the message Loading Kernel . . . appears before it hangs, then there is probably a bug in the kernel. Perhaps an included driver is probing an I/O port or reserved memory addresses that is incompatible with the system. Try the reserve= and exclude= kernel parameters (passed via the LILO prompt or on the LOADLIN.EXE command line, and so on) to isolate and work around such problems.

New Kernel Gets "kernel too big" Message

When compiling a kernel, the make target zlilo will create a compressed kernel. On newer systems, the target bzlilo will use a compression method called *bzip2*. If bzlilo was used and this message is still generated, upgrade the version of LILO.

It's also possible to build a smaller kernel—especially by moving more of the desired features into loadable modules. However, for servers, particularly for exposed servers where security is a concern, consider avoiding the use of loadable modules. See Chapter 10, "Configuring and Building Kernels," for more about creating modules, and Chapter 8, "Enforcing Security," for some of the dangers.

Kernel Gives "VFS Panic: unable to mount root"

The Linux kernel has a default root filesystem address (device and partition) encoded into it. This can be changed with the rdev command. There are a number of other defaults that are "hard wired" into a kernel at compile time—and various options to rdev can be used to patch new values into such a kernel without requiring a recompilation.

If the root filesystem value is wrong for a given kernel, then this message may appear as it tries to mount its root filesystem. Possibly the kernel was built on a different machine, built wrong, or the machine has been changed "underneath" it (such as upgraded from IDE to SCSI).

The easy solution is to override the kernel default while booting by providing it with the root= parameter (from the LILO boot loader's prompt) or on the LOADLIN.EXE command line.

After successfully booting, run the rdev command and/or modify the /etc/lilo.conf file to add an append=''root=...'' directive to it.

Kernel Reports "Unable to open an initial console"

This error appears if the root filesystem doesn't have a valid set of device nodes. Perhaps a filesystem other than a "root" filesystem has been mounted on the root mount point, or perhaps someone or something has trashed the /dev directory and/or some of its nodes.

Boot from a rescue disk, and then use it to mount and repair either the /etc/fstab file (if the partition chosen for / is not a root device) or the /dev directory and its nodes. The MAKEDEV script (located in the /dev directory of most LINUX distributions) can be used to make the requisite nodes. The mknod command can be used to perform these operations selectively.

Note that new versions of the LINUX kernel support a mechanism for dynamically managing tty nodes through a dispatcher (called ptmx, which uses the /dev/pts filesystem). The user space support for these is supplied by GNU glibc 2.0 and later. Binaries linked against older libraries may fail if there are no available static tty nodes available, and new binaries may fail if there is a problem with the ptmx system (such as the kernel was compiled without UNIX98 PTY support).

Screen Flickers and No Login Prompt Appears

If you have a workstation configured to use xdm or the GNOME program gdm (to provide a graphical login screen to X WINDOW) and you see the system trying repeatedly to start X and dying before it can display anything, check the mouse.

First, make sure that the mouse is plugged in. Then bring the system up manually in single-user mode and check that the appropriate device node exists under the /dev directory. Then try the gpm command to ensure that the system can "see" the mouse—or manually run startx to see the errors displayed. Check the configuration files upon which X WINDOW depends (/etc/XF86Config and /etc/X11/XF86Config are most common) to determine whether the mouse for which it is searching is the one that you found.

Another common problem in getting the X WINDOW system started correctly is ensuring it is correctly accessing its font directory, or its font server is working and accessible.

If all of that works, then you may have a problem with your xdm configuration.

"Unable to load interpreter"

If you get this repeatedly and immediately after boot, it is likely that /etc/ld.so.cache is corrupt and that you need to run the ldconfig command to rebuild it, by reading

/etc/ld.so.conf for library paths. Library paths can also be controlled with the LD_LIBRARY_PATH environment variable.

Otherwise, you might have exhausted all of your memory (real and virtual) or all your process table entries (which are needed to launch new tasks). Find a way to kill some processes from a running task in order to recover the resource, and then see what you can do to prevent a recurrance. If it was a runaway process, find its creator and have the program corrected.

In a worst-case scenario, you may have to follow procedures for shutting down a system without access, as described in the "Lost Root Password," section.

Extra swap files, as well as partitions can be used, so it is possible to add swap to a system without adding drives; see the mkswap man page for details. Note that adding more physical memory is always preferable to adding swap space.

Program Launch Troubles

This section provides information about the problems that may arise while attempting to launch programs. It is organized by the manifestation, with an explanation of the causes and solutions.

Only root Can Execute Commands

Check the permissions on the /etc/ld.* files.

Damaged or Accidentally Removed Shared Libraries

It is generally necessary to reboot the system with a rescue floppy in cases where the shared libraries have been damaged or libc.so has been removed.

Unfortunately, in the search for efficiency, many modern LINUX systems depend so completely on shared libraries that normal utilities cannot work without them. Very few binaries on a modern LINUX (or other UNIX) system are "statically linked." This is why the File Hierarchy Standard (FHS) requires that there be a /lib directory directly under the root directory and recommends that this should *not* be a mount point.

Large installations that develop their own system profiles should consider statically linked utilities if reliability is more important than performance.

Because programs used during the shutdown process also may be dynamically linked, the best chance for rebooting safely is the Magic SysRq method described in "Lost Root Password"—if it is available on your system (see page 252).

Otherwise, you will need to boot from a rescue disk or alternative root partition and then restore access to the correct shared libraries. If the affected system has a chroot environment prepared by the use of hardlinks, the files still reside on the disk and can easily be assigned their expected links again.

Be sure to run the ldconfig command any time shared libraries have been added, updated, replaced, or restored. Of course, /etc/ld.so.conf may need to be updated.

Can't Load Shared Library Even Though It Exists

This is likely to be caused by a more subtle bit of corruption to the /etc/ld.so.cache file. Just go to a root shell and issue the ldconfig command.

If that doesn't work, and you're running an RPM system, use the rpm -qf command to find out which package the library "belongs to" and then use the rpm -V command to verify the status of all files in that package.

"getcwd: cannot access parent directories"

This happens when a process (usually a privileged or SUID program) has changed into a restricted-access directory and then dropped its privileges or performed a setuid() or setgid() to an identity that has no access to one of the parents along the path to the current working directory.

Typically, the unprivileged child process cannot use ls or even echo * in this situation. The child process cannot open any files or directories below the current one—though it can access those outside of the current tree (subject to its normal permissions descriptions).

One of the most likely causes of this is to have a directory leading to the home directories set to the wrong permissions for some of the users listed thereunder. For example, if you set /home to be mode 771 (world executable, but not world readable), then you would get these error messages on every bash operation until you changed to the root directory and then back to your home directory.

You still wouldn't be able to do an ls of the /home directory (to see the names of the home directories of other users, for example). But, at that point the internal bash command would have the cwd (current working directory) in its environment.

Trying to execute the /bin/pwd command (the external binary form of the pwd command that's built in to bash and many other UNIX shells) will result in an error message like this:

```
/bin/pwd: cannot get current directory: Permission denied
```

Note that the permissions on each and every directory, from the root of the file tree to the cwd, are considered in the access control. Normally, a user cannot access a file unless he or she can traverse (execute) each of the components of the path to the directory containing a link to the inode that describes that file. A user would, therefore, need to have access to some SUID or SGID program (or some process running under one of the permitted user or group identities) in order to access such a file, even if it was owned by the user.

This facet of the UNIX permissions mechanism is rarely useful. Usually, it is a bug to have any file owned by a user who has no access to any of the links that lead to it.

Programs Are "dumping core" (SIG 11)

When a program reports that it has "dumped core" in response to a SIG 11 it means that the program attempted to execute an instruction that referred to memory that was not allocated to it.

This is usually the result of a progamming error. Often this is caused by attempts to dereference (use) an unitialized pointer, or as a result of errors in pointer arithmetic. (Pointers are variables that refer to memory addresses.)

However, when you see these errors coming from widely-used and well-tested programs, while performing common operations with well-known data sets, it usually indicates a hardware failure.

For example, if an attempt to recompile the LINUX kernel using the current version of gcc fails with a message like "internal compiler error" and references to SIG 11, an it's probably caused by unreliable memory.

Unfortunately, it can be very difficult to detect intermittent failures in modern RAM chips. The systems are so complex that simple sequential "write, read, verify" passes over memory may fail to exorcise real hardware problems. Compiling kernels, and compressing, decompressing, and archiving/de-archiving large data sets can access memory in ways that simple diagnostic software will not.

For more information on this topic, visit the "SIG 11 Problem" page: http://www.bitwizard.nl/sig11

Try running the software on other systems (if it fails on one and not others, it is very likely to be a hardware problem).

If it is hardware, then to fix the problem, try installing new or different memory into the affected system. If it seems to stem from bugs in the software, have a programmer fix them (or report them to the software's maintainers). (Try linking the program with Electric Fence and running that. Electric Fence is a bounds-checking version of the standard memory allocation functions.)

root's $PATH Is "Broken"

This may seem like a silly thing to call an "emergency," but some people are completely at a loss as to how to fix it. They should know that you can start any program by providing the full file specification to it—and that /bin/vi will get them into an editor. Also, a command like

```
export PATH=/sbin:/bin:/usr/sbin:/usr/bin
```

should suffice to get root back up and running (for one session). Naturally, the /etc/profile and/or /etc/csh.cshrc (for csh) files will need to be edited. These are the files used by most common shells to configure their initial PATH settings. Usually the PATH settings will be reasonable, even in the absence of these files. There are defaults compiled into the init program, which is the ultimate ancestor of all UNIX processes.

It is possible, even wise, to create a ~/bin directory and create hard or symbolic links from there to every file that root should ever use. Then root's PATH can consist of just that directory and nothing else.

While this may seem like a silly exercise, it may help discourage operators from unnecessarily running programs as root might even prevent some trojan horsess from working (some odd case where an attack can add a new file to one of the bin directories while they can't overwrite any of the files thereunder).

Maximum Files Opened

The kernel has a built-in limit, rarely reached in normal use, for how many files may be open at one time. Encountering this limit may lead to file open failures even when no other user is in contention for use of the file.

echo new values into /proc/sys/kernel/file-max and into /proc/sys/kernel/inode-max

For example:

```
inode-max = 32768
file-max = 5120

NR_TASKS = 1024 (linux/tasks.h)
MAX_TASKS_PER_USER = 128 (linux/tasks.h)
```

Also ensure that at least 256 ptys/tty nodes exist under the /dev directory; many distributions create only 64 (use the mknod or the /dev/MAKEDEV script).

Some settings related to the maximum number of tasks (system-wide) and maximum number of tasks per user can only be modified at compile time in the kernel sources. Look in /usr/src/linux/include/linux/tasks.h for those settings.

Filesystem Troubles

This section details various difficulties that a filesystem can present.

"unable to find swap-space signature" Error

Use fdisk to double-check the partition types of the entries in the partition table. After verifying that the partition type settings are correct, use the mkswap command.

It is possible to cause this error while trying to share swap space with other operating systems. See the Linux+FreeBSD HOWTO for an example of proper swap sharing.

Filesystem Out of Space

If a user exhausts the space available from a filesystem, you should find that root has a bit of "breathing room" courtesy of the reserved-space feature of Unix filesystems.

The tune2fs command can be used to set the user and group IDs permitted to use this reserved space.

The obvious answer is to remove some files. Another is to move (migrate) some to another volume (leaving behind a symlink). Compressing some with gzip or another compression utility is another option.

If root, or a process running with root privilege, overruns a disk volume, the disk's reserve space will be filled. For this reason, root mail should always be sent to an unprivileged account, and logfile rotation should be carefully maintained.

To proactively protect filesystems from reaching capacity, install some form of monitoring system like SLEW (a copy of which can be found in Chapter 4, "Capacity Planning").

Filesystem Out of Inodes

It is possible to run out of inodes even when ample space remains on a filesystem. Note that this is much different than the kernel's maximum number of concurrently open inodes (which is tunable via an entry under /proc/sys/kernel). If a filesystem has a large number of files that are less than 4KB, it might run out of inodes before running out of disk space.

The ratio of inodes to data blocks on any given filesystem is set at the time that filesystem is created (using the -i option to mke2fs). News spool partitions always require a greater proportion of inodes.

Suspected Bad Cluster/Sector

Some filesystem formats such as ext2 support the -c option on their fsck and/or mkfs commands. LINUX supports different versions of the fsck and mkfs commands for each of the filesystems that it supports.

For example, you'd use e2fsck -c to detect bad blocks and add them to the appropriate filesystem list (the bad blocks inode).

System Locked Up During mount Command

Occasionally a process can get into a "wedged" state—for example, if the mount command is used on a filesystem whose underlying device is not reponding. This can also happen if SCSI devices are detached or powered off from an active SCSI chain.

It should still be possible to switch to other virtual consoles, log in via serial terminals, via telnet, and so on. A ps command will show these "wedged" processes in the D state. A kill -9 has no effect (since signal processing is disabled while the process is processing a kernel system call—in *kernel* mode).

The most common case is when an NFS server becomes unavailable. See the section "System Inaccessible Via Network."

A system can safely run for many hours in this state, as long as no attempt is made to use the wedged processes or device (mount, for instance). Most services can be cleanly shut down and the system safely rebooted.

Become root and read /etc/mtab to see the presently mounted filesystems. Don't use the mount command itself, as it might also wedge. Arrange for a manual orderly shutdown by closing processes in their expected fashion. The scripts in the init.d directory can be given the stop parameter to aid in this. Avoid running scripts that will access mount and (if applicable) the affected network. This will significantly reduce the number of open files that may be affected by the hard reboot that will have to be performed.

Routinely enabling the Magic SysRq option when building kernels is recommended for situations like this. (See page 252 for details.)

Accidental File Deletion

When all links and file handles to a file have been removed, and the last open descriptor to the file is closed, then the space occupied by the file is available to be garbage-collected by the filesystem driver. Once it has been cleared by that driver, it is gone.

There's an Undelete HOWTO, and there are several LINUX hex editors. The ext2ed and debugfs commands are a couple of tools that are suitable for this sort of problem.

However, these heroics are best avoided by regular backups, data replication/mirroring, version control, good computing practices, and proper enforcement of security policy.

Accidental Recursive chown/chmod of ..

One of the more subtle ways of breaking a system is by using a command like this:

```
chown -r foo .*
```

A system can also be ruined by incomplete parameters during a restore command. In such cases, correctly reissuing the command (if you haven't ruined your own access to that program, or to chmod) will correct the problem.

However, recursive use of commands like chown and rmr -fr .* is *very bad* and should be issued by root with *extreme* caution. Here are some possible methods to prevent shell globbing from giving you extra trouble.

One solution is to do a ls -ald .* to find an alternative glob. For example, ./.[a-z]* is usually sufficient. In some shells you can use a "negated character class" of the form: ./.[^.]* to get everything that doesn't start with two dots. In other cases you might use ./.??* to get all links that start with a dot followed by at least two other characters.

In yet other cases it may be fastest to use ls -A (almost all)—which does not recurse—but it is not safe for use in a pipe as some directory names may be malformed.

In many cases it is safest to use a find ... -type f ... | while read command to explicitly recurse over the intended files.

Also with chown there is the danger posed by symlinks. It is probably wise to routinely use the -h (--no-dereference) flag when using chown as root.

With chmod there are similar concerns regarding symlinks. chmod will dereference those symlinks named on its command line (possibly as a result of glob expansion)—but *not* those that it encounters as a result of recursing through a directory. This is another of those annoying subtleties that can nail the unwary system administrator.

With the find command, you need to add the -follow option to follow symlinks—or just add a trailing slash to the symlink/dirs as you list them on the command line (forcing the shell to glob on a "zero length" trailing filename).

As they say, "The devil's in the details."

Corrupted Data

fsck has excellent filesystem recovery abilities, and it can in fact have additional success when run multiple times against a dismounted filesystem. Recovered inode blocks will be placed under the reserved directory lost+found, which exists on every physical partition of type ext2. With a good hex or binary viewer, you may be able to recover some valuable data even though the original file remains unrecoverable.

If you are willing to put the energy into such recovery heroics, consider using the dd command to make a sector-by-sector copy of the entire disk partition to another device, a tape drive, or through a network pipe into an rsh or ssh process that redirects its output to a remove device, partition or file (if your remote filesystem supports files that are large enough to hold your whole partition; remember the 2GB file size limit on 32-bit versions of LINUX!).

Network Problems

This section covers problems that are manifest when a network is misconfigured, misused, or broken.

NIS Access Does Not Work

Change /etc/nsswitch.conf to read

        passwd: compat

for the +/− entries in /etc/passwd to work.

Note that libc5 uses /etc/host.conf rather than /etc/nsswitch.conf and that a copy of libc5 with NIS support compiled in must be installed.

Also see Chapter 21, "Managing NIS."

System Inaccessible Via Network

Check the TCP wrapper settings, as controlled by /etc/hosts.allow and /etc/hosts.deny. Any other aspects of firewalling that apply to the machine should also be checked, and then the Ethernet or other network cable and the points at which it is connected to the network.

It is also possible that a nearby system is flooding the network connection. If this is the case, several neighbors on the segment will be affected erratically, and it will not matter what kind of service they are attempting to access.

TCP Traffic Is Slow and/or Erratic

There may be filtering problems with ICMP packets at either end or along the way. To block ICMP pings, you want to do something more like this:

```
/sbin/ipfwadm -Ia accept -P icmp -S 0/0 0 3 11 12
/sbin/ipfwadm -Ia deny   -P icmp
```

Note that type 3 is for path-MTU discovery!

This will accept these ICMP types:

0. echo reply so that outbound ping works

3. destination unreachable (for path-MTU discovery and to eliminate wait for a timeout on references to nonexistent hosts and domains)

11. TTL exceeded for traceroute

12. IP parameter error (very rare)

Input Problems

Many applications have the ability to select their own valid keystrokes for special functions. If a complex application such as emacs is the only program having difficulty, its own commands can be used to provide more comfortable keybindings.

One place to look for detailed information on this is: http://www.ibbnet.nl/~anne/keyboard.html

Key on Physical Keyboard Has Failed

In most circumstances the best repair for this is to replace the keyboard. However, if you're looking here, it's an emergency, in which case the loadkeys command can be used to work around the problem on text consoles, and xmodmap within X WINDOW sessions by remapping the needed keystroke to another key.

Backspace Key Does Not Backspace; Generates Control Character Instead

Check that the TERM variable is set correctly for the console you are using. Be sure to export the variable so subshells and child programs have it in their environment.

If that's correct, issue the command sttyerase and press the Backspace key to generate its control code as a second parameter. The Backspace key will now be assigned the deletion function, taking it away from whatever other key had the function (often DELETE or the now-rare RUB OUT). If this is the only terminal you use, you can commit the change to your shell login scripts.

Text Is All Displayed as Binary Characters

The most common cause for this is using a simple utility like more or cat to read a binary file. The terminal has accepted one or more of the binary codes as a command to change to a symbolic font; you now cannot easily read whatever it was trying to say. Even though you cannot see it, type the command reset and your terminal characteristics should be restored to their defaults. In rare circumstances, you may need to run the command twice.

System Does Not Appear to Respond to My Keystrokes

If the system is still accessible via the network, then restore the system default keymap by running loadkeys-d. Also, check that the keyboard is properly plugged in, and in the case of PS/2 keyboards, not accidentally swapped with the mouse port.

A Particular Key Does Not Work with X

The utility xmodmap allows a great deal of flexibility in remapping keys on the keyboard. Its man page contains useful examples, such as swapping CTRL and CAPS LOCK keys, and so on. However, it only affects an X WINDOW session. You will need to use loadkeys in order to affect text console sessions.

X Does Not Appear to Respond to My Keystrokes or Mouse

There's an X call to grab input focus; if the application or task that has done this gets wedged, the window manager may get confused, after which all input is ignored as far as the user can tell. (It sometimes happens that it is gathering in the input queue, then the wedged process times out or dies, and all the "ignored" input happens at once.)

You may or may not be able to get CTRL-ALT-Fx working to escape to another virtual console.

ssh or telnet in, or otherwise get text mode access, and then kill-9 the offending task (you can usually tell which one it is in a ps listing). If this does not suffice, continue up the process tree (psf will display processes by family). In the worst cases, killing the X server will force init to garbage-collect its resources and the discoverable resources of its children—there's no chance to save editor sessions, or for any programs to close open files. Usually, killing the broken task and its parent is sufficient.

Miscellaneous

Of course, some emergencies don't fit nicely into catagories. We list some of them here.

Parallel Device Not Working

In this modern age, there may be lots of parallel devices: ZIPs, printers, scanners, CDs, and goodness knows what else. With the PARPORT team working on good drivers, it is *occasionally* possible to get multiple devices working on the port. But in older systems, or for sanity's sake, you might load parallel device drivers as modules. If so, use `lsmod` to check that the loaded module is the correct one for the device you are attempting to access.

It is highly advised that you do not attempt to unload modules while filesystems dependent on those devices are mounted. The kernel should resist your attempt because the drivers are in use.

System Seems Slow with More Than 64MB of RAM

This was a problem in some chipset designs that were unable to cache memory beyond 64MB addresses. The problem is exacerbated under LINUX because LINUX allocates memory from the upper address downward.

Some suggestions: replace the motherboard or use an `mem=` kernel setting to limit the memory usage.

System Seems Unstable with More RAM

Some systems (chipsets/BIOSs) use a small chunk of address space at the "top" of their memory. Try using a kernel setting of `mem=`*xxx*`M` , where *xxx* is 1 megabyte less than the actual installed amount of RAM.

More Places to Look for Aid

The Tips HOWTO and the "2 Cent Tips" column in issues of the *Linux Gazette*[4] contain many nuggets of helpful information. Many software packages also maintain a README or ERRATA file mentioning the most commonly discovered errors. See also the "Further Reading" sections in many of the chapters.

There are a few companies that offer professional technical support for LINUX systems. (At least one of the authors can personally recommend Linuxcare Inc.[5].)

The Answer Guy at the *Linux Gazette* has been known to help people with technical questions.

---

4. `http://www.linuxgazette.com`

5. `http://www.linuxcare.com`

Glossary

A system administrator should understand these terms in order to make sense of most of this book and of technical discussions in NetNews, on mailing lists, in man pages, and in many other contexts.

Some terminology involves relatively obscure and subtle nuances (see the definitions of *NAT* and *IP masquerading* for example). System administrators must understand these differences and often need to be very precise in their use of terms. At the same time, they should be relatively forgiving and flexible in their interpretations of these terms, especially with users.

For different, possibly conflicting, definitions of the terms listed, look at the FOLDOC (Free OnLine Dictionary Of Computing) at `http://wombat.doc.ic.ac.uk/foldoc/`, "The Linux Glossary Project" at `http://glossary.linux-support.net/`, or "Internet User's Glossary" (RFC 1983) at `http://www.cis.ohio-state.edu/htbin/rfc/rfc1983.html`.

For a broader, often humorous, compendium of terms and an extensive commentary on hacker culture in general, see the Jargon File at

> `http://www.tuxedo.org/~esr/jargon`[1]

a.out The default filename for a newly compiled program. More commonly (in contrast with *ELF*) it refers to the COFF binary executable file format, which was a predecessor to ELF. LINUX kernels can (optionally) be compiled to support (either directly or via a loadable module) binaries in this old format. Although it is a bit of a misnomer, these COFF binaries are said to be "in a.out format."

access control lists Lists of users and access modes that are checked by an operating system during attempts to access filesystem objects (such as files, directories, devices, processes, sockets, and so on). As of kernel version 2.2, LINUX does not support ACLs on its filesystems or other objects—there are projects to add support for them.

> See also *meta-data*.

ACL See *access control lists*.

archive A file containing other files. Most forms of archive also contain *meta-data* about each of the files that they contain. There are many types of archives; these are usually named after the command that is principally used to create, access, and manipulate

---

1. esr is Eric S. Raymond (see Foreword).

them. Thus, the tar command creates tar files, various implementations of the zip and unzip commands work with zip files, and cpio creates cpio archives.

Conventionally, an archive file is given a *filename extension* to indicate its format. However, there is no prevailing convention regarding the naming of cpio and dump achives, since these are rarely (almost never) used to publicly distribute files.

artistic license   The alternative copyright license provided for the Perl programming language. It gives the copyright holder artistic control and provides a fairly generous set of rights for users to copy, modify, and make derivative works, but still encourages making them freely available. Contrast *BSD license*, *GPL*, *NPL*.

attributes   (ext2fs-specific) In addition to standard UNIX *permissions*, the *ext2* filesystem contains additional attributes, which the filesystem driver honors whenever the file is accessed or modified. Attributes are set or unset by the chattr command, and it is common to refer to the bits set by name. The "immutable" bit is particularly popular among system administrators trying to protect critical files from unintentional destruction by an inattentive root.

background   A task that is detached from a console (even a *virtual console*) but continues to operate, usually at a slower pace than a *foreground* task. See also *job control*.

backup (or archive)   Both of these terms are used as nouns and verbs. The noun form refers to any copy of a set of files (and the *meta-data* associated with them) on some form of removable media. The verb form refers to any process of creating such a set. An extra copy of a set of files to non-removable storage is sometimes referred to as "a backup"—but this is more precisely referred to as "replication" or "mirroring" or (in some cases) "version control."

big red switch   (colloquial) The reset button or the power switch. This is the last-resort method to reboot a system when it is "hung" (unresponsive).

binaries   Executable binary files. This is a jargon term that distinguishes between compiled programs and scripts, or sources. Although any non-text file can be referred to as a *"binary"* file, the term typically refers to *executable* non-text files. Non-executable non-text files are usually referred to as raw data, or by the name of their file format (such as GIF files or Laserjet data). The term may also be used in the context of *archives* to refer to archives containing binaries rather than source code.

binary   As an adjective, this is used to distinguish between text files and non-text files (those containing non-printable characters generally not suitable for editing with normal text editors, such as NULs). As a noun, singular of *binaries*.

BIOS   Basic Input Output System. This is the *firmware* of a *PC*. Originally, the BIOS provided routines that were used by MS-DOS to access the hardware. This allowed some details of the hardware to be abstracted into a set of "BIOS calls" (similar to

Unix/Linux "system calls") so that the same version of MS-DOS (or other early PC operating systems) could be run on different systems without modification.

However, in modern computing (using any 32-bit operating system, such as Linux, or even Windows NT) the BIOS is used as a boot loader and as a means to set the *CMOS* values.

A BIOS is necessarily written in *real mode*, while most modern operating systems require the processor to be in *protected mode*. The memory addressing of these modes is incompatible, though a 386 or later processor in the family can emulate "real mode" to create a "virtual 8086." Thus, the "toolkit" of BIOS calls is no longer useful during the normal operation of the system.

The PC BIOS also provides a set of "power-on self tests" (also known as *POST*).

block special   As opposed to *character special* file, *named pipes*, or normal files, block special files are direct links to devices that work with many bytes at a time. That is, a "block" of several bytes, or perhaps a very large block of bytes, could be either written or read, depending on other features of the device it is linked to. These are also sometimes referred to as *block devices*.

blocked I/O   When a process is writing to or reading from any file device, it can do so through "blocking" I/O system calls. These prevent that process from receiving any CPU cycles from the scheduler until more input is available or the output buffers have been flushed. This allows a program to work very efficiently.

Proper use of non-blocking system calls can allow an interactive program to appear very responsive. Knowing when to use blocking versus non-blocking calls is a desired skill for a Unix programmer.

BogoMIPS   MIPS (Millions of Instructions Per Second) are a common measure of a CPU's efficiency. BogoMIPS are a measure of speed—but not really MIPS, so it's "bogus." This calculation is made during the kernel's initialization so that it can use the resulting timing for certain short "busy loops" (as for delays during some I/O operations).

See the BogoMIPS-HOWTO for details.

BSD license   The copyright license found in prducts related to the Berkeley distribution of Unix-like operating systems. It grants very generous rights to copy, distribute, and modify for free and commercial derivatives as long as all changes to the code give the original authors their due credit. Because of its consideration to corporate needs, products under the BSD license are popular for businesses to use as a base for internal projects from which they might eventually profit. Contrast *GPL*, *artistic license*, *NPL*.

byte   Although this usually refers to an 8-bit data structure, it technically refers to the smallest directly addressable unit on a given computing architecture. For most architectures this is 8 bits. However, the term *octet* is more precise.

character special   As opposed to *block special* files, *named pipes*, or normal files, character special files are direct links to devices that can work with only one character at a time. These are also sometimes referred to as *character devices*.

CISC   Complex Instruction Set Computer. A CPU (microprocessor) design philosophy that emphasizes the availability of a large, complex, and "powerful" machine language instruction set. The Intel line of CPUs from the 8080 through the Pentium are generally categorized as CISC designs.

   Most other modern processors are considered to be *RISC* designs.

CMOS   Complementary Metal Oxide Semiconductor. With the introduction of the PC AT (80286-based systems), a real-time clock and battery backup system was added to the systems. These chips used CMOS technology because of its low voltage requirements and low current draw. (A watch battery can run a CMOS chip for years—most digital watches use CMOS.)

   This chip had extra registers for alternative timers, alarms, and so on. So the designers of these PCs used the extra registers to store system configuration data. These values are accessed via a firmware Setup program.

   See also *PRAM, nvram, firmware, BIOS, PC.*

COFF   Common Object File Format. A format for executable binary files (also called *a.out* files) that is obsolete in modern UNIX and LINUX systems. Most programs compiled on modern LINUX systems are in *ELF* (Executable Linking Format).

   A LINUX kernel can concurrently support a.out, ELF, and other executable file formats (such as *Java* byte-compiled files). These must be enabled by compile-time options, or (with a *kernel* configured to support them) via *loadable modules*.

compiled   A program that is written and then read by a compiler and transformed into platform-specific code. Although such code can be made portable, it must be recompiled on each new hardware platform, creating *binaries* that cannot be interchanged between platforms. Contrast *interpreted*.

data set   A list of the files and directory trees that are to be included in a given backup plan. A "comprehensive" data set would include "all" of the files on a system. (This actually should still exclude the "pseudo-files" under /proc and usually some others). Other data sets can be more specific. One might have a "system" data set consisting solely of system files (*binaries*, libraries, man pages, icons, and other resources). This could include a system's configuration files or specify those in a different data set. One might have "user data sets" for all users or "application data sets" for specific applications, such as databases.

   The key point is that a data set is a description of *what* is to be backed up. One can usually restore subsets of a backup. So, it is common to back up the "comprehensive" data set. However, as previously noted, that is not always desirable or feasible.

device nodes   An entry in the filesystem that provides access to a kernel device driver. Usually located in /dev and created as either a *block special* or *character special* file.

differential   This is a backup of all files in a given *data set* that have been added or modified since the last *full backup*. To restore a data set, one restores the most recent *"level zero"* and the most recent differential. A differential includes all the same files as the previous differential. So, in the typical case, the size of each differential will grow until the next "level zero" is performed.

directory   A special file containing a list of links to files. A link consists of a file's name and an *inode* entry. Some filesystems can store small *symlinks* in a directory, while in other cases the destination of the symlink must be stored in data as allocated by an inode.

distributions   Since LINUX is a free system, anyone who chooses to do so can combine it with other free software, package it, build products around it, and sell or give them away.

The term "distribution" is commonly used to describe any collection of software built around LINUX and other free software. Some distributions also include some non-free components.

LINUX distributions can be roughly divided into two categories There are "general-purpose" distributions such as Red Hat, Debian, and Slackware, and there are special-purpose "mini-distributions" such as Tom's Root/Boot, LRP (LINUX Router Project), and others.

dynamically linked   A program with some of its function calls and variables stored in *shared libraries*. Such programs are common, and gain a number of extra benefits, such as reduced memory overhead, by using functions stored elsewhere on the system. Contrast *statically linked*.

ELF   Executable Linking Format. The most common file format for storing executable binaries under LINUX. All recent kernels should be configured and compiled with support for running ELF files. Some may also (optionally) be configured with support for a.out (*COFF*) and *Java* byte-compiled files.

The differences among executable file formats should not be confused with the distinction between *dynamically* versus *statically* linked files.

endless loop   See *loop, endless*.

error messages   Usually text or other output from a program when it fails, to indicate the nature of its failure. Contrast with an *exit code*, which may not indicate an error.

exit code   When a typical shell script or function is finished, it may return an integer between 0 and 255 to let its parent process know whether it was successful (or, in some cases, what sort of action it performed). If it does not, the exit code is usually set to 0.

ext2, ext2fs ext was an extended filesystem improving on what was available to *minix*. ext2 has further extensions to enhance its performance, both in terms of CPU effort and speedy response time.

FIFO As opposed to *character special*, *block special*, or normal files, FIFO (First In First Out) queues allow for the filesystem to aid in using a program's output where an ordinary file is expected. For example, the `finger` dæmon accesses an ordinary file called `.plan`, but if it were a FIFO, a program would dynamically generate responses to any read request on that file. (It would be wise for such a program to use *blocked I/O*.) These are also sometimes referred to as *named pipes*.

file An operating system abstraction through which streams of data are accessed and stored. Under LINUX and other UNIX operating systems, these may take the form of *regular files* or may be represented as *device nodes* (*block special* or *character special* files), *FIFOs*, *sockets*, and so on. A *directory* is a special type of file that contains *links* (between any *filename* and its associated *inode*).

There are a couple of notable exceptions to the UNIX paradigm that "everything is a file." Network interfaces cannot normally be accessed as files. Also, the contents of a tape can contain multiple files. Any of these files can be an *archive* containing other files. Normally, the `mt` command is required to access any but the first member of a tape. See Chapter 12, "Backups" for more about tapes and their use.

file "holes" See *sparse files*.

filename Another term for a *hard link* or *symlink*. LINUX filenames on *ext2* filesystems can be quite long and can contain almost any characters (except slashes and NUL characters). However, there are other constraints imposed on filenames on other filesystem types.

filename extension If it exists, the characters after the last dot (.) in a filename. It is often used to indicate the type of data the file contains. To be sure, use the `file` program to actually read a small amount of the data in order to report what kind it is.

firmware Programs stored in *ROM*, usually a special set of routines in a computer that allows it to load any operating system (to load the system software). This also may include some diagnostics and utilities for manipulating the *nvram* or *CMOS* values that are used to store system-specific data (such as the boot device and some administrative preferences about the boot process).

On a *PC*, the firmware is referred to as the *BIOS*. Other systems may have much different firmware. Most of the recent workstations, including the Apple PowerPC, have some derivative of *Open Firmware*—which is a specification for a *Forth*-like programming language. This allows vendors to create platform-independent initialization and boot drivers for most hardware.

foreground A task that is attached to a console (even a *virtual console*) and operates interactively, as opposed to a *background* task. See also *job control*.

Forth A stack-oriented "threaded" programming language, noted for is extensibility and compact implementation footprint. Sun Microsystems used a byte-compiled form of Forth called FCODE, which eventually evolved into the Open Firmware specification (IEEE1275).

free When people in the *Open Source* community speak of free software, they could mean one of several things: the software is "freely available" to be downloaded and is easily given to anyone; it is "free for personal use," but a fee applies for businesses; individuals and businesses can review the source code, and need not fear if the software becomes unsupported by its originator. The first definition is most similar to the usage in "free beer," and the last is most similar to the usage in "free speech" and is especially favored by advocates of and participants in the *GNU* project.

full backup This is probably the most confusing term that relates to the subject of backups. It often does not mean "comprehensive." A "full" backup does not necessarily mean that it includes every file on a whole system. "Full" in those cases means "including all files in a given data set without regard to previous backups." In other words, it means "not incremental" and not "differential."

It is better to use the phrase "level zero" to make this distinction.

General Public License See *GPL*.

glibc The GNU C libraries version 2.x is used/ported to LINUX as their libc version 6. The term glibc refers to those libraries. Earlier versions of the LINUX C libraries were more derivative from the earlier GNU libraries.

glibc adds support for the shadow password suite, modular naming services (including NIS, and allowing for the development of LDAP, NDS, Hesiod, and other directory and name services modules), and internationalization (NLS).

Most modern LINUX general-purpose distributions are based on glibc 2.x (LINUX libc version 6.x). However, some special-purpose distributions, particularly the floppy-based "micro distributions," still use earlier versions of libc because of its smaller size and "lighter" weight.

GNU GNU's Not Unix, a recursive acronym. This is the name of a project started by Richard M. Stallman, and is the mission of the FSF (Free Software Foundation), which he founded.

The purpose of the GNU project is to produce a "*free*" operating system and suite of applications, utilities, and programming tools that are non–proprietary and unencumbered. Some might say they are encumbered by the *GPL*, the license that protects their free code from becoming proprietary.

When Linus Torvalds created and released his first version of LINUX, it was no accident that there was a large body of freely available utilities, and programming tools that could be incorporated into LINUX *distributions*—it benefitted from the ongoing and as yet incomplete GNU project's interim development.

It is the goal of the GNU project to have their own kernel. Several beta releases of this (the *HURD*) have been released and are available for interested programmers. For more information on the GNU project, see their web site: `http://www.gnu.org`

GPL   To protect the GNU project software from being appropriated for proprietary use by hardware vendors, the Free Software Foundation releases their software under the *GPL* or *General Public License*. This license specifies that derivative works that are made publicly available or sold must also be provided under a similar license. This is the governing license of most, but not all, of the source code in a common LINUX distribution. Contrast *BSD license, artistic license, NPL*.

hard link   An entry in a directory that contains a pointer directly to the *inode* bearing the file's *meta-data* (which then points to the data blocks containing the file's contents). All non-*symlink* directory entries are "hard links."

Note that the initial creation of a file using `open()` (with the O_CREAT flag) creates one hard link. The `ln` command (without the `-s` option) creates additional hard links. There is no concept of "primary" or "secondary" hard links in UNIX. All hard links to a given inode are essentially equivalent.

Also note that a directory name is a hard link to a directory inode. The "dot" (.) in that directory and the "dot-dot" (..) entries in all of its subdirectories are all hard links to that same inode. Thus, the link count on any directory should be equal to the number of subdirectories it contains plus two (one for the parent's directory, the only "normal name" to it) and one for the directory's own "dot" entry.

This is why the `ln` command specifically does not allow the creation of hard links to directories under LINUX. Note that `root` is permitted to create a directory hard link under some other forms of UNIX (but not under LINUX using the GNU `ln` command).

hung   Refers to an unresponsive system. If there appears to be no productive activity from a system, it is referred to as being "hung."

This diagnosis should not be taken lightly by the LINUX system administrator. It is relatively rare for LINUX systems to hang. Getting no response from the console (X WINDOW or text mode) is not conclusive. Generally, it is useful to also attempt to `ping` the system and access it remotely (via `telnet`, `ssh`, or any interactive network login service that should be available on that system). It can also be useful to enable `getty` on a serial port so that a *null modem* and a laptop, or other terminal or terminal emulator, can be connected.

When a system is diagnosed as hung, it should be rebooted using the *big red switch*. After the system comes back up (and completes its `fsck` filesystem checks), then the system administrator should inspect the logs in `/var/log/messages` and make a note in any manually maintained system logs (that is, /etc/README) in an effort to understand why the hang occurred.

HURD   Quoted from the HURD homepage at http://www.gnu.org/software/hurd/hurd.html: According to Thomas Bushnell, BSG, the primary architect of the Hurd, "'Hurd' stands for 'Hird of Unix-Replacing Daemons'. And, then, 'Hird' stands for 'Hurd of Interfaces Representing Depth.' We have here, to my knowledge, the first software to be named by a pair of mutually recursive acronyms."

The HURD is a set of servers designed to run under the MACH microkernel; it forms the basis of the FSF GNU kernel.

IETF   Internet Engineering Task Force. A body that adopts and recommends standards for the protocols (and some APIs) used on the Internet. They have no legal or regulatory power and operate by "rough consensus and running code." Their recommendations are published in the form of RFCs (and STD and FYI documents). See the home page at http://www.ietf.org

incremental   This is a backup of all files within a given *data set* that have changed since the last backup (of any kind). Thus, a *"level zero"* backup on Monday, then an incremental on Tuesday would only get the files that are new or changed since Monday. An incremental on Wednesday will only include files that were added or changed since Tuesday. This is in contrast to a *differential*.

The important thing to remember about incremental backups is the restore order. You must restore the "level zero" first, and then restore each and every incremental in the same sequence as they were created in order to fully restore the data set.

infinite loop   See *endless loop*.

init   The initial process launched by the kernel, of which all other userspace processes are children. The normal program serving in this role, /sbin/init, contains garbage collection routines to "reap" abandoned resources and parentless processes. When a system is properly shut down, init is the last program to close, after freeing all resources used by other programs. Under special conditions, it is possible to use another program as the initial process.

inode   Analogous to DOS "clusters," inodes are the basic units of stored data on an ext2 filesystem.

Internet Engineering Task Force   See *IETF*.

interpreted   A program that is written, then executed immediately when read by a shell or other interpreter. Also called scripts, such programs run more slowly than *compiled* code but are generally simpler to create, and very portable among operating systems and hardware.

IP masquerading   A particular form of network address translation (*NAT*), where activity from any number of IP addresses is forced to appear to another network (typically the Internet) as originating from a single host.

> This is done by rewriting the source IP address and source port fields of outgoing packets and the destination IP address and port fields of incoming response packets.

> It is essentially a form of transport layer transparent proxying. In some other forms of NAT (one-to-one), only the address fields are rewritten, and the IP port numbers are left unchanged.

> IP masquerading has been a standard compile-time option in LINUX kernels since version 1.2. There are also modules to handle some protocols (such as FTP, IRC, and those used by RealAudio and CUSeeMe). Those protocols require special support due to their own quirks. For example, FTP requires coordination between TCP connections, for data and control.

> IP masquerading should not be confused with the use of "masquerading" in sendmail. The sendmail option rewrites mail headers, the apparent "From" addresses, in order to implement mail routing policies. IP masquerading operates on TCP/IP *packets* at a much different level in the communications protocols.

> It should also not be confused with "IP aliases" (also known as "subinterfacing"), which is a process of assigning multiple IP addresses to a single interface. IP aliasing does not involve any rewriting of packets, as these are routed through an interface— it merely affects which packets are accepted by a given interface and routed through it. There are also mail aliases, shell command aliases, and many other uses of that term.

> See also *NAT*.

ISO9660   The most common filesystem found on CD-ROMs.

Java   Once called "Oak," Java is a language designed to be easily portable to new hardware architectures. *Interpreted* with a properly implemented Java *virtual machine*, or *compiled* with a compatible Java language compiler, these programs could run on any hardware. That dream has not yet been perfectly realized, but the rise of the World Wide Web and the use of Java "applets" through browsers has brought it much closer to that goal. It is also seeing increased use in "NC" machines—single-purpose networked computers.

jiffie   This is a small counter (32-bit on x86 systems) that is incremented on every context switch and used by some device drivers for very small timing loops. It "wraps around" (overflows the 32 bits and returns to a value of 0) after about 490 days of uptime.

> There has been concern that these jiffie overflows might cause problems for some LINUX device drivers. However, no significant problems have occurred on the many systems that have been up for more than 500 days—nor on those where

a premature jiffie overflow was patched into a kernel for testing. Any such bugs should be easy to fix as they are discovered.

job control   A mechanism for temporarily suspending interactive or *foreground* tasks, allowing tasks to operate in the *background*, and the ability to launch multiple processes from one console session. LINUX and most modern forms of UNIX support job control. This requires support in the kernel and the shell.

Job control involves the way that a shell or other process responds to certain *signals* (asynchronous events that are dispatched to routines, "*signal handlers*" in a program). Most terminal drivers are set to intercept CTRL/Z by dispatching a SIGSUSP (suspend) to the currently connected process. The shell bg and fg commands also dispatch signals to these jobs.

Job control is one of the oldest forms of task switching and multitasking available under UNIX. Other common techiques are to use a windowing system such as X WINDOW or the screen program.

kernel   UNIX systems have a kernel that provides a system call interface (including ioctl() I/O device control interface) to allow programs to interface indirectly with hardware and files.

The LINUX kernel provides filesystems, networking support for TCP/IP and other protocols, and device drivers. These can be built into a kernel "statically" or as *loadable modules*.

See Chapter 10, "Configuring and Building Kernels," for more about the LINUX kernel.

level zero   Although this term should only apply to dump and restore (programs that support numbered backup levels), it is common to implement backup levels using tar and cpio scripts and to refer to them in the terms analogous to those used by dump.

See also *full backup*.

libc   The fundamental library that implements most of the functions of the C programming language. On most systems, this is installed both as a shared library (libc.so.*) and as an archive of object files (/usr/lib/libc.a).

The *shared libraries* (or "shared object files") allow a relatively small program to dynamically load the library and call functions therein. This is analogous to the DLLs (*dynamically linked* libraries) on some other platforms.

The static archives are suitable for static linking—the objects archived into a *.a file are copied into a program's binary file during its compilation.

There are many libraries on a typical LINUX or UNIX system. libc is the set that is linked into most C programs (anything with a #include <stdio.h> and/or a #include <stdlib.h> in its sources).

LINUX can support the concurrent installation of many versions and revisions of any given shared library. The most widespread major versions of libc are libc4, libc5, and libc6. libc6 is also known as *glibc2*. G<small>NU</small> libc version 2. libc5 was a heavily modified and adapted version of G<small>NU</small> libc version 1.x, while L<small>INUX</small> libc6 is an unmodified port of G<small>NU</small> libc version 2.x.

Thus, many L<small>INUX</small> users use the term "libc" to refer to libc5.n and "glibc" to refer to L<small>INUX</small> libc6.n.

library Files containing groups of functions for other programs to use. *Shared libraries* are most common, but this also includes static libraries—created by using the `ar` command on a list of `.o` object files. Static libraries are suitable for creating *statically linked binaries*.

LILO LInux LOader. This package consists of a small chunk of boot loader code (which can be placed on a floppy, into a system's *master boot record* or *MBR*, or into the *superblock* of any L<small>INUX</small> *ext2* filesystem) and the `/sbin/lilo` command. This command reads a configuration file (`/etc/lilo.conf` by default), builds or "links" the boot loader and map files, and installs the needed code into the specified disk blocks.

LILO is probably the single most confusing element of a basic L<small>INUX</small> installation. It helps to think of the `/sbin/lilo` command as a "compiler" and the `/etc/lilo.conf` file as a program that gets compiled, with a set of "directives" that affect where the resulting code gets put. The primary boot block is outside of the filesystems on parts of the disk that cannot be accessed using filenames. Since L<small>INUX</small> does not dictate the type of filesystem on which its kernel must reside, the LILO boot loader must be able to load the kernel independent of filesystems.

This is why `/sbin/lilo` builds a "map" file and links it into the boot loader. The map contains a set of low-level addresses, which point at each fragment of each kernel that is referenced by the loader. Thus, it can find and load the kernels as long as they have not been moved. After the kernel is loaded, it can find and mount the filesystems to manage them.

A consequence of this is that the L<small>INUX</small> kernel is not required to be located on its root filesystem, nor even on the same disk. In fact, it is possible to have a L<small>INUX</small> system with no copy of the kernel to be found on any of its filesystems.

There are a number of alternatives to LILO for loading L<small>INUX</small>. A popular one is `LOADLIN.EXE`, which can load L<small>INUX</small> from MS-DOS.

link Either a *hard link* or a *symlink*—an entry in a directory that has a *filename* and points either directly or indirectly to an *inode*.

link count U<small>NIX</small> filesystems keep link counters in each *inode*. They count the number of *hard links* that point to it. When the link count is zero (and the number of open file descriptors in the kernel is zero), then the filesystem driver will clear the inode and return to the free list all data blocks to which the inode referred.

It is not usually possible to recover files whose link count has become zero. In other words, `rm` *is forever!*

Linux Presumably the reason you picked up this book. Once upon a time (about August 1991), a Helsinki student posted in comp.os.minix that he was building a new *Minix*-like operating system around a kernel optimized for his 386. It was a few years before Linus Torvalds became famous for the UNIX-like operating system that grew from those humble beginnings. Pronounced like "Linus" with an "x" on the end—in Finnish, so with a short "i." This is somewhere between LIH-nucks, rhyming with "Tux," the mascot penguin drawn by Larry Ewing using the GIMP, and LIH-noocks, rhyming with "books." Most people do just fine with LIH-nicks, rhyming with Minix.

loadable modules Portions of *kernel* code that have been compiled separately and that can be loaded during normal operation using `modprobe` or `insmod`.

LOADLIN.EXE An MS-DOS program that can load a LINUX kernel (stored as a normal MS-DOS file) and pass it parameters. This is an alternative to *LILO*. It is particularly handy for running LINUX on a laptop or from some hard drive that the system's *BIOS* cannot access.

  `LOADLIN.EXE` (and some similar programs for the WINDOWS NT console) can be used to launch LINUX as though it were an MS-DOS program. It should be noted that this is a "one way trip," and that the only way back to MS-DOS (or WINDOWS 95 or 98 or WINDOWS NT) is by shutting down LINUX and rebooting.

loop, endless See *loop, infinite*.

loop, infinite See *infinite loop*.

media set One or more tapes, diskettes, or other backup media that comprise a single backup. One normally maintains several media sets per data set. Providing alternatives addresses the risks of loss, theft, or corruption of any one set. It also allows the system administrator to restore older versions of a file in cases where the damage to the file was not immediately detected, and the corrupted version of the file was backed up.

meta-data Information about a file rather than in it. This includes the file's *ownership*, *permissions*, *link count*, time stamps (*mtime*, *ctime*, *atime*), and any filesystem-dependent *attributes* and/or *ACLs* that might apply to a given file. In some contexts, the filename or *inode* can be considered to be an element of its meta-data. However, it is usually convenient to think of the meta-data as the contents of the *inode*, and the data as the contents of the blocks (to which the inode points) that are the contents of the file.

Minix A minimal microkernel operating system with a vaguely UNIX-like set of programming and user interfaces. It was written by Andrew S. Tannenbaum for use by students of computer science. The source code is included in the textbook *Operating Systems: Design and Implementation*.

Minix was notable in that it could run on systems as primitive (by today's standards) as the XT. Popular among students, its use was limited to educational and academic purposes.

The early versions of LINUX were built under Minix, and LINUX still supports the Minix filesystem, which is usually used for floppy diskettes.

Andrew S. Tannenbaum is one of the world's most respected professors of computer science—his textbook is used worldwide. He and Linus engaged in a legendary "flamewar" (actually, more of a reasoned debate) on USENET's alt.os.minix newsgroup in the early days of LINUX development (before the creation of the alt.os.linux newsgroups, which was before the creation of the comp.os.linux.* *hierarchy* of newsgroups).

Professor Tannenbaum also wrote an interesting distributed operating system called Amoeba, which employs features like process migration and a capabilities security model to make a cluster of workstations act as a single virtual computer.

named pipe   See *FIFO*.

NAT   Network Address Translation. A feature of several routers and implementations of TCP/IP routing software, NAT allows for IP addresses in packets to be "translated" (patched or changed) while the packet is being routed.

The most common form of NAT is *IP masquerading*. This allows a whole network of systems to connect to the Internet or some other network while apparently only using a single IP address (as far as "outside" network systems are concerned). IP masquerading has been supported in the standard LINUX kernels for several years.

There are other forms of network address translation, including one-to-one mapping and one-to-many, used for some load sharing and/or load balancing applications.

There are experimental LINUX kernel patches to support some of these other forms of NAT. For details see: http://www.rustcorp.com/linux

network address translation   See *NAT* and/or *IP masquerading*.

NPL   The Netscape Public License, developed when Netscape released the source for their browser software under the Mozilla project. It provides special rights regarding commercial use of the code to the copyright holder and has some requirements regarding the requirement that modifications to the source code be provided to the copyright holder, but otherwise encourages free use and availability. Contrast *BSD license*, *GPL*, *artistic license*.

nvram   Non-Volatile Random Access Memory. This is a small chunk of RAM or set of registers (like the PC *CMOS* values) that stores some boot parameters for a system. This term is generally used on RISC workstations. On Macintosh 68000 and PowerPC systems, this is referred to as *PRAM*.

octet 8 bits. On most architectures, this is equivalent to a byte. It is most commonly used in reference to the representation of IPv4 addresses, as four octets in decimal form.

Open Firmware Open Firmware support is recommended as part of the *PCI* specification. Defined by the IEEE 1275 specification, this is used as the firmware for many UNIX and *RISC* workstations and for Apple PowerPC systems. It is derived from Sun FCode, which is a byte-compiled form of *Forth*.

More information on Open Firmware can be found at `http://www.openfirmware.org`.

Open Source Programs for which the original source code is available, for which relatively permissive opportunities to modify the code and share the results with others exist, and which are developed by people whose primary means of communication with each other is the Internet.

There was a trademark application filed on this term, which was rejected. At any rate, the capitalized form should be applied only to programs, applications, hardware, or other things that meet the "Open Source Definition," which can be found at `http://www.opensource.org/osd.html`.

See also *free*. Many of the issues raised there continue to be hotly debated whenever there is some question of whether a particular project is really open source, with or without capital letters.

Of particular interest might be `http://www.gnu.org/philosophy/words-to-avoid.html`

OpenBIOS A project to create an *Open Source*, modular, and advanced *BIOS* for PCs.

OTP One-Time Passwords. Any system of one-time passwords. The most common OTP methods for UNIX and LINUX are based on the S/Key/OPIE suite.

ownership The user (UID) and/or group (GID) that is associated with a file, directory, process, or process group.

paging The use of disk partitions and/or files as *"virtual memory."* This differs from *swapping* in granularity, since individual memory pages can be "swapped" in and out, rather than requiring that whole processes be read or written. The LINUX kernel does *paging* and generally does not perfrom true swapping.

To add to the confusion, however, the "paging" files and partitions under LINUX are called "swap files" and "swap partitions"—the system calls and utilities (`swapon` and `mkswap`) also misuse the terms.

PC Personal Computer. Originally a reference to any microcomputer that was intended for "personal" or "single user" use. The term was appropriated by IBM with the introduction of their first "personal" (micro) computer. As "clones" appeared, the term came to refer to any "IBM PC-compatible" microcomputer. It still refers generically to the platform and architecture of systems built around the x86 and derivative processors.

The term PC can be used to distinguish these systems from Apple MacOS-compatible systems and various *RISC* workstations. It is occasionally used in the obsolete sense to refer to microcomputers in general.

LINUX was originally developed on a 386-based system, although it has been ported to many others, including Apple 68K and PowerPC, Sun SPARC, and other workstations.

PCI   Peripheral Component Interconnect. A self-configuring local bus. Originally proposed by Intel for PCs, PCI can now be found on PowerPC systems and RISC workstations. PCI is now the dominant bus in modern computing.

permissions   Access control to UNIX files and directories are evaluated along three categories—user, group, and others or "world"—for three forms of access—read, write, and execute. All UNIX files have an owner and belong to a group. The group is usually the primary GID of the owner at the time that the file was created, or another GID of which the file's owner is a member and to which the file was assigned using the chgrp command.

These access "modes" are stored as three sets of three bits each. They are usually represented as a string like rwxr-x--- or in octal (750). The chmod command is used to modify a file's mode (permissions). Only the owner of a file (and root) can change its mode. Default permissions on newly created files are determined by the umask of the creating process (as set by the shell built-in *umask* command and/or the umask() system call).

The read (r), write (w), and execute (x) permissions have obvious meanings when applied to regular files and device nodes. However, their application to directories is not intuitive. The write permission conveys the ability to create, modify, and remove links in a directory regardless of the ownership and permissions on the inodes to which those links point. The read permission allows a user/process to perform ls commands and other read accesses. The execute permission allows "traversal" of a directory. It is not possible to access any point under a directory (including subdirectories) without execute permissions on each and every parent directory. This implies that the root directory must be world executable.

There are three additional settings that can be set on standard UNIX files: setuid (SUID), setgid (SGID), and "sticky." (The term sticky is frequently misused to refer to SUID and SGID settings.) The SUID bit on an executable file indicates that the program will execute with the effective privileges of the *file's* owner, rather than the normal permissions of the process/user that launched it. The SGID bit has an analogous meaning with respect to the group to which a program file is assigned.

SUID and SGID executable binaries are one of the oldest and most widely used forms of delegation under UNIX.

The SUID and SGID bits are ignored on non-executable files and on "scripts" (text programs in sh syntax or starting with a *shebang* #! line). This latter fact addresses historical security implications (race conditions) of such scripts.

SGID directories under LINUX force new files created thereunder to have a group assignment matching that of the directory, regardless of the GID and supplemental group membership of the user/process that creates such files. The SUID setting is ignored on directories, as it is on non-executable files. The semantics of the SGID directory can also be accomplished using the mount command's -o bsdgroups option on filesystems that support it.

The sticky setting on files is ignored under LINUX. Historically, it marked certain executables for preferential caching. However, sticky directories modify the semantics of write access to that directory. In a sticky directory, only the file's owner (and root, of course) can unlink (remove) file links.

pid   Process identifier. A number used by the kernel to keep track of the system-level resources necessary to switch between this process and others running on the system. It is easily visible to a system administrator by use of the ps command.

POST   Power On Self Test. When PC-compatible hardware is turned on, a set of minimal programs in its *BIOS* tests the system to verify that it has the minimum functions necessary to launch the boot loader. Failures of the tests that precede video access result in *error messages* in the form of a pattern of beeps.

PRAM   Parameter RAM. This is what Macintosh users usually call the *CMOS* or similar chip and its contents.
See also *nvram, firmware*.

process   An instance of a running program. *init* is the first process and is the ancestor of all others.

protected mode   On Intel microprocessors in the 8086 (x86) family, a mode of the 80286 or higher processor that has special memory addressing and protection features, allowing it to address much more memory than was previously possible on the 8088/8086 models. The first *Linux* kernel took special advantage of the protected mode features found in the 80386. Although its code has been revised and made portable to many architectures, LINUX is not compatible with the 80286, whose implementation of protected mode is rather unusual.

real mode   On Intel microprocessors in the 8086 (x86) family, a mode of the processor that is backward-compatible with the original 8088/8086 memory addressing model. This term was introduced to distinguish that mode from *protected mode*.

recursion   See *recursion*. When you get tired of following the references there, return to whatever you were doing before.

regular file   A file that is completely ordinary. It is neither a *character special* nor *block special* file, nor a *FIFO*, nor a *socket*.

RFC   Request For Comments. These are documents that propose standard practices and protocols for all Internet practices. They are drafted by interested parties and submitted to the *IETF*, where they are assigned to working groups and subjected to a relatively simple and open review, refinement, and adoption process.

All of the major Internet protocols and formats are defined by RFCs. This is primarily of interest to programmers who write clients or servers to implement these protocols. Thus, a programmer working on a new mail user agent (MUA) or mail transport agent (MTA) should pay close attention to RFC 822, which defines mail header formats and options.

Most RFCs are not directly relevant to system administrators. However, system administrators should be familiar with how to find and read RFCs, because some are essential. More information is available at `http://www.ietf.org/rfc.html`

Note: Some RFCs are written and never adopted, and some are adopted and never implemented by any significant number of sites. The intent of the RFCs is to promote and ensure interoperability among packages that implement a given protocol, and stable interaction between sites that are using these protocols.

RISC   Reduced Instruction Set Computer. This is a class of CPU designs including the SPARC, PowerPC, and MIPS processors. It is distinguished from *CISC* (Complex Instruction Set Computer) by a design philosophy that emphasizes high-speed execution of relatively simple instructions over availability of a large set of "powerful" machine language instructions.

This design philosophy holds that the complex operations are best done in software, saving more space on the CPU chip for registers, caches, pipelines, and other performance-enhancing features.

shared library   Shared libraries are object files that are dynamically linked to executable binary programs (*binaries*). These are analogous to Microsoft WINDOWS DLL files. Under LINUX, shared libraries can be stored in a number of directories (usually listed in `/etc/ld.so.conf`). Shared libraries typically include files under `/usr/lib` and `/usr/X11R6/lib`. If the shared libraries are deleted or become damaged, or if the `/etc/ld.so.cache` file is corrupted, then programs that rely on them (see *dynamically linked*) will fail to execute. Almost all normal programs on a system rely on libc (see *libc*), so a damaged libc usually requires a reboot (with a rescue diskette) for recovery.

There are three principal advantages to shared libraries. They reduce program size, saving disk space. They reduce the memory footprint, allowing more programs to run in less real RAM, because the LINUX kernel's memory management system can use page aliasing such that the shared library is actually loaded only once and is then shared among all processes using it. They can allow for "drop-in" upgrades and local customization without requiring re-compilation and re-installation of the many programs that are linked to them.

Thus, with shared libraries a system administrator can move from file-based directory services to NIS, NDS, LDAP, or some future or custom set of services without changing the rest of the programs that use these services.

See also *libc*, *library*.

signal   Under UNIX and LINUX, the signal is the most fundamental and common form of interprocess communications (IPC). It is also the basis for "event-driven" programming under these systems. Each UNIX implementation defines a set of signals that are associated with various asynchronous events, such as a terminal sending an "interrupt request" (SIGINT) or a change in window size (SIGWINCH).

signal handler   A code routine within a program that serves the special purpose of responding to *signals* provided by its parent or other processes. A common example would be SIGINT, described above, or SIGSUSP as described under *job control*.

skulker   A script that periodically removes unwanted files (such as core files) or kills specific processes.

These must be carefully written to avoid "false positives"—erroneous matches to the criteria used to determine which files to remove or processes to kill.

sockets   A socket is the primary form of interprocess communication (IPC) introduced by BSD. There are two major sorts of sockets. A "UNIX domain socket" is a node (directory entry) in the filesystem, such as /var/run/printer, /dev/log, or /tmp/.X11-unix/X*. The other major sort of socket is in the TCP/IP or "inet" addressing family. Sockets are the normal form of connections and transactions performed over TCP/IP address. In either case, they allow a client to communicate with a server, locally in the case of UNIX domain sockets, and across TCP/IP networks in the case of Internet domain sockets.

An "Internet domain socket" is uniquely identified over the entire Internet by a combination of source IP address and port, and destination address and port.

sparse files   Under many filesystems, a file can be stored in such a way that large, "blank" portions are "skipped," not stored as long streams of NUL characters. Any normal operations on these files will behave as though these regions of the file *are* filled with NULs. The amount of data stored on disk is significantly less than the entire file. This is especially useful for large databases.

Programs that perform seek() and lseek() calls past the end of an existing file may then create a file "hole" (depending on how large the seek gap is, and on the filesystem type and its block size settings).

Information about how utilities such as cp, tar, and similar commmands can affect the "sparsity" of files on which they operate can be found in Chapter 12, "Backups."

statically linked   A program with all of its function calls and variables resolved within itself. Such programs are rare but useful, because they operate even in the absence of valid *shared libaries* elsewhere on the system. Contrast *dynamically linked*.

swapping   Technically, the LINUX kernel provides *paging* rather than "swapping." However, all of the utilities that support these paging services (from the fdisk "type" option to mark a portion of a hard disk as a "swap partition" and the /etc/fstab term for identifying these devices, through the swapon and swapoff commands) use the nomenclature of swapping. See *virtual memory*.

symlink   Symbolic link. An entry in a directory that is not a file, but contains the name of another file that should normally be accessed instead (unless lstat or some other command that works on links is used). Contrast *hard link*.

tarball   A common way to refer to a file created with the tar command. This applies to compressed and uncompressed archives. This is often used to distinguish among package management systems. Slackware and some other distributions use "tarballs" as their package format. These come as separate archives of source code and binaries. The Red Hat derived distributions and some others use RPM, while Debian GNU/Linux and Stampede use their own package format.

thread   Also known as a "lightweight process." LINUX supports *kernel* threads (kthreads) in addition to pseudo-threads (pthreads). These allow multitasking within a single *process* context.

Kernel threads are a LINUX-specific feature, supporting separate units of execution (CPU scheduling) that share a single memory/*processs* space. Multithreaded programs entail the use of "threadsafe" libraries.

Pseudo-threads are supported under most forms of UNIX and provide cooperative multitasking among different lines of execution within a process, without kernel support. They use the pthreads library.

trap   See *signal handler*.

troll   A posting to USENET netnews or to a mailing list that is intended to generate discord and flamewars, or a person engaging in this activity (which is called "trolling").

UFS   One of the BSD filesystem types. LINUX has limited support for these, currently read-only. By the time you read this, perhaps it will have more advanced support for these filesystems. It is unclear whether UFS offers any advantages over *ext2fs*. However, the support may be useful in those rare cases where you might need to connect a BSD or Solaris hard disk to your LINUX system. It is probably far more common under S/LINUX (the SPARC port), where you may want to access other filesystems.

umask   A setting in a UNIX process that modifies the permissions on newly created files. It is generally represented as a three-digit octal number that will be logically ANDed against the mode 666 (rw-rw-rw-). Note: execute bits are not on newly created files in any case.

Thus, a common setting of 022 will result in files created with a mode of 644—world and group readable, with only the owner having write/modify access. A umask of 027 will result in files that are read/write to their owner, readable by members of the group to which these files are assigned (usually the owner's primary GID, but see 287 on SGID directories for more details).

When working in SGID directories, a umask of 007 or 002 is reasonable. For most other cases, 077 or 027 is prudent.

UMSDOS   A variant of the MS-DOS filesystem driver for LINUX, which provides support for UNIX filesystem semantics through the use of special DOS files to contain the necessary *meta-data*. UVFAT is a variation of the LINUX VFAT driver, which supports WINDOWS 95 or 98 long *filenames*.

Details can be found in the mount(8) man page, and in the kernel sources and documentation.

Unix   The operating system after which LINUX is modeled. Although often used to refer to any operating system that provides features and programming interfaces that emulate UNIX, the term is a trademark legally held by The Open Group.

VC   See *virtual console*.

VFS   Virtual Filesystem. An abstraction layer in the LINUX kernel that enables it to support a common interface to multiple underlying filesystem types. This allows the LINUX kernel to support many types of filesystems, such as its native *ext2fs* and *xiafs* types, the MS-DOS FAT and WINDOWS 95 or 98/WINDOWS NT VFAT types, and many others, while allowing most user programs and utilities to work with the files thereon.

virtual   Not real, but visible anyway; provided as an emulation by the computer. The term is used as a prefix. See *VFS*, *virtual console*, *virtual memory*.

If it's there and you can see it—it's real.
If it's not there and you can see it—it's virtual.
If it's there and you can't see it—it's transparent.
If it's not there and you can't see it—you erased it!

—An old IBM VM statement, Scott Hammer

virtual console   Linux and most implementations of Unix for the PC platform support this feature. It allows the console (keyboard and video monitor) to be treated as several "virtual terminals."

Each of these has its own device node (/dev/tty??) and can run its own copy of getty. Someone at the console can log in to each of these under any valid user name, just as he might if he had several separate terminals at hand.

By default, the Left Alt+F1 through Left Alt+F6 keys can be used to switch among the first six of these. Most distributions are configured to support six VCs with gettys on them. Additional getty sessions can be added by editing the /etc/inittab file and ensuring that the appropriate device nodes exist (possibly adding them using the mknod command).

If more than twelve VCs are used, the thirteenth through the twenty-fourth can be accessed by using the Right Alt key with the various F? keys. It is also possible to "cycle" among the active VCs using the Left Alt+Left Arrow and Left Alt+Right Arrow keys.

When xdm and startx start X Window sessions, they are bound to the first available virtual console (the one right after the last getty). It is possible to start multiple concurrent sessions of X using a command like: startx-- :1 and to switch from them to other VCs using Ctrl+Alt+F?.

It is possible to use VCs without running a getty on them by redirecting output to the appropriate device node. By adding an entry to the /etc/syslog.conf, one can configure syslogd to copy or redirect messages to a VC. One can start interactive programs on a VC using programs like open.

virtual memory   Memory beyond what is actually available, but which programs believe is actually available in the system. See *paging*, *swapping*.

virtual terminal   See *virtual console*.

xiafs   An early Linux native type of filesystem. Although it offered numerous advantages over the *Minix* filesystem that was first supported by Linux, it was later supplanted by the extfs (extended) and *ext2fs* (second extended) filesystems. It is named after its creator, Frank Xia.

Linux supports many filesystem types; any programmer can write a new set of drivers to link into the Linux VFS interface.

zombie   An entry in the kernel's process table that is preserved until the parent process performs a wait() system call on it. This is how the *exit code* is stored and returned for all Unix and Linux processes. A zombie is also known as a *defunct* process.

The process that results in a zombie has already exit()ed, and all resources (allocated blocks of memory, open files, and so on) that were assigned to it have already been reclaimed by the kernel. To get rid of a zombie, kill the parent (which can be discovered by searching the PPID column from the ps command's output).

To prevent zombies, the programmer can use a "double fork()" as part of the exec(), leaving the "grandchild" process as an orphan that will then be "adopted" by the init process (see *init* for details). Another option is for the programmer to create a *signal handler* to respond to the SIGCHLD event, which is how the kernel informs a parent of the demise of any of its children.

In short, only the programmer can prevent zombies.

References

[1] Paul W. Abrahams and Bruce R. Larson. *Unix for the Impatient, 2nd Ed*. Addison Wesley Publishing Company, 1997.

[2] Martin R. Arick. *Unix for DOS Users*. John Wiley & Sons, 1995.

[3] Frederick M. Avolio and Paul A. Vixie. *sendmail: Theory and Practice*. Digital Press, 1995.

[4] Bill Ball. *Teach Yourself Linux in 24 Hours*. Sams Publishing, 1998.

[5] Peter L. Bernstein. *Against the Gods: The Remarkable Story of Risk*. John Wiley & Sons, 1996.

[6] John D. Blair. *Samba: Integrating Unix and Windows*. SSC Inc, 1998.

[7] Philip E. Bourne. *Unix for VMS Users*. Digital Press, 1989.

[8] Robert M. Bramson, M.D. *Coping with Difficult People*. Dell Publishing, 1981.

[9] Fred Butzen and Dorothy Forbes. *The Linux Database*. MIS:Press and M&T Books, 1997.

[10] D. Brent Chapman and Elizabeth D. Zwicky. *Building Internet Firewalls*. O'Reilly & Associates, 1995.

[11] William R. Cheswick and Steven M. Bellovin. *Firewalls and Internet Security*. Addison Wesley Publishing Company, 1994.

[12] Hewlett Packard Co. *The Ultimate vi and ex Guide*. Addison Wesley Publishing Company, 1990.

[13] compiled by J. Purcell. *Linux Complete Command Reference*. Sams, Red Hat Press, 1997.

[14] Michael C. Donaldson and Mimi Donaldson. *Negotiating for Dummies*. IDG Books Worldwide, 1996.

[15] edited by Eric S. Raymond. *Linux Undercover*. Red Hat, Inc., 1998.

[16] Æleen Frisch. *Essential System Administration, 2nd Edition*. O'Reilly & Associates, 1995.

[17] Simson Garfinkel and Gene Spafford. *Practical Unix & Internet Security, 2nd Edition*. O'Reilly & Associates, 1995.

[18] Simson Garfinkel, Daniel Weise, and Steven Strassman, editors. *The UNIX-HATERS Handbook*. IDG Books Worldwide, 1994.

[19] Donald C. Gause and Gerald M. Weinberg. *Exploring Requirements: Quality Before Design*. Dorsett House Press, 1989.

[20] Barbara Hemphill. *Taming the Paper Tiger: Organizing the Paper in Your Life*. Kiplinger Books, Washington, DC, 1992.

[21] Barbara Hemphill. *Taming the Office Tiger: The Complete Guide to Getting Organized at Work*. Kiplinger Books, Washington, DC, 1996.

[22] David B. Horvath. *Unix for the Mainframer*. Prentice Hall, 1998.

[23] Bruce H. Hunter and Karen Bradford Hunter. *UNIX Systems Advanced Administration and Management Handbook*. Macmillan Publishing Company, 1991.

[24] Mark F. Komarinski and Cary Collett. *Linux System Administration Handbook*. Prentice Hall, 1998.

[25] Evi Nemeth, Trent R. Hein, Scott Seebass, and Garth Snyder. *Unix System Administration Handbook, 2nd Edition*. Prentice Hall, 1995.

[26] U.S. Bureau of Labor Statistics. *Dictionary of Occupational Titles*. U.S. Government, Washington, D.C, 1990.

[27] Ivars Peterson. *Fatal Defect*. Times Books, Random House, 1995.

[28] SAGE. *Job Descriptions for System Administrators, 2nd Edition*. USENIX Association, 1997.

[29] Peter H. Salus. *A Quarter Century of UNIX*. Addison Wesley Publishing Company, 1994.

[30] Tsutomu Shimomura and John Markoff. *Takedown: The Pursuit and Capture of Kevin Mitnick, America's Most Wanted Computer Outlaw—By the Man Who Did It*. Warner books, 1996.

[31] Mark G. Sobell. *A Practical Guide to Linux*. Addison Wesley Publishing Company, 1997.

[32] Clifford Stoll and Julie Rubenstein. *The Cuckoo's Egg : Tracking a Spy Through the Maze of Computer Espionage*. Pocket Books, 1995.

Index